Singing Up the Country reveals that Bob Trubshaw has been researching a surprising variety of different topics since his last book six years ago. From Anglo-Saxon place-names to early Greek philosophy - and much in between - he creates an interwoven approach to the prehistoric landscape, creating a 'mindscape' that someone in Neolithic Britain might just recognise. This is a mindscape where sound, swans and rivers help us to understand the megalithic monuments.

Continuing from where scholarship usually stops and using instead the approaches of storytelling, the final chapter weaves this wide variety of ideas together as a 'songline' for the Avebury landscape. This re-mythologising of the land follows two 'dreamtime' ancestors along the Kennet valley to the precursors of Avebury henge and Silbury Hill.

Few writers have Bob Trubshaw's breadth of knowledge combined with a mythopoetic ability to construct a modern day story that re-enchants the landscape. *Singing Up the Country* will be an inspiration to all those interested in prehistory, mythology or the Neolithic monuments of the World Heritage Site at Avebury.

Previous books by Bob Trubshaw
published by Heart of Albion:

Explore Folklore

Explore Mythology

Sacred Places: Prehistory and popular imagination

How to Write and Publish Local and Family History Successfully

Little-known Leicestershire and Rutland

Rutland Village by Village

Good Gargoyle Guide: medieval carvings of Leicestershire and Rutland

Leicestershire Legends retold by Black Annis

Previous books edited by Bob Trubshaw
published by Heart of Albion:

Explore Phantom Black Dogs

To Gail

Singing Up the Country

The songlines of Avebury and beyond

[signature]

Bob Trubshaw

[signature]

Heart of Albion

Singing Up the Country:
The songlines of Avebury and beyond

Bob Trubshaw

Cover photograph by Bob Trubshaw

Sunrise at south entrance to Avebury henge with jackdaws, November 2007

Two ravens sit on Odin's shoulders and speak into his ear all the
news they see or hear. Their names are Hugin [thought] and
Munin [memory]. He sends them out at dawn to fly over
all the world and they return at dinner-time. As a
result he gets to find out about many events.

Snorri Sturluson, thirteenth century

ISBN 978-1-905646-21-0

Published by
Heart of Albion Press
113 High Street
Avebury
Marlborough
Wiltshire
SN8 1RF

albion@indigogroup.co.uk

Visit our web site: www.hoap.co.uk

Printed in England by Booksprint

Contents

Acknowledgements

Parts of this book draw heavily on the research of Andy Collins, Michael Dames, Alan Garner and the late Margaret Gelling. In those sections I have listed their relevant publications but my debt to them is deeper – without pondering over their insights I would not have been able to bring many of these ideas together.

Understanding the prehistory of the upper Kennet valley owes everything to the work of the many archaeologists who have excavated here – a full list would read almost like a who's who of notable British archaeologists. Avebury is largely how it looks today as a result of Alexander Keiller and, given his interest in early modern occultism, I hope he would at least partially approve of my approach. The published works of Aubrey Burl, David Field, Mark Gillings, Jim Leary, Josh Pollard, Andrew Reynolds and their various collaborators (see References for details) have both given me an understanding of the prehistory of the area and also provided some limits on my imagination. I am grateful to David Field for an email discussion about rivers and sending a copy of the published version of his thesis. Thanks also to Ros Cleal and Nick Stanshall for sharing their understanding of the Avebury archaeology and helpful discussions. My interpretations undoubtedly differ from all these academics – while their aim is broadly to use the evidence to establish what is probable, I have used their work more to avoid what is implausible.

A number of people have, knowingly or otherwise, been of great help in the development of ideas presented here. To each of the following a big 'thank you'.

Jamie Blackwater for, among much else, sharing his understanding of the spirits of place. Janet Bord very promptly offered a selection of photographs from the Fortean Picture Library archives. Jill Bourn for helping me understand place-names over the last twenty-or-so years, detailed discussions about Leicestershire and Rutland toponyms, and for loaning Ann Cole's thesis. Ben Fernee for drawing my attention to the role of Frederick Hockley in promoting the idea of Holy Guardian Angels. Alan Haylock for his splendid illustration of swans. Peter Knight for his detailed knowledge of West Kennett chambered long barrow. Alan Latham for information about farmers buying and selling at different markets, following their fathers' precedents. Heather Smith for bringing my attention to the Pearl poet. Helen Ward for describing the singer at St Ouen in Rouen.

Shaun Ogbourne for sharing relevant parts of his vast experience and knowledge of the Wiltshire landscape, and for unwittingly instigating this book – preparing a talk about prehistoric journeys for the Wyvern Dowsing Society (which he chairs) opened the proverbial floodgates to ideas which came together as this work.

Alby Stone for his long-standing friendship and much needed advice on Proto-Indo-European etymologies. He has helped me avoid several major errors – and pointed out that the dog was inexplicably missing – although any remaining blunders are mine. He probably does not entirely agree with the published version but we can agree to differ as only good friends can.

Adam Stout for being on a personal journey that seemingly started as a passenger when I edited *At the Edge* and going on to become a much better engine driver than I ever could be. Oh yes, also for most helpful discussions and encouragement. His comments on the draft of this book were pertinent, not least for his own keen interest in both Avebury and the confluence of the Kennet and Thames at Reading. My discussion of the 'otherness' of the initial burials in West Kennett long barrow incorporates some of Adam's ideas.

Adam also spotted the spectre of John Barrett's ideas of a 'mobile Neolithic' wandering, uncredited, in my opening chapters. In his 1994 book *Fragments from Antiquity,* Barrett was the first to see the Neolithic people moving across a landscape made up of a myriad of places each with their own social and religious significances. This idea had become so integral to my own thinking that, truth to tell, I had forgotten its origin. Due thanks to John Barrett – and to Adam for spotting my oversight.

Ian Brown has, as for many previous Heart of Albion titles, provided some stunning illustrations; he also read a draft and offered a number of constructive suggestions, notably on the origins of Guinevere's name.

Alison Skinner stepped in at the eleventh hour to provide much-needed proofreading and also corrected a few wonky facts.

I am especially grateful to the various *land wights* of the upper Kennet valley for 'singing' their songs to me – if only my hearing was more attuned to their ways this book would have been much better. The ghost of Ted Hughes walks through this book in his manifestations as the twentieth century's most insightful bird shaman; hearing a radio version of *Cave Birds* broadcast on 26 May 1975 was the first major WTF moment in my life, and one which still resounds. The jackdaws nesting in the trees around this house, disturbed from time to time by rooks, noisily remind me that this alchemical drama continues, several thousand years 'off key'.

Lines from songs by Laurie Anderson, Nico Case and Sam Genders have inspired short sections of the Kennet dreaming. The blessing for peace at the end of the final chapter is from the Yajur Veda.

Finally, my greatest thanks is to Judi Holliday, without whom this book would most certainly never have happened.

Prologue

Dear Diary

Today Grandma and I went in the boat up the River Kennet to the White Lady's country. Grandma chanted lots of songs about the White Lady and swans and white dogs and bulls and many other things. Sometimes she sang too quietly for me to understand the words. We are going to stay here with lots and lots of other people for several nights. Grandma said next year when we come up the Kennet she'll tell me why she chants the songs. I want her to tell me now but she won't!

Kenna

OK, perhaps a young girl living around 3,500 BCE might not have left a diary quite like that. Nevertheless, by the end of this book, I hope her Grandma's songs will make sense to us – although perhaps not in exactly the way young Kenna might have been told.

To understand what such 'songs' of the upper Kennet valley might have been back then we need to understand what early Neolithic people might have been thinking – especially their myths and legends. That requires some fairly wide-ranging rummaging around various academic specialisms, together with a certain amount of looking beyond the slowly-changing horizons of academic preconceptions, plus a modicum of imagination. My aim is not to create the most probable view of early Neolithic thinking – there are too many unknowns – but rather to re-create a viewpoint which, based on current scholarship, is plausible.

We look at the past according to modern day knowledge and predilections. The past will change as future archaeological discoveries are made. What I offer here is perhaps a different collection of such 'predilections' to most. My overall aim is to inspire you to widen the way you think about the past, especially the Neolithic monuments of the Avebury area.

Facing page: *The author's shadow. Photograph taken in the north-west sector of Avebury henge at dawn, November 2007.*

Preface

During two trips in 1983 and 1984 writer Bruce Chatwin (1940–89) visited the Australian outback to research the Aborigines' Dreamtime myths and legends that, after 1987, would become well-known by the name he gave to the resultant book, *The Songlines*. Most people reading *The Songlines* assume it to be a factual book, ignoring how little contextual information (such as the dates of his travels) is included. Judging by the responses to Chatwin's other works we should, however, assume that – whatever facts are there – the author's innate abilities as a storyteller often take the upper hand. Chatwin himself later described the book as a work of fiction. (See Shakespeare 2000 and Travers 2002, especially pages 38–67, for detailed discussions of Chatwin's blending of fact and personal interpretation.)

Right at the start of the book Chatwin acknowledges that he followed in the footsteps of Arkady Volchok, who he presents as the first white man to gain the trust of the understandably secretive Aborigines about their sacred sites and the paths which link them together. Chatwin provides an elaborate biographical 'back story' for Arkady, including playing Buxtehude on the harpsichord in the middle of the Outback. However Arkady only existed in Chatwin's mind. Toly Sawenko, the land rights worker who – in the course of a meeting lasting only a few days – did provide Chatwin with his much-needed information, lived a life which had little in common with this imaginary Arkady. And presumably Chatwin had read Charles Mountford's pioneering study (Mountford 1968) which remains one of the most detailed accounts of specific Dreamtime myths.

With Chatwin's fictionalising abilities in mind, ponder on this quote from near the opening of *The Songlines*:

> 'Sometimes,' said Arkady, 'I'll be driving my "old men" through the desert, and we'll come to a ridge of sandhills, and suddenly they'll all start singing. "What are you mob singing?" I'll ask, and they'll say, "Singing up the country, boss. Makes the country come up quicker."'

> (Chatwin 1987: 16–17)

Whether there ever was a 'mob' of Aboriginal elders in the back of Toly Sawenko's Land Cruiser who said they were singing up the country I'm happy to leave as an open question, especially as it has provided an appropriate title for this book. One thing is for sure – they would not have used the word 'songlines'. This is part of Chatwin's convenient fictionalising. Aborigine terms translate as 'Dreaming tracks', 'footprints of the ancestors' and 'way of the law' (curiously reminiscent of Indian concepts of *dharma*). Ethnologists have adopted the term 'song-routes'.

All this notwithstanding, I have also used Chatwin's term 'songlines' in the subtitle because this has, since 1987, popularised awareness of such mythopoetic relationships with the landscape. The downside is that it popularised the assumption that only traditional cultures (such as the Aborigines) possess such myths and they have long-since been lost in Western societies such as Britain. While such a mythopoetic relationship has been lost to the extent we have no handy word such as 'songlines' to describe these place-related myths and legends, in this book I hope to show that such myths of place have been lost more because too few people recognised what there was, rather than because they were never recorded.

I feel a need to apologise for using 'songlines' and the quotation from Chatwin, 'singing up the country', as attention-getters for my own work. Yet his work, with all its fictionalisation, succeeded in getting Aboriginal culture widely valued in the West. Like Chatwin, I too attempt to synthesise a wide range of ideas in a manner which is readable. I too will allow storytelling to take over the facts as this book develops – although, unlike Chatwin, I hope it will be easier for the reader to recognise where facts become speculation, and speculation becomes invention. Imaginative narrative structures about past and place – 'singing up the country' if you will – not only makes the country come up quicker but, as the Aborigine elders would have implicitly understood, also makes the *past* come up 'quicker'.

For many people today, Britain's past and its rural landscape are deeply woven together by a mutual nostalgia (as outlined in the opening chapter of my 2005 book, *Sacred Places: Prehistory and popular imagination*). We may know legends and myths for some of these places, and historians and archaeologists have added their arguably less-mythic narratives in recent centuries. And we have always had a dreamtime – every traditional tale which starts 'Once upon a time… ' occupies this timeless temporal zone. However only a few pioneering explorers in the British Isles have 'sung up the country' in a manner we normally associate with much more exotic climes. This book draws upon their expeditions and outlines some charts where future path-finders can venture.

In a number of places this book continues ideas in *Sacred Places: Prehistory and popular imagination*. Towards the end of that work I introduce the idea of the past as something not simply to be studied or known but rather as something that we have a 'conversation' with. And, depending who we are conversing with at any given time, strongly colours not just what we talk about but the way we discuss it too. The different – and distinct – chapters of this book may be thought of as an example of this metaphor. Each chapter aims to offer an introduction to a particular area of scholarship; my aim has to make them as self-contained as possible, although overlaps are inevitable. If you prefer, think of each chapter as a conversation with several experts in a specific aspect of the past.

In the final chapter I try to weave all these ideas together into a 'Dreamtime' narrative, a 'songline' to explore a journey that is both in the physical landscape and in the 'mindscapes' we create for those landscapes. Whether this narrative follows the 'footprints of the ancestors' or simply creates a new set of tracks through the Dreamtime I am happy to leave unresolved.

You are quite welcome to skip chapters or read them out of sequence. Indeed, feel free to read the final chapter first to see where it's all going – although you will probably find many of the ideas over-speculative until you have read the 'whys and wherefores' in the earlier chapters. But if you do read from start to finish in the ol' fangled way, then I am well aware you may wonder at times where this book is heading.

While this is not the sort of book where it is appropriate to put too much emphasis on the reflexive process of situating myself in my writing, suffice to note the 'life as a journey' metaphor has been particularly relevant to the gestation of this work. After twenty-five years of living in Leicestershire I felt the need for a significant change and, as a result of a combination of 'coincidences', moved to Avebury towards the end of 2010. While the prehistoric monuments in and around Avebury have deeply inspired me since my first visit thirty years ago, arriving in that most special of landscapes encouraged me to explore it anew on foot. This book was drafted in February to May 2011 in the midst of all the excitement.

While walking the footpaths and bridleways some of my previous research began to take on a life of its own – 'the ideas had ideas', so to speak. These new thoughts about the upper Kennet valley were given to me either while walking through that landscape or sitting at my desk looking out at the north-east sector of Avebury henge from inside the only house built on the line of the prehistoric henge bank. Before this part of the bank was all-but flattened in recent centuries, the earth of the bank would originally have been a few feet above my head as I sit here in the first-floor office. I do not make any claims to have 'channelled' these new thoughts – but at the same time am quite happy to acknowledge that they might not be entirely my own creation… After all, when writing about this country's 'dreamtime' from a liminal location on the boundary of a principal 'dreamtime' place, some blurring of time and place, self and not-self, real world and 'dreamtime' seems only natural.

Just two small items of pedantry and a suggestion to take on our journey:

The compilers of Ordnance Survey maps and the Wiltshire Victoria County History volumes spell the River Kennet with one 't' and the names of the villages with two 'tt's – so West Kennett and so forth. Archaeologists invented a different convention for their publications, but that will be ignored here. This book is mostly concerned with the upper reaches of the River Kennet valley or the origins of the name of the

River Kennet so I have usually spelt Kennet with one 't'. The exceptions are references to a parish or an archaeological site which takes its name from a parish (such as West Kennett chambered long barrow).

As the abbreviations AD and BC are inconsistent (one a contraction of Latin and the other English; one appears before the year and one after) I have followed the growing use of CE (Current or Common Era) and BCE (Before Current or Common Era) for dates. Simply substitute AD and BC if you prefer an explicitly christo-centric worldview. Archaeo-astronomers usually talk in terms of thousands of years Before Present; in the relevant section I have converted their dates to BCE to make the correspondences with archaeological dating more obvious.

The examples of place-names are mostly from Leicestershire and Wiltshire simply because these are the counties I know best. If you are not familiar with either of these counties then do some homework and find the equivalents where you are – it is an excellent way to start to get to know the history of an area better!

Chapter 1

Prehistoric Wayfaring

We almost always travel to get from A to B. The bit in-between is usually a necessary evil or, at best, secondary to the destination or return home. But this book is predominately about pre-modern and prehistoric ways of life. Modern notions of travel as a means to an end, dominated by the destination and the 'task' of getting there, fit poorly. Leaving and arriving may be important; but the experiences along the way are usually more significant. Indeed some journeys may not have an anticipated destination – or the expected end may not be reached. To avoid contaminating our thinking with modern perceptions, perhaps we should think less about 'journeying' than 'wayfaring'.

Before the Iron Age, when horses and animal-drawn vehicles became an option – at least for the posher sort of folk – such wayfaring would typically be by 'shanks pony'. Other options for land-based travel would have to wait for the invention of mechanised transport. So, if horses were not an option, then everywhere was 'only' walking distance away. But everywhere is in walking distance if – as the American humourist Steven Wright observed – you have the time. One suspects pre-modern people simply wouldn't get the joke. Life was just places in walking distance put end-to-end, as it were, so 'walking distance' was as long as your life. And 'life as a journey' is a metaphor that has become ubiquitous, so much so that it is difficult to think about life except as a subsidiary of that metaphor. Answers to the question 'What is life if not a journey?' are usually more than a little off-beat. We find it easier to comprehend the visionary insight of the seventeenth century Japanese poet Matsuo Basho, who wrote in his travel diary 'each day is a journey, the journey itself is home... '

Such metaphorical journeys readily encroach into more spiritual domains. As long ago as the fourth to sixth centuries CE the famous Indian writer Vatsyayana observed 'It's not the road you walk, it's the walking.' Yes, he is famous. We may not know

Small rivers would have been important prehistoric routes. The 'Little Avon' near Bottlesford, Wiltshire, August 2009.

1

An idyllic beach on the north side of the Isle of Coll, July 1985.

exactly when he lived, but most people have at least heard of his best-seller, the *Kama Sutra*. The metaphorical and spiritual – not to mention sometimes erotic – aspects of journeys will feature in later chapters of this book. For the moment I'll just bring in my own experiences of walking through the countryside which seems to set exactly the right pace for more meditative 'ruminations' – or 'walking Zen' as Alan Watts once called it. This book owes its origin to just such ruminations as I explored the landscape around Avebury in early 2011. But they go back to when I was much younger. Travel diaries I kept on walking holidays in 1977 and 1980 (my first trip to Avebury) reveal all sorts of ideas that 'came to mind' along the way. Such mental detours are not matched by later diaries for holidays made by bicycle and, latterly, car. My experience of the spirits of place 'inspiring' quite profound insights also includes the day after Midwinter solstice in 2000, when (for no more spiritual reason than the office party having taken place the night before in a hotel down the road) I found myself walking near Alderley Edge. And I wasn't even seeking any sort of insights…

Life as a road trip

Prehistoric people did not simply go from place to place for the sake of getting from one location to another locality. For hunter-gathering people life was one long road trip. Although hunter-gathering people have now been squeezed to the margins of the inhabited world – such as the Arctic or the deserts of Africa – we can see parallels to this in the way traditional Saami lifestyles involve following reindeer herds over hundreds of miles, or Inuit people skilfully use overland and waterborne transport to hunt seals. We have at least some evidence of the extensive travel needed for native Americans to successfully exploit the vast bison herds. While the parallels with Europe in the Mesolithic and early Neolithic may only be approximate, we can infer much about how life might have been before agriculture 'took off' in the later Neolithic and onwards.

Although for most of us walking is the only sensible-paced transport option, it was not the same in prehistory. But as far back as 9,000 years ago we have direct evidence for waterborne transport being at least as important as walking. Mesolithic hunter-gatherers on the inner islands of western Scotland left evidence of hunting seal and red deer and also collecting 'industrial' quantities of shell fish and hazel nuts. Clearly this was part of a seasonal travel routine which enabled different foods to be collected – and presumably some of it stored. But crucially these remains are from different islands (Coll, Colonsay, Oronsay and Jura) which, then as now, were separate. And, at the time of writing, archaeologists have been excavating a Mesolithic log boat in the waters of the Solent which is only slightly more recent than the evidence from the Scottish islands.

Despite modern mental baggage to the contrary, mobility and travel could not have been exceptional in prehistoric societies – they were integral aspects of those societies. Without travelling between the islands our Mesolithic antecedents would have starved. And every now and again they must also have travelled further away to meet other 'tribes' – genetic diversity is not an optional extra for long-term human survival. To live in the British Isles before – and during – the Neolithic was to be part of a society which relied on boats as much as legs.

Early watercraft – whether log boats or skin-covered 'kayaks' or 'coracles' – clearly follow rivers and sea-coasts. The routes are largely determined by the geography. But 3,000 or more years ago walking was constrained less by the terrain – we can, if we really want to, ascend the steepest hills – than by trees. Or, more accurately, a combination of trees and the animals that lived among them. Nowadays when we are out in the woods there is little prospect of encountering wild boar or wolves. This was not the case 1,000 or more years ago. In the Neolithic there were also bears and

The Ridgeway near Wayland's Smithy, Oxfordshire, March 2011.

aurochs, the formidably large wild cattle. While woodland can make overland travel exceptionally difficult, it is rarely completely impassable as wild animals – pigs, cattle and deer – made tracks through while foraging or escaping predators. These tracks become used and adapted by humans as they too forage or travel through the woodland.

In the modern age where a footpath is defined clearly on a map, and may even be fenced in, we think of paths as something that have always been there. And, to all intents and purposes, some indeed have. But in pre-modern societies, particularly those living before widespread enclosure of fields, a path existed only because it had been created by those who went before you. 'Paths are made by walking' as the Spanish poet Antonio Machado observed. In open countryside – heathland and the like – they may also be more akin to a 'skein' of almost-parallel tracks, rather than one narrower way.

Following in the steps of those who have established an accepted or 'best' way to go is a profound statement of human culture. The generations of people who went before went to tend animals, plant and harvest crops, travel to market, meet up with relatives and friends, find spouses and – ultimately – were carried to their final resting places. Little wonder then that following a path became such a widely-used metaphor for the passage of one's life.

Examples of early Neolithic polished stone axes.

Ethnographic studies of nomadic and semi-nomadic cultures confirms that the whole of life 'happens' while travelling. All manner of subsistence activities are accomplished. Goods are traded. Relatives and other people are met. Children are born. Illnesses are overcome – or not. And travel fulfils a love of change and exploration – which are not merely modern aspirations but seem to be an enduring aspect of human nature since earlier times.

Once farming makes us more sedentary then journeys are necessary to enable the more material aspects of culture to be traded or given as gifts – and, as always, gift-giving is either immediately reciprocated or places some longer-term 'onus' on the recipient. People trade food, whether to overcome shortages in hard times or simply to add diversity to their diet. People trade specialist raw materials, such as flint, salt and the ingredients to make pots – especially the 'grogs' mixed in with the clay, which in earlier Neolithic pottery seemingly are always white and, where sources can be ascertained, apparently from somewhere which must have had 'cultural significance' as well as simply being suitable for the task. They also traded or gifted high-status objects, such as polished stone axes.

Probably the highest-status of these non-functional axes were those made from pale green jadeite quarried at high altitude on Monte Viso and Monte Beigua in the Alps. Examples have been found in Brittany, including the chamber tombs at Gavrinis and Carnac. Thirty known examples have been discovered in Ireland, Scotland and especially near the Hampshire and Dorset coasts – confirming that these were important locations for cross-Channel trade even five thousand years ago.

Just over a quarter of British-made examples of similar axes came from a difficult-to-access quarry on the upper slopes of Great Langdale in the Lake District where a band of green volcanic tuff is exposed. Almost certainly the quarry was chosen as much for the mythic significance of its dramatic location rather than simply because of the quality of the stone. About two dozen other quarry sites spread widely through Britain have also been approximately located. Yet hand axes from all these different places have been found widely distributed, often many hundreds of miles from whence they came. Given that something in the order of a month's hard work was needed to make just one of these, then something equally 'valuable' must have been expected in exchange.

A great many less-conspicuous exchanges must also have taken place, but these have left little or no trace among the material culture that archaeologists discover. And for all the material clutter that does or does not survive, there was something even more valuable that would be shared – ideas. The deeper meanings and significance of journeys and the places along the routes would be retold in legends and myths.

Bothies and nightclubs; Apaches and Scots

In a web page explaining the title of his CD *Bothy Culture*, the musician Martyn Bennett (1971–2005) makes the observation that:

> … in some ways bothies have the same, familiar atmosphere to
> urban nightclubs – arriving for the sound-check when they are
> merely cold, empty shells is always a spooky experience. Perhaps
> the same spirits of so many fire/spot-lit, whisky/drug charged
> nights have somehow imparted a memory of the ghosts of those
> people you have never met and can only imagine.
>
> (Bennett c.1997)

The words of Apache storyteller Dudley Patterson illustrates the deeper aspects of this:

> How will you walk along this trail of wisdom? Well, you will go
> to many places. You must look at them closely. You must
> remember all of them. Your relatives will talk to you about them.
> You must remember everything they tell you. You must think
> about it, and keep on thinking about it, and keep on thinking
> about it. You must do this because no one can help you but
> yourself... Wisdom sits in places. It's like water… you also need to
> drink from places. You must remember everything about them.
> You must learn their names. You must remember what happened
> at them long ago. You must think about it and keep on thinking
> about it. And your mind will become smoother and smoother.
> (Basso 1996: 70)

Within the British Isles the only surviving evidence for this is the Scottish Travellers' tradition, especially as maintained by Stanley Robertson (1940–2009). For Robertson 'places "become" through memory, and memory teaches through place.' (Reith 2008: 81)

> Within Traveller culture, the pervasive themes of cyclical renewal or life as a journey reflect a worldview instilled by the practical, descriptive, and symbolic richness of Traveller education in which the guidance of family, tradition and nature is always accessible when sought.

(Reith 2008: 95)

'In the concealed Traveller topography of North-East Scotland', as Sara Reith calls it, '[...] Stanley's expansive worldview encompasses the material, ancestral, ethereal and eternal as ever present resources.' (Reith 2008: 81–2) The remaining chapters of this book are devoted to such expansive worldviews, those 'mindscapes' through which our ancestors and antecedents made their way.

Wayfaring needs waymarking

Having established in this broad manner the way that travel – wayfaring as I prefer – was integral to pre-modern and prehistoric people this in turn raises a related issue. When we pop to the shops we rarely turn on the sat nav. Yet to get to there we need to know that we turn left at the end of the road, cross over at the zebra crossing, then take the second right. To go somewhere less familiar we normally rely on sat navs, maps or just verbal descriptions – "Go straight over three roundabouts, go past where the petrol station used to be, turn left at the Red Lion – no, it's the Slug and Lettuce now... '

So too pre-sat nav societies made cognitive distinctions between familiar and unfamiliar landscapes, and between local and distant destinations. Natural, manmade and man-modified landmarks would have to be committed to memory for less familiar journeys. Place-names linked by a mythical narrative – a 'song line' of some kind – would be an effective mnemonic (Chapter Six looks at this in more detail). For some journeys, what might be thought of as more 'ritual' ones in some respect or another, the mythic narrative might re-enact the time of primordial creation, or the progressive settlement of the region by ancient ancestors, or be part of a rite of passage – and such journeys are most likely deeply immersed in the mythic narratives of the society. Indeed, the re-enactment of the myth, or a fragment of it, might be the *reason* for the journey. The memory of such myths would be passed on with these 'ritual' retellings. The tales would become integral with the places where they were retold.

Perhaps such mythic meaning and significance was once so prevalent there was no such thing as a purely 'mundane' journey in prehistory. Nevertheless there would have been a distinction between longer 'walkabouts' and shorter 'shopping trips'. But even if all journeys were richly embedded in a dominant world view, presumably some journeys resonated more deeply with spiritual and ritual matters than others.

Navigational landmarks in relatively familiar landscapes need not have been monumental – they could have been as minimalist as placing a small distinctive

The remains of one of the two chambered cairns at Cairnholy, above Wigtown Bay near Dumfries, July 1985. The sea is visible to the left of this photograph.

stone on top of a large boulder – although clearly only some of the more monumental markers – chamber tombs and standing stones – have survived since prehistory in most places. And, although the term 'landmark' covers all these, were such guides always intended for the land-based traveller? How did users of coastal waters navigate? How prevalent were such 'sea marks' on the coasts of Britain, and what do they tell us about the prevalence of prehistoric waterborne travel?

King's Quoit chamber tomb, Manorbier, September 1995. One of many Neolithic chamber tombs in Pembrokeshire which seem to have been sea-marks as well as sepulchres.

Each of these questions has been addressed by at least one – and in some cases several – academics who took part in an academic conference session at the end of 2004. Their papers appeared in a book called *Prehistoric Journeys* (Cummings and Johnston 2007). Those who have prior experience of such collections of academic papers should note that this book greatly surpasses the usual expectations of insufficiently-overlapping viewpoints which typify books of conference papers.

Being 'dropped' by helicopter for week-long surveys of areas of Western Greenland abandoned by modern hunters as being unduly inaccessible may seem as remote from British archaeological practice as it is reasonable to imagine. Yet the researchers were able to reliably reconstruct hunting routes not used since about 1200 CE simply by looking for landmarks such as a small (typically head-sized) distinctively-coloured rock placed on top of a boulder near the skyline, and larger cairns in the lower-lying areas. These routes led to evidence of four different types of shelters, corresponding to ethnographic evidence for four types of hunting camps. However not all the landmarks were mundane – some 'arrangements' were clearly part of the old hunting magic condemned by the christian missionaries to Greenland.

So when, in the two following chapters, the discussion turns to the survival of prehistoric artefacts at British Neolithic sites there is a sense that the 'sites' should be interpreted as part of a spectrum of different types 'camps' which were once linked by landmarks perhaps little more distinctive than cairns or even head-sized stones on bigger boulders. Only the bigger monuments – such as tombs – would have been sites of social interaction.

Back in 1976 Aubrey Burl augured that British prehistoric henges were associated with places easily accessed by water, or on other routeways. So what should we make of chamber tombs (a little older than these henges) which are situated a short, often steep, climb above the sea? Was it so Grandad got a good view of the waves in the afterlife? Maybe that as well. But three of the contributors to the *Prehistoric Journeys* book take a detailed look at the surviving prehistoric sites on the coasts of Ireland, Wales (especially Pembrokeshire), south-west Scotland (the area of Dumfries and Galloway which includes Cairnholy), Dorset (especially Poole harbour) and the Isles of Scilly. The overwhelming conclusion is that these tombs were not sited simply to overlook the sea (although this too is true) but to act as reliable navigation aids for sea-borne travellers. Interestingly the tombs are sited to act as sea-marks just where underwater features make the water most hazardous, for example where submerged sand banks create locally-faster tidal races. Not only could our Neolithic ancestors knock up a nifty henge, here is evidence that they also nipped around the treacherous waters of the British Isles.

Just to prove they weren't in the least bit daft, given a sensible alternative to the most treacherous inland seas of the British isles they made for the source of rivers that linked together via a short overland trek rather than risk the more extreme coastal tidal races. So Kilmartin valley was preferred to going around the Mull of Kintyre. The Upper Clyde also connects conveniently with the sources of the Tweed (and thence the east coast) and the Nith to the south. Dunragit provides another alternative to the extreme waters of the Mull of Galloway. All these prehistoric Scottish overland routes 'filled up' with monuments such as henges – and then remained important until the present day; indeed, some are now dominated by motorways. The same argument links the two Avons of Wessex (the Bristol Avon flowing west and the Christchurch Avon flowing south, which passes near Stonehenge and has its headwaters near the Marden mega-henge). This river and land 'short cut' avoids going the long way round the undisputedly tricky waters off Land's End. Furthermore the headwaters of the River Kennet, a tributary of the Thames, are at Avebury, adding a third major routeway to the east. No surprise then that, Wessex 'filled up' with prehistoric monuments on a scale that is on a par with the contemporary routes in Scotland. (See Noble 2007 for a more detailed account of the correlations between Neolithic monuments and routeways.)

Recently-published research reveals that such early seafarers could also construct navigation aids to ensure they made it back to their boats after venturing overland. Roger Hutchins has suggested that the prehistoric stone rows (associated with the tin-producing areas of the British Isles, which would presumably attract sea-borne traders) act as both direction finders and 'mnemonics' for the journey back to the nearest natural harbours (Hutchins 2011). More work needs to be done to confirm his ideas but this suggestion is consistent with the settings of contemporary megalithic tombs as sea marks – and the reality that all monuments act as landmarks.

The experience of journeying

Walking, as with other ways of moving our bodies such as crawling, climbing, jumping, stumbling, and so on, is an 'embodied experience'. We use our whole bodies, not just our legs, when we move about. Our perceptions – the 'response' of the ground to our weight, our use of visual cues to maintain balance – are also integral to even the most basic acts of movement. And, at the risk of being overly-profound, what we do with our bodies – and what we perceive – is in every respect key to what makes up our culture – material or mental. Movement is not in some sense separate to the rest of human activity, it is by and large what makes human activity possible, in all its cultural diversity (See Noë 2004).

And when we are journeying or wayfaring what we experience, and the values we give to those experiences, depends on the season of the year, time of day, quality of the light, the weather and much else. Misty or clear, windy or still, sunny or rainy – they all affect not only what we can see (and hear and smell) but also affect our own visceral responses to the act of walking. Walking uphill into strong wind-driven rain is a far more challenging experience than skipping along a firm sandy beach in the full sun with just a gentle cooling breeze. While we may walk further along the idyllic beach, we have a greater sense of achievement from having 'beaten' the tougher terrain in inclement weather.

What we see while walking depends on the terrain – difficult stony outcrops or dense tree roots require all one's attention to be directed downwards. Slippery or boggy ground requires one to test each step, using leg muscles in different ways to when walking on either gravel or smooth tarmac. In contrast, a smooth sward of pasture grass means that – give or take dodging the odd cow pat or sheep poo – one can devote most of one's attention to the distant panorama and the clouds in the sky, often associated with a greater sense of oneness with the world. Walking on a well-maintained riverside path may require as little attention to one's feet – but the views will usually be much more constrained by the valley sides and denser vegetation associated with valleys.

Entering the Otherworld

Since the age of eighteen I have been fortunate to live in close proximity to countryside eminently suited for rambling – successively West Yorkshire, Sussex, Surrey, Leicestershire and now Wiltshire. Back in the 1970s one wore 'sensible shoes' – although, as a cash-conscious student, I have to admit mine were not always sensible enough for the hazards of Brontë country in the winter. But for most people a day's walking is topped and tailed by a drive from and back to a more urban or suburban life. Walking in the countryside is 'other' to their day-to-day world. Certainly, to judge by the activities in a typical pub car park in, say, the Peak District or the Dales, one would have to assume that such ramblers are about to undertake an Otherworld journey. They don a shamanic costume of special trousers and special jackets. Most essential are the 'mercurial' boots and socks deemed essential for this Otherworld expedition. Other parts of the ritual attire may include special

'... all one's attention... directed downwards.' The exposed roots of the beech trees on the bank of the eastern entrance to Avebury henge, August 2008.

thermos flasks, maps or mobile GPS systems. And this magical attire is adorned with words of power – such as Berghaus, Rab, Regatta, North Face, Cragghopper or (for those who desire the most empowering sigils) Rohan.

Just why the English in particular have such powerful myths about the countryside is a story in its own right – and one I have already summarised in the opening chapter of *Sacred Places: Prehistory and popular imagination* (Trubshaw 2005a). Suffice for the moment to note that the old adage about 'Other people have myths, we have religion' can also be reworded to reflect our relationship with 'wayfaring' in the landscape. You don't have to live in Papua New Guinea or wear a bone through your septum to see the world through the lenses of myths. You're simply so used to looking through the lenses to notice that they're there (and if that idea is novel to you then read Simon Danser's *The Myths of Reality* [Danser 2005] for an accessible overview of the way myths shape our modern world).

Nevertheless, ethnocentric myopia notwithstanding, our antecedents probably had a richer and more varied sense of mythic journeys. A quickly-assembled list of ethnographic parallels includes:

- journeys re-enacting primordial creation
- journeys re-enacting primordial migrations

'... a smooth sward of pasture grass means... one can devote most of one's attention to the distant panorama and the clouds in the sky, often associated with a greater sense of oneness with the world.' The summit of Waden Hill – less than half-a-mile from the photograph on the facing page – looking towards Silbury Hill, West Kennett chamber tomb and Swallowhead Springs, October 2008.

- initiatory quests (either sent or led)
- quests to seek visions
- quests to 'meet' – or follow – deceased ancestors
- quests for healing or psychoactive plants
- quests or hunts for totemic animals
- Otherworldly quests
- open-ended 'walkabouts'

Any experienced ethnographers reading this list will probably think of many more examples. But that would be to miss my point. Which is that most, if not all, of these examples are somewhat alien to dominant Western culture. Indeed to have personally explored even the *idea* of any of these would be deemed somewhat 'alternative'. We're a long way from popping to the shops or taking the M25 to visit Grandma. We would share Dorothy's thoughts when she said to Toto, 'I've got a feeling we're not in Kansas anymore.'

But some such journeys are associated with so much cultural baggage that they are best conveyed in a separate chapter.

Chapter 2

Journeys with Significance

There are many words for walking. We amble. We stroll. We march. We trudge. We perambulate. Best of all, perhaps: we saunter. This last word is from the French, *Saint Terre* meaning 'Holy Land'. It derives from the Middle Ages, when pilgrimage was all the rage. Everyone was going to the Holy Land. Some people took it up as a profession. They would wander from town to town, from church to church, begging for alms, like sadhus and holy men do in India today. When asked where they were going, they would say, 'to Saint Terre…' – to the Holy Land.

They would never actually get there. It was the journey itself that mattered. Perhaps they were already in the Holy Land in some sense. Perhaps it was the walking that took them there.

(Stone 2009)

CJ. Stone's evocative writing conveys the sense of Vatsyayana's observation cited in the previous chapter: 'It's not the road you walk, it's the walking.' However, although the derivation of saunter from Saint Terre sounds intriguing, this is actually an example of 'folk etymology' dreamt up about two hundred years ago. No one is certain, but the word saunter probably derives from the Middle English *santren*.

Nevertheless, C.J. has plenty of personal experience of walking every day, at least of a secular kind – when not writing he is a postman. We can say with confidence that prehistoric people would find the concept of postmen entirely alien. But would they have had close encounters with experiences that we associate with the word 'pilgrimage'? We do not know how far back these traditions go, but, significantly, the earliest European literature reveals that pilgrimage was widespread in Classical Greece. The pilgrims were known as *theoros* (the unlikely origins of our word 'theory') as they visited shrines in the expectation that the deities (*thea*) would reveal themselves. This tradition was maintained throughout the Roman Empire. Likewise planned pilgrimages were clearly commonplace in ancient China. They are also encountered in ethnographical accounts – for example, Peter Jordan described how the Khanty of Siberia only enter sacred areas and burial sites at certain times of year and approach them along specific paths (Jordan 2001).

Indeed, as well as ritual journeys, there were rituals *of* journeys. Although, according to Hesiod, everybody could read omens from the spontaneous activities of birds, anything observed when setting out on a journey was especially significant. Movement from left to right was more favourable than right to left, and the type of bird was significant – for example, woodpeckers were especially auspicious for carpenters. (Johnson 2008: 128–30)

The formation of the Holy Roman Empire from the ruins of the military Roman empire simply shifted the destinations of such pilgrimages to christian – or, in some cases, christianised – sites. Starting in about the eighth century a complex package of ideas, originating in Constantinople and the eastern Mediterranean, is imported into British christianity. These ideas instigate a 'cult of saints' which, among other influences, adds a further layer of meaning to the veneration of founding saints who characterised pre-Augustinian christiantity in the British Isles. And some of these – especially the Welsh and Cornish saints – are forever travelling from place to place– at least according to their early medieval hagiographers. Their lives are portrayed seemingly as an endless sacred journey, akin to Indian sadhus or Sufi 'wandering dervishes'.

Pilgrimage is all-but synonymous with Islam and the *hajj* to Mecca, and the many other lesser-known destinations sought out by devote Moslems. But, as with so many other Moslem traditions, there are pre-Islamic roots. The *Ka'bah* at Mecca was sacred to Al'Uzza, a mother goddess associated with the full moon, before being 'claimed' by Mohammed as the place of Allah. The priests of the sacred shrine are still known as *Beni Shaybah* or 'Sons of the Old Woman' – Shaybah being, of course, the famous Queen Sheeba of Solomon's times. (Camphausen 1989; Trubshaw 1993; Bey no date).

We have few first-hand accounts of medieval pilgrimages. But we do have Indian photographer Raghubir Singh's accounts of his pilgrimages around the Ganges valley (Singh 1974; 1992). He recalls his emotions rather than the epic narratives which 'shape' the pilgrimage route. The movement, fasting, veneration all generate specific kinaesthetic feelings – the full range of tactile, olfactory, visual and auditory senses. He reports that often here and there, now and then, I and not-I all become blurred – through dreams, offering Ganga water to his dead father, even hallucinations and being under spells. However these novel experiences are assimilated within the Hindu worldview he inhabits collectively with other pilgrims. The emotional responses aroused during this period of liminality on pilgrimage eventually became incorporated into his long-term sense of self and the purpose of life.

Hindu pilgrimage manifests in many other manners. One of the more exotic – and indeed erotic – was devised in the sixteenth century near Braj in what is now Rajastan. A series of groves, each around a large stone-lined 'well' or cistern, are linked together by a ritual perambulation which takes twenty-three days to complete. The narrative which links these groves together is a long sacred poem which describes Krishna's seduction of Radha. The result is a powerful blending of the landscape with devout devotion, poetic literature and the erotic. Sadly this once stunningly beautiful sixteenth century precursor to secular theme parks has been overrun by the expansion of Braj into a modern city.

In Japanese Buddhism the week-long *akimine* pilgrimage has some of these same aspects. As Carmen Blacker, who completed this pilgrimage twice in the 1960s reports, 'In a week, we had undergone death, conception, gestation and rebirth in the heart of a mountain which stood for a mother's womb. (Blacker 1975 (1986: 233)).

Poets are perhaps best-placed to record the emergent emotions which pilgrimages are wont to expose. As Japanese haiku poems are all about suggestion and allusion perhaps it is no surprise that one of the most renowned haiku writers, Matsuo Basho (1644–94), left a series of ambiguous travel diaries which allude to his 'interior' feelings as he travelled the pilgrimage routes of seventeenth century Japan (Heyd 2008).

Back in the Occident

Although first-hand accounts of traditional christian pilgrimage may not be as revealing as their oriental counterparts, we can be certain that the emotive aspects of such long journeys formed enduring memories. One key aspect of medieval pilgrimage was that it enabled a person to escape the monopoly their parish priest had over their spiritual welfare. Until little more than a hundred years ago, all aspects of one's sense of identity and 'place in life' were much more closely determined by where one lived. To a much greater extent than now, changes in identity – and indeed perception of the world – were only possible when 'away from home'.

With the Reformation the opportunity for pilgrimage disappears. But, at least for the social élite, it evolves into tourism – and all the near-synonyms such as excursions, jaunts, trips, expeditions and tours. Which means especially the Grand Tour, the Enlightenment's secular continuation of the medieval devotion, with coaches to Classical Italy and Greece replacing the saunter to the Holy Land. But the transformations were equally formative for later life. The Grand Tour was initiatory and transgressive for young gentlemen, as visits to European cities of culture were not restricted to art galleries and cathedrals but would include the delights of the 'women of the night'. They would come back to settle down and find themselves a wife, with packing cases of antiquities to decorate their stately homes in the best possible taste.

The Grand Tour evolves – albeit discontinuously – into 'sun worship', manifesting most clearly in the transgressive and somewhat initiatory experiences of Club 18–30 holidays, where an excess of popular culture eclipses the expectations of encountering high culture on the Grand Tour. Even if most people's holidays are at least a little more demure than the anticipations of Club 18–30 clientele, holidays are always about leaving home for a liminal period – whether for a long weekend or a

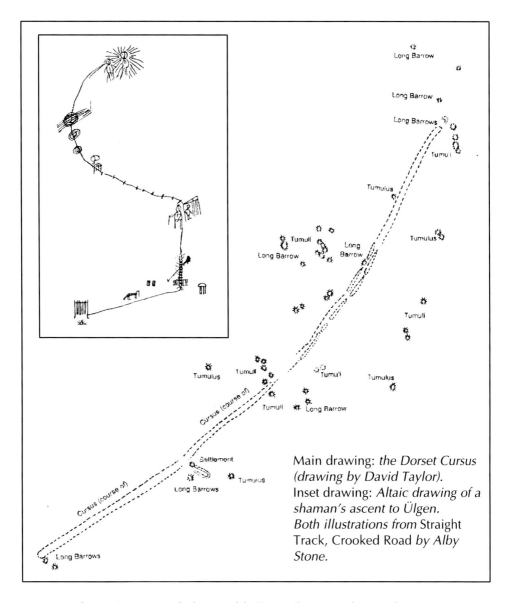

Main drawing: *the Dorset Cursus (drawing by David Taylor).*
Inset drawing: *Altaic drawing of a shaman's ascent to Ülgen.*
Both illustrations from Straight Track, Crooked Road *by Alby Stone.*

gap year bumming around the world. Even if we neither seek nor attain any transgressive or initiatory experiences nevertheless we will seek to bring back some enduring 'happy memories'. This is the perhaps the lowest level of the emotional transformation which travel provides. And, when the travel is fuelled by a heady mix of spiritual belief and devotion, we can readily see that something much more transformative than 'happy memories' is quite likely to ensue.

We never miss the last journey 'home'

Some might think I am stretching things by including holidays as examples of ritual journeys. But key aspects of holidays, including the journeys, are 'ritualised'.

However the same can be said for shopping trips and, with the possible exception of such special instances of the worship of Mammon as toy shops on Christmas Eve or the first day of the New Year sales in Oxford Street, then the ritualised aspects are deeply secular.

But there is one journey that each of us has yet to make which, no matter how secularised or otherwise, retains a profoundly liminal and transformative role – both for us and those who survive us. At some time our bodies – or, for some, first their bodies and later their ashes – will be taken to their final resting place. Funeral processions are an integral aspect of human culture. They assist in soothing grieving relatives and friends with their largely conservative repetition of time-honoured traditions. They provide an acceptable way of sanitising the process of bodily decay – whether by burial or cremation, or (as may have been the case in, say, the Neolithic) by excarnation.

Widespread yet all-but spontaneous expressions of collective grief accompanied the final journey of Princess Diana in 1997; a smaller scale tradition arose at Wooton Bassett in 2009 when Royal British Legion members paused to salute war dead repatriated from Afghanistan to RAF Lyneham. Quickly this impromptu recognition grew to involve the entire town, who were often up to three deep in the town's High Street. By the time RAF Lynham closed over 150 such repatriations had passed along this route. In recognition of this Wootton Bassett was awarded the honour of becoming the third town in Britain to have the name 'Royal'.

If in modern secular Britain such a large proportion of us feel it necessary to honour the dead by lining the route of the cortège, little wonder that more historic 'corpse ways' have acquired a rich folklore, often linked to such paranormal phenomena as ghosts or phantom black dogs. Since the mid-1990s Paul Devereux has published extensively about corpse ways and what he calls 'spirit paths' and collected examples from both the old and New World (e.g. Devereux 2003). Many of these are straight – 'dead straight' if you like – others have deliberate kinks to throw off the Devil (there was a widespread belief in eighteenth and nineteenth century Britain that the Devil could only travel in straight lines; ethnology and mythology provides plenty of other 'kinky' examples of either travelling to or thwarting the Otherworld – see Stone 1998a&b).

Despite the thorough research of Paul Devereux, Alby Stone and a number of co-researchers, the origin of this tradition seems lost in the proverbial mists of time. Bronze Age burial mounds sometimes – although not always – are associated with linear alignments. And the early Neolithic so-called 'cursus' monuments are undoubtedly linear and probably processional ways – but conclusive evidence that they were funeral routes is lacking.

Little imagination is needed to assume that deep mythological meanings were in the minds of the makers of such monumental Neolithic earthworks such as cursuses and henges (many of which are linked to known cursuses, or – as with Avebury – have double avenues of stones forming what appear to be processions frozen in time).

The Dawn Watcher. One of many simulacra on the sarsen stones at Avebury. This megalith is one of the few surviving stones of the north inner circle, Avebury henge. Photographed at dawn, August 2008.

These monuments acted as 'mirrors' – microcosms – of the relationship between the living and the dead, the realm of mortal humans and immortal deities, either sculpting the earth itself to emulate, say, the act of primordial creation, or providing a ritual setting for the annual re-enactment of key cosmological events, such as the rebirth of the sun each winter solstice. And, as ever, one of the Big Questions which seemingly all human cultures attempt to answer, is 'What happens to our 'souls' after death?' Further, if – as many people in a great many different societies do – we find the concept of reincarnation simpler (or at least more reassuring) than other alternatives then the next Big Question is 'Where do our souls go between death and their next incarnation?'

Chapter Nine looks at myths which suggest that migrating birds – notably swans – might hold the key to this question, but for the moment we might want to consider that the stones of henges 'stored' the souls. The large number of 'simulacra' faces on Avebury's megaliths cannot be simply accidental (Meaden 1999). Walking around Avebury at dawn is a magical experience as face after face looking at the rising sun 'appears' on the stones – faces that are difficult to discern later in the day.

British archaeologists have been rather dismissive of these faces, probably because they rarely walk around Avebury at dawn to see them. Standing stones and other megalithic monuments of north-western France include a number of man-modified stones which are anthropomorphic. Standing stones in Madagascar are known as *vatolahy,* literally 'man stones'. And British folklore tells of numerous stone circles, such as the Rollright circle on the Oxfordshire border or the Merry Maidens in Cornwall, which are held to be people turned to stone. While the origins of such legends are difficult to date, the prevalence of this trope does argue for some antiquity.

If, as at least some Neolithic people might conceivably have done (and Chapter Nine may convince you), I deeply believed that Avebury's massive sarsens in some way 'trapped' the spirits of my immediate ancestors, or held within them the souls of an as-yet unborn offspring, just how much more 'magical' could such an early morning saunter become?

In recent years two senior academic archaeologists have criticised their colleagues for putting too much emphasis on the importance of ancestors in British prehistory, as ethnographical parallels suggest that – while honouring the dead in various ways is important to many traditional societies – this does not usually, if at all, extend to a modern Western sense of 'ancestry' over many generations (Whitley 2002; Scarre 2008). However these professors do accept that a more focused interest in ancestors was part of British prehistory – without, it has to be said, offering too many clues as to what such a 'focused interest' might have been.

These academics are seemingly unaware of the deep relationship between kinfolk and places among Scottish Travellers – especially the places encountered on the annual cycle of travel associated with seasonal agricultural work. Stanley Robertson has evocatively described how just one of these sites – a green lane to the west of Aberdeen known as the Old Road of Lumphanan – resonates with multiple personal and cultural associations (Reith 2008: 81–92).

The worldview of the Scottish Travellers offers a different perspective on the human remains in West Kennett chambered long barrow. The primary burials were all within a few generations of each other – although 'secondary' burials and associated ritual activity continued for many hundreds of years afterwards. We do not have an accurate idea of when the construction of the Avebury henge began, but it is almost certainly later than the initial burials at the West Kennett barrow, but overlaps with these secondary burials.

While human remains were discovered in all five chambers at the eastern end of West Kennett long barrow it is unclear why so *few* people's bones were there. The bones include those from fingers and toes – suggesting that bodies de-fleshed inside the tomb, as such small bones are rarely, if ever, removed to other locations after de-fleshing has happened. But there are too few skulls and limb bones compared to other human skeletal remains. Yet in the ditches of Windmill Hill human skulls, lower jaws and long bones were recovered – but very few other parts of the skeleton, least of all the smallest bones. This strongly suggests that selected parts of people were taken from the chambered tomb to Windmill Hill.

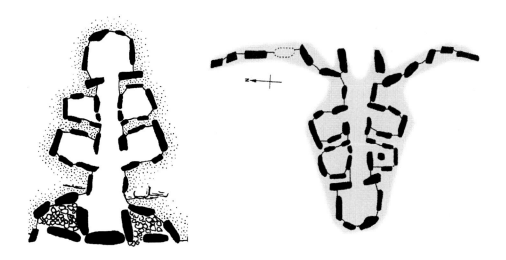

Left: *Plan of chamber and forecourt of West Kennett long barrow, with the entrance (and later blocking stones) at the east (bottom of this sketch). Is this intended to represent the head, arms and legs of a 'goddess'?*
Right: *Plan of West Kennett (without later blocking stones and with the entrance at the top of this sketch) 'interpreted' as a bucrania (ox skull with horns).*

Whatever the meaning and significance West Kennett had for its makers, it was not the final resting place for the whole community. One deformed female skull and five women with spina bifeda or spina bifeda occulta suggest that these were closely-related people, either a ruling élite or 'liminal' to the rest of society (discussed further in Chapter Nine). But a tomb – or at least ossuary chamber – the monument undoubtedly was. Yet the five chambers are also like a human figure laid down, with the five recesses corresponding to the head, arms and legs. That this is intended to be recognised as a Goddess, the Great Mother, is left in no doubt – the entrance is between the legs. West Kennett was as much a womb as a tomb. And there are plenty of parallels in non-Western religion of powerful female deities who are both live-givers and death-dealers.

Whether or not the elongated shape of the barrow, extending about one hundred metres to the west, was intended to be phallic is less certain. However, if the plan of the chambers and façade is 'flipped' then (before the blocking stones were added) there is a striking resemblance to a horned bull's head – which in turn 'echoes' the shape of the uterus and Fallopian tubes. Cattle skulls and bones were found in the tomb and elsewhere in contemporary early Neolithic sites, sometimes in ways which clearly suggest ritual rather than casual deposition. Furthermore, at the time West Kennett chambered long barrow was built and used, wild aurochs – much larger than domesticated cattle – still roamed in British woodland (they seem to have been hunted to extinction during the Bronze Age).

Kali dancing on a corpse.

Using such clues as the construction of the monument provides, West Kennett can be 'read' as the home of the yet-to-be-reborn as well as of the spirits of the dead – perhaps a clearer precursor to my more speculative 'reading' of the later Avebury henge.

I will be returning several times to how we might consider the complex meanings that Avebury might have held in prehistory. For the moment at least I am happy to leave the thought that some Neolithic people considered that, if not the bodies of their loved ones then at least their souls, made their way up the River Kennet to find their 'home' once more in or among the sarsens of the henge or its avenues. I am quite willing to accept that this is out-and-out speculation. But it is one that is matched by the current thinking of a more august academic. My ally is Professor Mike Parker Pearson of Sheffield University who, since 2003, has been Director of the Stonehenge Riverside Project. Based on remarks made by Madagascan archaeologist Ramilisonina in about 1997 regarding the function of 'standing stones' (or *vatolahy*, literally 'man stones') in traditional Madagascan culture, Parker Pearson has since made frequently-published suggestions that Stonehenge was for its makers the realm of the dead, with nearby Durrington Walls mega-henge the corresponding realm of the living. (Parker Pearson and Ramilisonina 1998).

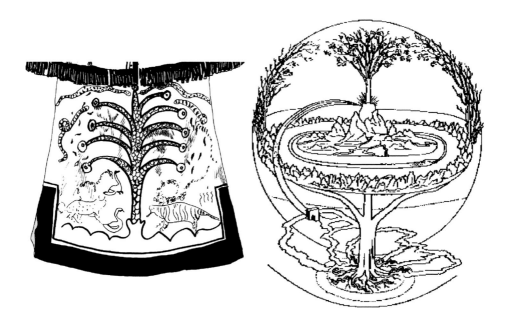

Left: *World Tree on a Siberian shaman's cloak.*

Right: *A classic depiction of the Scandinavian World Tree, Yddrassil.*

After drafting the above paragraph and needing the exact bibliographical details, I discovered that Parker Pearson has support from another person with extensive expertise about the prehistory of the Wiltshire landscape, Mike Pitts. And, in a rather obscure review that I had not previously encountered, Pitts also anticipated at least some aspects of my speculations about Avebury:

> Risking accusations of whimsy, I expanded on [Parker Pearson's] theme by pointing out that Woodhenge was to the east – the living where the sun rises – and Stonehenge to the west, where not only the sun sets but, over the horizon, was the distant source of the bluestones, which I suggested might then be envisaged as an embodiment of the land of the ancestors expressed in the living landscape. The famous midsummer alignment (of both Woodhenge and Stonehenge) indicates the rising and setting sun at their closest points on the horizon, a symbolic juxtaposition, I proposed, of the new-born and the ancestors.
>
> (Pitts 2002)

However I would not want to conclude this section with the presumption that 'cosmological' ritual journeys need be predominately about death or rebirth.

Members of Charnwood Grove calling the quarters, Beacon Hill, Leicestershire, summer solstice 2006.

Cosmological myths describe the *whole* of creation and the rituals which enact such myths therefore emulate, conceptually at least, the whole of the cosmos. As this is rather big it is often easier to focus on the centre instead – hence the World Tree, the cosmic axis or *axis mundi*, are commonly encountered in both myth and ritual. Or the sacred centre may instead be thought of as a navel or *omphalos,* as at Delphi.

Anyone who has taken part in a modern pagan ritual will be accustomed to casting a circle and calling the quarters as a way of both defining a temporary sacred space and simultaneously creating a microcosm. The oldest-surviving examples of such rites are perhaps when Taoist priests begin a ritual by pacing out a miniature world which also defines the boundaries of the sacred area. Some religious historians have argued that, as with so many other Taoist rituals, this cosmo-liturgical 'saunter' has been borrowed from Buddhist practices; others however accept that this may be one of the few Taoist practices which go back to pre-Buddhist shamanic traditions common to Central Asia and Siberia.

Interesting as such ideas of a 'sacred centre' and the relationships between ritual microcosms and the macrocosm may be, they are not the centre of attention for this book. Instead I will look at people whose sense of identity with particular places has been disrupted.

Chapter 3

Myths of Place

One type of journey which would have been familiar, at least from time to time, to prehistoric people would be that of moving to a new homeland. Usually because of human strife (perhaps caused by conflict for natural resources or the consequences of natural disasters) even settled farming communities find themselves as refugees seeking new territory. Inherently more nomadic societies would be even more mobile over the generations. Indeed, archaeologists and historians have established that all New World and sub-Saharan African tribes were repeatedly displaced further south until shortly before colonisation.

It is hardly wild speculation to assume that there were prehistoric parallels in Europe starting about 10,000 years ago as the last ice age retreated. Indeed the most recent major migration of Germanic-speaking peoples into the British Isles – principally the Angles, Saxons and Jutes – happened within historic times. Within just a few hundred years assorted Scandinavians aimed to settle throughout their new homeland – although a truce was brokered and the Anglo-Saxons retained control of south-west England. Lesser 'migrations' since then include the Normans in the eleventh and twelfth centuries and the Huguenots from the sixteenth to eighteenth centuries.

Even when detailed historical sources are not available, traditional creation myths based on epic journeys into uncharted territory reveal that such journeys were comparatively recent. The best example of such 'mythic history' can be found in Scandinavia where the early phases of settlement become the basis of myths first documented barely a dozen or so generations later. Although the time depth is much greater for Aboriginal Australians, their Dreamtime myths recount various aspects of creation which also seem to be based on migration – and are re-enacted by those walking the relevant 'song lines'. The exodus led by Moses – perhaps the memory of an event over three thousand years ago – remains a defining part of Jewish identity. And, while the original migrations may have been forgotten, the Roma people are aware that they came from outside Europe – probably not Egypt as the term 'Gypsy' infers (or even from Bohemia, as the French believed when they termed them

'Bohemians' – a word which has entered English with different connotations) but via several different migration routes from northern India.

In my own childhood during the 1960s a much more recent 'Dreamtime' myth was frequently retold on British television. Cheaply-made 'Westerns' were scripted around stereotyped images of cowboys, Indians and sheriffs, which we now – but less so then – recognise as historically inaccurate portrayals of any of these protagonists. The plots of specific films were firmly rooted in an overall narrative – the colonisation of the American Midwest a mere hundred years or less before the films were made.

Mythologised wagon trains to the Wild West frontier similarly became valorised in South Africa as the wagon treks from the coast headed northwards into the Transvaal. In the late 1960s a pilot television sci-fi programme with the working title 'Wagon Trek to the Stars' was renamed *Star Trek* and space took over as the final frontier for Hollywood-style heroes to conquer. *Star Wars* took similar mythic agendas to a more imperialising level, with the one-to-one combat of a Western shoot-out transferred into zero-gravity, and a horse called Silver now morphed into a silvery sky rocket. The main difference was, in contrast to the rampantly racist meta-narrative of Westerns, the scriptwriters for *Star Trek* were willing to transgress media prejudices – the first white man to kiss a black woman on prime-time American television was when Captain Kirk kissed Uhura.

Countless documentaries act as proxy journeys to, and through, real places we might not have the time, inclination or – in some cases – physical ability to ever make for ourselves. Add to this the prevalence of 'road movies' and train journeys as a trope in cinema, and the ubiquitous use of journeys – metaphorical or literal – in the music of songs of all eras. Western popular culture has an obsession with travel, and much of it comes packaged as 'journeys with significance'. And, seemingly, so it has always been. We can trace the precursors of such television series as *Coast* back through the early twentieth century travel writers such as H.V. Morton or Arthur Mee and his Kings England series of county-by-county guides. They too were preceded by the likes of William Cobbett in the 1820s, William Gilpin in 1770 and the previously-unprecedented *A Tour thro' the Whole Island of Great Britain* written (based on first-hand travel) by Daniel Defoe and published in several volumes between 1724–6). They all owed a debt to John Leland who toured England between 1536–45, recording the medieval monasteries shortly before Henry VIII would commit most of them – and their invaluable libraries – to Reformation-fuelled oblivion.

And the antecedents continue as far back as history itself. Izaak Walton's *Compleat Angler* of 1653 is structured around a secular 'pilgrimage' – a fishing trip – which parodies Chaucer's *Canterbury Tales* (itself hardly the most devout account of medieval pilgrimage known to us). Writing almost at the same time as Chaucer, the anonymous author of *Sir Gawain and the Green Knight* begins his poem with a 'travelogue' of Sir Gawain's journey from Snowdonia to Cheshire (this will be discussed further in Chapter Seven). Bear in mind that *Canterbury Tales* and *Sir Gawain* are the oldest surviving examples of literature in Middle English – for several centuries previously all writing had been in Norman French or Latin. Old English, the language of the pre-Conquest Anglo-Saxons, regales us with poems about travel and quests – for example, one called *The Wanderer*. And, while not part of British culture, the oldest literature of Classical Greece is Homer's mythologised travelogues, *The Iliad* and *The Odyssey*.

But establishing historical precedents for wanderlust are not the main purpose of this chapter. Rather I want to look further at the legends which we tell about the places we return to at the end of epic journeys – the places we think of as in some way 'ours'.

'If you own this place, then tell me the stories of these places'

Just as we should not take our own Western myths about the Midwest or the Transvaal at face value we should not take the settlement myths of traditional societies any more literally. A great many tribes will say that they have lived in the same place since the beginning of time, yet archaeological and historical evidence begs to differ. But what we and they all share is something which seems all-but universal – the need to create myths and legends which link a society to a place or region. It is as if in the absence of land charters and other such paraphernalia of legal ownership then knowing these narratives amounted to ownership.

This is illustrated wonderfully by, a perhaps purely apocryphal tale, which recounts how a British Columbian chief met with a British official who was claiming that the Crown now owned his tribe's lands. The chief challenged the coloniser: 'If you own this place, then tell me the stories of these places.'

Clearly the British official could not meet the chief on his own terms. But interestingly so much of the ethnology that we have for First Nation peoples was recorded because Western people were curious about the 'stories' of these traditional people – not merely the stories about their landscape, it has to be said, but the entire exotic 'package' of their lives and worldview. And we are not immune. When we move to a new home then many of us are interested in getting to know the locality. Local history societies are rarely set up and run by the 'indigenous' locals but almost always by in-comers. The writing of this book, a few months after moving to Avebury, is being interrupted by research into previously-published archaeology and history about this part of Wiltshire, and trips out along the footpaths and bridleways to explore it further for myself. I too want to find out what 'stories' the 'natives' tell about this place – even though rather too often they are the colourless narratives of academic archaeologists rather than anything as exotic as we regard ethnographical accounts.

Indeed, no matter how much some academics may wince, they too are constructing narratives about the places they research. While today's academics may hold the belief that 'the truth' of at least certain aspects of the past is but another few research grants away, we only have to look back to the 1960s and 70s, or further back to the 1920s and 30s, to see that the leading academics of those times came up with narratives which are more akin to legend or myth in their substance. Adam Stout has tellingly described how, during Mortimer Wheeler's excavations in the late 1930s at Maiden Castle near Dorchester, Wheeler interpreted the evidence for Neolithic conflict in a manner which can now be seen as a 'child of its time', as the sabres of the imminent Second World War rattled resoundingly in the pages of the national papers that at the same time followed his dig with considerable fascination (Stout 2008).

Wheeler's contemporary O.G.S. Crawford, in his 1957 book *The Eye Goddess*, revived the myth (started by Johann Jakob Bachofen in 1860) of a pan-European Great Goddess – an idea further developed by Gordon Childe (1958) and Glynn Daniel (1958). No matter how deeply-rooted this idea now is among many feminists and pagans, such speculations about a universal Neolithic goddess were dismissed as an imaginative 'myth' by a new generation of academic archaeologists in the 1980s.

We all own the past – but who 'owns' the past's stories?

I am unfairly picking on Wheeler and Crawford, as a whole book could be devoted to the myth-making of earlier generations of eminent prehistorians – with a good chance that a new chapter could be added with the passing of every academic generation hereafter. Honest error is the inevitable consequence of attempting to interpret the ambiguous available evidence. All such archaeological interpretations attempt to create some sort of overall narrative – or, at the very least, fit a minor 'dig' into the regional or national narrative currently in favour.

While few, if any, archaeological undergraduates are formally trained in the arts of storytelling and myth-making – and indeed many would consider such activities as beyond the pale of the meta-narratives of 'scientific endeavour' – the widespread popular interest in archaeology judges archaeologists on their ability to 'tell the story' of the places they excavate. Mick Aston may only have three days in real time for his team to do their 'geofiz' and trenches, but the goodies that are revealed in the holes are recruited by Tony Robinson to tell a good story about a much longer duration of time. Neither Mick or Tony presumably associate with the British Columbian chief, yet all three are bound together by the need to recount – or, for *Time Team*, in large part invent – the stories of a place. And these specific stories are located within a meta-myth which, for the Canadian elder, represents ownership of territory and, for modern day television audiences, sustains our beliefs about who 'owns' the past, who is deemed to have the necessary knowledge to 'invent' the stories for places rendered silent by the partial or total absence of documentary history.

While it is easy to see the myth-making processes alive and well a few decades ago, we can hardly expect to recover the myths or legends of people living four or more millennia ago. Unlike the British coloniser in Canada, who – in the final analysis – didn't know the stories of the place simply because he did not see it as part of his

Facing page: *Llyn Tegid (Lake Bala) – the place of Taliesin's birth, as revealed by Michael Dames in* Taliesin's Travels *'which convincingly places this god-like hero into distinctive places in the north Wales landscape.'*

The sole surviving stone of Faulkner's Circle, Avebury, April 2011. Waden Hill is in the distance and the West Kennett Avenue runs parallel with the trees in the mid-distance. Mark Gillings suggests that this spot had mythic significance in the Mesolithic which was retained well into the Neolithic.

remit to find them out, the stories told by those who created the most distinctive monuments of prehistoric Avebury have been lost to us simply because they ceased to be retold. Nevertheless, as I have already shown for West Kennett, there may be clues – and I will explore many more clues in the following chapters.

As I have previously recounted in some detail (Trubshaw 2005a Ch.8) my love of Avebury was instigated in the late 1970s by a modern day attempt at rewriting the myths and legends of its landscape. Suffice for the moment to say that it was the first two books by Michael Dames, *The Silbury Treasure* and *The Avebury Cycle* (Dames 1976; 1977), which 're-mythologised' the Avebury landscape for me. Dames' subsequent research led him to also look broadly at the myths of the Irish landscape (Dames 1992) then to both re-locate Merlin in the Welsh landscape (Dames 2002) and reinterpret the tales of Taliesin in a manner which convincingly places this god-like hero into distinctive places in the north Wales landscape (Dames 2006).

'Good enough' legends

Whether or not Michael Dames has found the 'truth' about these places and their legends is of limited interest to me (although I am well aware that Michael himself would strongly disagree with that remark). For me he has succeeded in finding associations between legend and place which are more than 'good enough' to inspire me – and others – to visit the places. And, without a shadow of doubt, since the late 1970s a great many people have visited Avebury as a result of either reading his books first-hand or encountering his ideas filtered through any number of other writers. His ideas are now rarely credited – his 'legends' have entered into the realm of seemingly-traditional lore within his own lifetime.

This book too is concerned with legendary ways of seeing the land, especially the prehistory of the upper Kennet valley. As with my responses to Dames' writings, I am less concerned with finding some sort of 'truth' about the prehistory of Avebury. Instead I will offer a number of more-or-less compatible legends which have 'good enough' associations with the landscape.

But first I will note that, once again, I have allies among the archaeological élite. Mark Gillings, of the School of Archaeology and Ancient History at the University of Leicester, took a leading role in the excavation of the mostly destroyed so-called Faulkner's Circle 750 metres to the south-east of the main Avebury henge in the bottom of the dry valley between Waden Hill and Overton Hill. The evidence for the stone circle was ambiguous, suggesting that originally there might have been a natural arrangement of stones which was modified in the Neolithic. But what was not ambiguous was the unusual amounts of Mesolithic flint revealed by the excavation. This led Gillings to suggest that the location had mythic significance in the Mesolithic which was retained well into the Neolithic (Gillings *et al* 2008: 152).

Jim Leary and David Field in their recent book about the excavations associated with the 'restoration' of Silbury Hill, significantly called *The Story of Silbury Hill*, (Leary and Field 2010) include in their 'story' suggestions that the construction of Silbury took place not, as previous archaeologists had asserted, as one 'grand plan', but in successive campaigns of construction over maybe up to about one hundred years. Clearly the construction would have been in response to a myth deeply-seated in the builders' minds. Leary and Field note parallels to myths retold during the building of Hopewellian mounds in America (presumed to have been built between 50 BCE to 400 CE); the tenth century CE Krakus mound in Krakow, Poland, and the more recent Big Horn Medicine Wheel, Wyoming.

Other than noting that the chalk, soil, sarsen fragments and organic deposits from which Silbury is constructed may have come from significant places, Leary and Field do not get beyond concluding that 'the very act of [construction] was designed to be read and comprehended by the community' (Leary and Field 2010: 121). No doubt mindful of the way fashions for archaeological interpretation have proved to be fickle, whatever Silbury's big story might have been, these authors are not venturing to suggest.

Stepping into this breach, two enthnographical parallels come to the fore. Firstly, the re-enactment of creation as an 'island' formed from the primordial mud and water. New World myths frequently link this to an 'earth-diver' bird – and we will have good reason to look to the significance of swans on the River Kennet in Chapter Nine. Secondly, a symbolic act of fertilising the land (and effective fertilisation of the thin soils is an arcane art which must be mastered for sustained arable farming on Avebury's chalk). A moment's pause should allow the realisation that these two

Silbury Hill at sunset, August 2008.

concepts are not mutually exclusive – primordial creation could indeed be a Big Bang more anthropomorphic than the cosmogonies of modern day astrophysicists, perhaps more akin to Krishna's seduction of Radha at Braj.

Could Silbury be the accumulated ritual deposits of semen-like wet chalk? Or, as Michael Dames first proposed, was Silbury thought of as the womb of a Mother Goddess? What if the Neolithic people who built Silbury thought, like the Mexica (Bernal-García 2007), that sacred mounds were 'earth wombs' from which shamans set off on supernatural journeys? Or is Silbury's own creation story a complex mix of these and other ideas, perhaps interwoven with the belief that at West Kennett chambered long barrow to the north and Avebury henge to the south (approximately contemporary with the construction of Silbury) were the realms of as-yet-to-be-reborn spirits of ancestors?

I am happy to leave all these thoughts unanswered, at least for now. Indeed, if you have any interest at all in the Avebury prehistoric monuments, I would encourage you to weave your own story for Silbury. In the final analysis it can remain only your story – but however simple or complex, it is your link to this landscape, your tentative claim to sharing 'ownership'. In the final chapter I will return to this 'active' way of re-mythologising the landscape with thoughts about all the major prehistoric monuments of the upper Kennet valley.

Chapter 4

The King Alone Stood on the Mound

In the penultimate paragraph of the last chapter I asked 'What if the Neolithic people who built Silbury thought, like the Mexica, that sacred mounds were 'earth wombs' from which shamans set off on supernatural journeys?' But I could just as easily have worded it as 'What if the Neolithic people who built Silbury thought, like the Anglo-Saxons, that sacred mounds were places for their kings to access the Otherworlds? Indeed, not just the Anglo-Saxons but the entire north Germanic culture of their homelands, which is also the basis of most Scandinavian culture and myth.

Early medieval Germanic kings were inaugurated by standing on a sacred mound. Surviving examples of these mounds in southern Sweden are often associated with stone rows. And, although some of these inauguration mounds seem to be erected for the purpose – or at least as meeting mounds – more often than not they are reused prehistoric burial mounds. (Pantos and Semple 2004; Sanmark and Semple 2008). Surviving literature reveals that the king alone stood on the mound at the time of his inauguration as he alone could 'access' the Otherworlds at this liminal and transitional time. While the origins of Scandinavian kingship rituals are not known, several academics have argued that at least one aspect of them – the royal procession around regional meeting mounds, or *Eriksgata* – may be late prehistoric (Sundqvist 2001).

The relationship between these kings and their people was considerably more complex than those of the modern day royal family. In a detailed study of the origins of Irish kingship, Daniel Bray notes:

> According to the mythic ideology of kingship, then, the king
> appears to be an unique figure in the social order, on the one
> hand at its centre and on the other set apart from it; since just as
> the cosmos and the social hierarchy took form from the body of

> the first king, so the entirety of society and the cosmos is
> incarnated in the form of the king. In other words, there is an
> identification of the king with the body politic, as well as with the
> land, in the relationship of microcosm to macrocosm. The king
> was thus expected to reflect the characteristic qualities of each of
> the classes of society, as well as perform specific duties to ensure
> the welfare of each.
>
> (Bray 1999: 108)

A newly-settled Anglo-Saxon in the Kennet valley could not help but notice probably the most impressive double stone row in Europe in proximity to Europe's largest 'Otherworld' mound, Silbury. He understandably might well think that some very important kings had been inaugurated there. He was probably wrong, but within the understanding of history he would have had, the logic was impeccable. Add to the mix the round barrows that we know as Bronze Age which overlook the Avenue from the south-eastern skyline – which would be the dead spit of the mounds his ancestors were buried under back in the homeland – and the feeling of being 'at home' would be complete. Never mind that twentieth century archaeology would show such feelings to be based entirely on false chronologies, such knowledge was nearly 1,500 years in the future.

The same Anglo-Saxon would also notice a substantial number of smaller mounds in the area – the Bronze Age barrows which still survive on Overton Down and a great many more, not least those once on the summit of Waden Hill – and mounds which we now know to be Neolithic, such as the recently-recognised 'Silbaby' (a.k.a. Waden Mound) and 'Merlin's Mound', the prehistoric mound now in the grounds of Marlborough College.

Over the last one or two hundred years historical and archaeological understanding has greatly increased the 'depth' of the past. But we, as much as the Anglo-Saxons, continue to draw on the past to legitimise our emotional or mundane links to places. Much of our perception of the past is strongly coloured by an overly-romantic nostalgia (see Trubshaw 2005a Ch.1). We know with confidence that in both Britain and south Sweden during early medieval times meeting mounds and royal inauguration sites were likely to be linked to previously-important monuments (Sanmark and Semple 2010), which has to mean that a suitably 'mythologised' version of history was being retold. The past then, at least as much as now, helped legitimise the present.

Whatever the broader facts, there is no evidence that any Anglo-Saxon kings were inaugurated on Silbury. Although an intrusive burial was excavated on its upper slopes, nothing suggests that he was thought of as a king. Indeed, by the time we have any historical record of the local kingdoms Silbury was near the frontier of a war zone – the dispute between Wessex and Mercia which led firstly to the construction of the Wansdyke just to the south, and culminated in Wessex's favour at the battle of Kempsford, on the Thames, in 802 when what we now think of as

The king alone stood on the mound. Illustration by Ian Brown.

Silbury Hill seen from the Winterbourne, May 2008. Was this once known as 'King's Hill' which became distorted to a legend about King Zel?

northern Wiltshire was added to the original Wiltonshire (based around Wilton, an important early medieval town later all-but eclipsed by the building of nearby Salisbury). Silbury probably acquired its name during this dispute when it was pressed into service as a defensive 'fort' – a *burh* or 'bury'.

And yet, and yet... In the eighteenth century local lore held that Silbury was the burial place of an otherwise unknown King Sil or King Zel. Other legends say it was not the king himself buried here but a statue of him on a horse made from solid gold. You may even see the king – or maybe just a knight – in golden armour near the mound on certain nights, according to other accounts. Hearing a local say 'King Zil' or 'King Sel' in a West Country accent would be all-but indistinguishable from hearing one say 'king's hill'. So is the King Sil who – just maybe – gave his name to Sil *burh* instead a later personification of the Old English *cyning hyll* ('king's hill')? And, if so, why did the Anglo-Saxons' think this was the king's hill? What legends were they hearing the locals tell over a thousand years before the legend of King Sil was first written down?

Curiously, if Silbury was just maybe once taboo to anyone but the most élite, history repeats itself – the élite of English Heritage have deemed it taboo for commoners to walk on its slopes, although this time to protect the various rare plants growing there rather than for any Otherworldy concerns.

*The Lia Fáil (Stone of Destiny)
at Tara, February 1991.*

Legends of kingship

Royal inauguration sites are, understandably, commonly associated with legends. And the Irish are known for good *craic* and traditional tales. Little surprise then that the Hill of Tara (Irish *Temair na Rí,* 'Hill of the Kings') has a varied collection of myths. For example, legend holds that the Stone of Destiny (Irish *Lia Fáil*) – which since 1798 has been on top of the Forradh ('Inauguration Mound' or 'King's Seat') – cries out loudly when the rightful king of Ireland places his foot upon it.

Forgive me for going slightly off topic for a moment, but inauguration 'footprints' are an interesting topic in their own rite, sorry, right (see Bord 2004). Some, such as the one at Dunadd, have visible foot-shaped depressions. Such flattish stones (typically flagstones) – they were not upright standing stones – were known in Old English as *leac*, a word related to the phallic-shaped leek plant (Welander *et al* 2003: 107; Pantos and Semple 2004: 85; Pollington 2000: 485), suggesting that *leac* had connotations of potency. 'Putting your foot in it', as the king literally did at these inaugurations, must be a bowdlerised version of an earlier, more blatant, act of potency.

Tara was one of a number of royal centres in medieval Ireland but, because of its near-central location and the survival of extensive earthworks which in part go back

The Tynwald, Isle of Man in the early twentieth century. By permission of Fortean Picture Library.

to the Neolithic, it has become the focus of national identity and associated mythmaking. Indeed much of the 'accepted history' of Tara is now being re-assessed as more akin to myth-making than accurate accounts.

At around the same time as the Irish kings were being loudly greeted by the Stone of Destiny, Scottish kings were inaugurated on the Stone of Scone Until 1296 this was originally on the summit of Boot Hill at Scone Palace. Since then it as mostly been at Westminster Abbey, where it became the Coronation Stone for British monarchs – apart from a few months walkabout starting at the end of 1950, and its transfer to Edinburgh castle in 1996.

The Stone of Scone has its fair share of history and legends – and a good mix of the two (Welander *et al* 2003). Just as interesting is the legend of Boot Hill. The name is a corruption of 'moot hill' – the name by which Anglo-Saxons knew all meeting mounds. Indeed the modern word 'meet' is the modern pronunciation of 'moot'; later the influence of Scandinavian settlement meant the Old Norse word 'thing' was also used, as for the Tynwald on the Isle of Man, still the site of the national parliament.

Facing page: *The foot imprinted on a rock at Dunadd fort. Photograph from Janet Bord's* Footprints in Stone *by permission of Fortean Picture Library.*

Legend maintains that Boot Hill is made up of all the mud brought on the boots of the Scottish barons when they came to meet the king. And, although it's not right, this is not as daft as it might seem as Boot Hill is indeed a man-made moot mound. What the barons needed to do was swear allegiance to the new king while standing on their own ground. As this is long before roads were built through most of Scotland, and sailing around the coast was at least as tricky then as it is now, the barons would have rebelled long before the king had completed his journey to all their estates. Instead, the barons brought a turf from their lands in a leather satchel and, while kneeling on this turf, swore allegiance at Scone. So Boot Hill is – in part at least – made from the turves the barons brought (and just maybe a little bit is the mud off their boots!). And, to twist this tale on itself, the Tynwald mound is also known to be made of turves brought from the four 'quarters' of the island.

Before you begin, take a hundred turves

Perhaps it was always so. Perhaps every meeting that took place at Anglo-Saxon moot mounds required those attending to bring a turf from their land. Because everyone always did it there was no need to ever write about it – the clerks of the day would safely assume that all their readers knew such things. Most of the meetings which took place at moot mounds up and down the land were the monthly 'Hundred moots'.

Hundreds were set up around 450 CE, about five hundred years before counties came into recognition around 1000 CE. They were the 'borough councils' of their time in that they brought together elected representatives from nominally one hundred dispersed 'farmsteads'. Hundreds may have been akin to borough councils but clearly the speeches were not about cutting the cost of rubbish collection. Their main purpose was agrarian, not least agreeing on how shared common grazing should be managed. This is not as simple as it sounds. Even a non-farmer can appreciate that over-grazing will lead to poor quality livestock. But *under*-grazing also needs to be avoided as this would allow unwanted shrubs and trees to take hold. Indeed the invasion of bracken in upland areas in recent decades is an example of just such under-grazing. Clear evidence that discussions about the management of commons was frequently on the 'agenda' is that many of the oldest hundred moot sites are at the centre of such inter-commoned heathland or upland woodland.

As the Anglo-Saxon population grew then hundreds were divided and otherwise redefined. By 1086, when details of hundreds can be established from the entries in the Domesday Book, some counties – such as Wiltshire – have a large number of fairly small hundreds whereas others – such as Leicestershire – have only a handful.

Leicestershire provides an example of a once-large hundred which split. The original Goscote Hundred met at Six Hills on the Fosse Way where eight parishes come together like the slices of a pie – an excellent example of an early moot in the middle of an inter-commoned grazing, in this case the upland wood pasture of the Leicestershire Wolds. However the Hundred stretched from places west of Ashby-de-la-Zouch (and now in Derbyshire) to the edge of Rutland in the south-east. At a later

The Moody Bush Stone, Leicestershire, in the late 1980s.

date, which is not known, the hundred was split into West Goscote and East Goscote. While the moot site for West Goscote is not known (but might have been the Swannimot Rocks near Whitwick) the moot site for East Goscote was marked by a standing stone which still survives near Queniborough. On the boundary of three parishes and (ignoring eighteenth century hedges) with good views to high east Leicestershire one way and across the Soar valley in another, the stone is inscribed in what may well be eighteenth century lettering with the words 'Moody Bush'. This is indeed the Moody Bush Stone. 'Moody' is a corruption of the word 'moot' and the stone clearly replaced a bush that once served as a distinctive landmark but died.

What is most interesting about the Moody Bush Stone is that it was still being used as a meeting place in the eighteenth century. A local landowner brought his tenant farmers together there for what he called a 'court'. And early folklorists tell us that

Another view of the Moody Bush Stone, Leicestershire, in the late 1980s.

each tenant brought with him a turf from their land. Each turf was placed on the top of the Moody Bush Stone and only when all turves were present did the 'court' formally commence.

I have looked hard in folklore accounts for any similar examples of turves being taken to meetings but, so far, have failed to find any. Was the eighteenth century Moody Bush Stone custom a local quirk? Or was it the continuation of a custom which was once commonplace at every hundred moot? So taken for granted that no one ever mentioned it? After all no one at the time took the trouble to explain the Scandinavian name for hundreds – wapentakes. The word – meaning ('take' or 'count' of weapons) – confirms what is known, that each man present would be carrying the spear which denoted the status of a free man. So only men bearing spears would be counted.

A similar tradition has survived in the conservative Swiss canton of Appenzell where the annual meeting to agree local legislation requires, at least according to tradition, men to be wearing a sword before they can vote. (Women literally didn't count – indeed only in 1991 were women in the canton allowed to vote on local issues.) Antique shops around the town hall square were well-stocked with antique-looking swords when I visited about twenty years ago.

Indirect evidence that the eighteenth century custom at the Moody Bush Stone might go back before the time of the similar turf custom at Boot Hill in Scone comes from the curious 'Land Ceremonies charm'. This comes down to us from a manuscript of the early eleventh century. But it was recorded as an anachronism, already a curiosity. Basically if you think your fields have been bewitched and you want them blessed then it's no good expecting the priest to put his wellies on and come over to your muddy farm. No way. Instead:

> By night before it becomes dawn take four turves from the four
> sides of the land [...] and then carry the turves to church and let
> the priest sing four masses over the turves; and one should turn
> the green side of the turves towards the altar and one should
> replace the turves where they came from before the setting of the
> sun…

The whole text is a work of 'christian magic'. Despite plenty of priestly patter (literally, as the officiant is required to recite the *Pater Noster*) it still betrays its origin in pre-christian practice. At one point there is a three-fold evocation of 'Erce, erce, erce.' As this is not the obvious corruption of a Latin word, the best guess is that it is the name – perhaps misheard – of a one-time local pagan deity, presumably an Earth Mother.

Whatever the real origins of the Land Ceremonies charm it once more suggests that turves were deeply symbolic of land rights as far back as the pre-christian period. Were the tenant farmers meeting at the Moody Bush Stone the last surviving participants in a tradition which would have been familiar at every Anglo-Saxon hundred and as far away as Scottish barons and the Manx Tynwald? Just conceivably could the turf mound tradition have an echo in the turf and chalk construction of a mound we have already discussed – Silbury? Could it – as I shall explain in Chapter Ten – go back to the beginning of time itself, or at least to rituals re-enacting primordial creation?

Chapter 5

Do you ken the queen of the Kennet or her kith and kin?

To answer this last question I need to take a close look at a river. Or at least look closely at its name. The River Kennet has been spelt in many ways but the older versions are usually 'Cunnit', although the earliest is 'Cynetan'. Older still is the name of the Roman small town on its banks, Cunetio (to the south of Mildenhall, which is to the east of Marlborough). But does the Kennet take its name from Cunetio or does Cunetio take its name from an early name for the river? River names tend to be rather slow to change and rarely take a new name from one settlement along their length. Towns do however take their name from nearby 'landmarks' – and Roman towns are no exception.

Partial confirmation that it is the river name which came first is that Kintbury (in west Berkshire, also in the Kennet valley to the east of Hungerford) also takes its name from the Kennet. There is another place called Kennett on the boundary between Cambridgeshire and Suffolk to the north-east of Newmarket. This also takes its name from the river that forms part of the eastern boundary, which flows into the fenland waterways and on to King's Lynn. Until it silted up in the fourteenth century, this was a useful trade route. Scholars are as perplexed by the origins of this East Anglian river name as they are for the longer Berkshire and Wiltshire river.

The following discussion assumes that the name Kennet is the continuation of a river name which goes back to pre-Roman times. Indeed the word seems to be part of a family of words which have a shared origin in the mists of linguistic time – a time and place which have yet to be historically established but which modern linguists refer to as 'Proto-Indo-European'. As the name suggests, the major languages of India and Europe had a shared ancestry. While the exact whys and wherefores are a matter for many scholarly debates, changes in pronunciation over the millennia can be tracked.

The site of the Roman small town of Cunetio, March 2011. The River Kennet runs between the willow trees in the mid-distance.

Until recently historical linguists and archaeologists shared the belief that in the Bronze Age Kurgan warrior-horsemen spread their culture and distinctive Indo-European language westwards. However this has been disproved by recent linguistic studies, instigated by John Colarusso's observation that –*ssos* place-name endings in the eastern Mediterranean and Balkan region were associated with settlements that existed before 5,000 BCE. If the names are that old too then a whole new time-frame opens up. This is consistent with other evidence indicating that Indo-European languages had spread to most parts of its range during the Mesolithic *at the latest.*

To all intents and purposes this means that my discussion of Proto-Indo-European words *in Britain* is referring to the language spoken here during the Mesolithic – although no doubt evolving over the millennia. But do not assume that it evolved smoothly into later Celtic 'dialects' – it is just as possible that the so-called 'Beaker People' of the Bronze Age (the Amesbury Archer, excavated in 2002, is the best- and earliest-known of such people in Britain) brought with them a Germanic language as a Celtic one, or that the Neolithic language was closer to Germanic than Celtic anyway. Think how much English has changed since the time of Chaucer and then multiply that by the time durations of prehistory – for example, early Neolithic people were as distant from their late Neolithic descendants by 1,600 years, which is two-and-a-half-times longer than since Chaucer was writing. And Chaucer's dialect, while closest to modern English, was only one of many all-but mutually unintelligible regional dialects at the time. Modern British culture has far more influences on linguistic change than the comparatively small 'insular' population of

Neolithic Britain, so rates of change are faster now – but the substantial time-scales and lack of standardising influences means that languages always evolved.

While the origins of Indo-European languages are still being argued about, what is more certain is how groups of modern words in the various Indo-European languages can be tracked back to a much smaller number of 'root' words. The expertise involved is formidable but, on the basis of the collective erudition of many decades of historical linguists, Kennet can be linked to groups of words that include:

- **ken** (with the sense 'to know', as in the nineteenth century popular song 'D'ye ken John Peel')

- **king** (*cyning* in Old English)

- **kin** (family or race; *cynn* in Old English)

- **kith** (native country, home – in the sense of the place you ken or know)

- Old English ***cennan*** 'beget, create'

- German ***kind*** ('child' – as in kindergarten)

- Greek ***gyne*** 'woman' (which gives us such modern words as 'gynaecology' and, rather indirectly, **'queen'**).

- **genus** (Before the sense of biological classification arose around 1600, the Latin and Greek origins of this word denoted 'race, stock, kind, family, birth, descent, origin, offspring. It originates with Proto-Indo-European and is related to old words which share the meaning of 'beget, birth, origin'.)

- **dogs** / kennels

- canals / ditches

The problem is that although the early versions of these words sound somewhat similar – in other words they are 'homophones', or nearly so – they cover several different Proto-Indo-European root words. So kin, cennan, kind and genus are all from the Proto-Indo-European root *gene-* meaning 'to give birth, procreate'. However ken, cunning and words meaning 'to know' are from Proto-Indo-European root word *gno-* and include know, cennan, cunning, canny, etc. Kith is a late development of this group, entering English from other languages where it had the sense 'people you know'.

As the concept of kingship came quite late to Germanic-speaking societies it is by far the 'late starter' in this list and the origins of the word are the most muddied. For reasons that will become clear later in the chapter, the origin of the word 'queen' (unquestionably from the Proto-Indo-European root *gene-*) is much more relevant than the origins of 'king'.

The facade – and later blocking stones – of West Kenett chamber tomb, November 2007.

The word 'know' comes from the Old English *cnawan* and, as may be guessed, the 'k' was not originally silent. So it would have sounded similar to 'ken' (Old English *cennan*). However, even though they sound similar, linguists suggest that these are derived from two different Proto-Indo-European words. Certainly the 'biblical sense' of 'to know' is not attested before about 1200. The modern word 'know' has three precursors in Old English – *cnawan, cennean* and *wit*. The latter, now used in such expressions as 'a witty remark', originally had a much broader sense of 'knowledge, understanding, intelligence, mind'. The national parliament of England in Anglo-Saxon times was called the *witan* – 'the meeting of the wise'. As the origins and modern meanings of the word 'know' are distinct from 'ken', I will use the latter rather than the former in this book, even though at first glance it may appear rather quaint usage.

And, yes, this group of words is also related to the word 'cunt'. The earliest written record of this indelicate locution was around 1230 and refers to an Oxford street evocatively called 'Gropecuntlane' (Briggs 2009); this usage suggests that 'cunt' was an established colloquialism by this time. Presumably it is a slang derivation from the Latin *cunnus* ('vulva'). The one-time word for rabbit, 'coney' (pronounced to rhyme with 'honey' or 'money'), has quite a different origin but became a dialect word, 'cunny', that was interchangeable with the word 'cunt' so too was dropped from polite conversation and the popular name for rabbits became 'bunnies' (a name formerly used for squirrels). Confused? Just think how we use the word 'pussy' today...

As a pure aside, when researching the etymology of 'cunt' I discovered that the word 'berk', nowadays used as a mild term of disaffection, is a contraction of the rhyming slang 'Berkshire hunt'. Presumably it is nothing more than coincidence that the river Kennet, which is a homophone, runs through Berkshire... Several popular authors have suggested that Kennet is not simply a homophone of 'cunt' but actually cognate. This could only be true if Kennet as a name is no older than the Germanic languages in which 'cunt' occurs – it could not have come through Celtic languages.

As the early sense of 'kith' is 'native country, home' some of you may be wondering if the word 'country' is also derived from these cognate words. It is not, simply a homophone which enters English in the mid-thirteenth century (with the sense of 'district, native land') as a borrowing from the Old French *contree* which in turn is a contraction from the Vulgar Latin *terra contrata,* 'land lying opposite' or 'land spread before one' (the Latin word *contra* meaning 'opposite, against', as in modern English coinages such as 'contraflow'). In the manner of thirteenth century aristocratic affectation, the French loan word replaced the Old English word 'land' which had a similar meaning.

While we're following through with these words and usages, the alliterative phrase 'kith and kin' is also fairly late (first recorded towards the end of the fourteenth century) and originally had the sense of 'country and kinsmen'.

'Kin' seems to be close to another Old English word, 'beget'. Indeed, deliberately using what was already an anachronism, the King James' translation of the bible tells that 'Abraham begat Isaac, and Isaac begat Jacob, and Jacob begat Judas and his brethren' and indeed a number of other lineages linked by the same word, 'begat'. These biblical accounts read as if only the men mattered to family history. Clearly that is not the case and Issac's mother also begat Issac, just as Issac's wife begat Jacob – not to mention any sisters Jacob might have had, who otherwise remain outside this account. The matriarchal line of descent matters at least as much as patriarchal lineage – which is probably why the Old English words *cynn* and *cennan* ('kin' and 'beget') sound so similar.

And, if for a moment we can ignore the insulting manner in which the word 'cunt' is normally used and instead consider it – as it might once have been – a 'neutral' term for the place from which we are all naturally begat, then this word too fits naturally alongside *cynn* and *cennan*.

The curious case of canines

At first glance the appearance of the word 'dog' seems out of place. Indeed it is not the English word 'dog' but the Latin word *canis* which belongs here. Dogs are distinct for their long 'canine' teeth, although using the word 'canine' to refer to dogs rather than teeth is a modern usage in English. As an example of how words evolve over many centuries, our word, hound, shares the same etymological origin even though 'canine' and 'hound' sound so different. We also use the word 'kennel' as a synonym for 'dog house'. Kennel enters English via the Norman French *kenet,*

Hound of Annwn. Illustration by Ian Brown.

meaning 'little dog' – which makes sense if you know that the modern French word for dog, *chien*, was once pronounced with a hard 'k' and '-ette' is the diminutive.

The oldest evidence for domesticated dogs is a skull and teeth from Kesslerloch Cave in Switzerland, discovered in the nineteenth century and recently dated to about 12,000 BCE. Another jaw bone, from a human grave at Oberkassel, in Germany, is about 11,000 BCE. Earlier dates for domesticated dogs have been claimed but these are more probably wolves.

By the Neolithic dogs had been man's best friend for over 5,000 years. So was the upper Kennet valley famous for its little dogs, '*kenets*'? The Welsh word for dog, *cwn*, (pronounced 'koon') fits the first syllable but I have no evidence for the –*et* ending prior to Norman French. Dogs were one of the first animals to be domesticated in the early Neolithic (and perhaps before then they symbiotically associated with humans as scavengers or hunters). A fireside hound would be a must-have companion in the early Neolithic fashions for home. And, whether or not that home was in the Kennet valley, its name most likely alliterated with 'ken-'.

As dogs are scavengers later myths would see them as Otherworldly psychopomps assisting the spirits of the dead to their final abode (Stone 2005). Indeed in cultures where excarnation was commonplace – such as the Neolithic – scavenging dogs may have been observed all-too clearly 'transforming' a corpse. In Welsh myth and lore, the Hounds of Annwn (Cwn Annwn) were the spectral hounds of the otherworldly paradise, Annwn. When escorting souls on their journey to the Otherworld they might be led by a fearsome hag called Mallt-y-Nos, 'Matilda of the Night'. However the same hounds are also referred to in Welsh folklore as Cwn Mamau ('Hounds of the Mothers'). This is a curious mix of death and birth, all the more curious because the hounds of Annwn were seemingly albinos – snow-white with red ears. So much curiosity that I will devote a section of Chapter Nine to exploring it further, after introducing yet more relevant ideas.

For the moment I will instead draw attention to a little-known homophone of our word 'kennel', also once spelt 'kennel'. This word goes back at least to Middle English, when it meant a 'gutter' or 'channel'. Indeed it becomes our words 'channel' and 'canal'. So was the upper Kennet valley famous for its watery channels – the river courses? Or the sometimes water-filled ditches of the henge and Silbury Hill? I really wouldn't want to push that suggestion too hard but whatever word the people who dug the amazingly deep ditches at Avebury used to describe the outcome of their efforts was as a word as likely to have sounded like 'kennel' as 'ditch' or 'dike' (both from the same Proto-Indo-European root word).

The composite sense of Kennet

Some of the modern English and Old English words which are cognate with Kennet, and their homophones, have counterparts in Celtic languages such as Welsh. This is especially clear for the cognates of 'know', 'family' and 'race' – and dogs. We are left with the sense of an earlier root word that seemingly encompasses:

Avebury henge ditch from the south-west sector of the bank, November 2010.

- a race of people with a shared bloodline;
- a country one knows well and thinks of as home;
- the ownership or 'kingship' of that country and its people;
- dogs.

Clearly these meanings are not exclusive but have an overlapping sense for which we have no modern word. However was this composite sense shared by the earliest forms of 'Kennet'? I have no way of proving this – but you have no way of disproving me either, so let us 'play' with this composite sense of Kennet for a few more paragraphs.

What this collective sense of kin/kith/king reflects is akin to the tribal and ancestral ties which prehistoric people had with the landscape. I am willing to concede that our concept of kingship probably originates in the Iron Age and would be anachronistic in the Bronze Age and Neolithic. But some sort of élite – whether regal or spiritual – is represented in early Neolithic burial practices, so more modern notions of kingship presumably evolve out of this earlier concept for which we have no surviving word.

Indeed, it is curious that none of these cognates seem to have a spiritual aspect. For Mesolithic and Neolithic people the land was not just 'home', not just where 'life happened', it was where all their food and all other resources came from. The same is still strictly true today, although we tend to focus more on the subsequent 'processing' of natural resources than their origin. But if you are fully aware that everything about your life and survival is intimately connected to the land then it is a very small leap of faith to assume that the same landscape is shared with the gods and goddesses. The same intimate association between the land and the people (the 'kith and kin' of the later expression) would have extended into the realms of the deities too. Did they too walk the land, as too the spirits of your ancestors?

Or was it rather that you walked *on* the deity – on the body of a goddess who was literally the earth mother? A goddess whose name was so sacred we still (although for seemingly different reasons) regard it as taboo – a goddess whose name sounded either like Cunt – or Kennet? I have no stronger reason for making this assertion other than it completes the interwoven set of meanings for the kith/kin/king/cunt group of cognate words in a manner that seems to reflect best the relationship prehistoric people – especially those of the early Neolithic – most probably had with their land.

Perhaps – and maybe I am again stepping where the more angelic fear to tread – the concept of kingship goes back before male-dominated majesty. Should we not be looking at the origins of the word 'king' but instead a word which denotes an élite honoured as much for being sacred as for their regal-ness, and much less gender-specific? Could the word be closer to the modern sense of 'sovereignty', especially the way sovereignty can be used to denote close association with a county – or, in recent centuries, an empire?

Enter the queen

Indeed, are we not looking so much at the king as his consort, the queen? The answer has to be a resounding 'Yes'. Despite the vagaries of English spelling, phonetically this is 'kween'. And the origins are clearly with the Proto-Indo-European word *gwen*, meaning 'woman or wife', with some scholars supposing that the sense was 'honoured woman'. As if we need confirmation, the Sanskrit versions of this word are *janis* 'a woman' and *gná*, 'wife of a god, a goddess'.

Somewhere in this word soup are lost the origins of 'quim'. It appears in written English in the 1610s as slang for vulva but is of unknown origin. While it may have descended from Old English words such as *cynn* and *cennan*, more likely it is related more closely to the Old English word *cwen*. From its original meaning of 'wife', early on in Old English it split into two more specific meanings – the wife of a king (modern 'queen') and a now-archaic word 'quean' which starts life meaning' "young, robust woman' but within the Anglo-Saxon era has shifted to denote a female serf or prostitute. By the sixteenth and seventeenth centuries quean had only the sense of a woman or girl who showed casual or improper behaviour. (For those who really need to know everything, using 'queen' to denote homosexuals appears to originate in 1930s Australia and is presumably a misspelling of 'quean'.) The absence of early written forms means scholars cannot be certain that it goes back much before the late sixteenth century. But it certainly sounds like it is one of the ken/kin/kith/king/queen/cunt and Kennet family. So, on the basis that if it looks like a

A man and cow, Bronze Age rock art, Bohuslän.

duck and sounds like a duck, then very probably it is a species of duck – quim appears and sounds like a 'species' of the Proto-Indo-European word which gave us, among other words, queen.

Do early records of inauguration rites betray any evidence of seemingly much older customs? Customs associated with the succession of tribal power, enacted at most every few years and of profound importance to the society, are exactly the sort of rites which change slowly. The British coronation customs, for example, are largely built up of symbolic objects and rites which go back many centuries. Indeed historians have long presumed that the early medieval accounts of Irish kings symbolically 'marrying' the (female) sovereign of the land as part of their inauguration rites may be archaic. The evidence is a late twelfth-century account by Giraldus in his *Topography of Ireland* in which he describes the Irish king mating with a white mare then bathing in a broth made from her flesh. It certainly seems archaic. It seems very akin to the ritual marriage of the tutelary goddess Aine and ritual marriage associated with Cnoc Aine in County Limerick (Binchy 1958, cited in O Duinn 2008: 211

It also has direct parallels to Vedic inauguration rites, the asvamedha, although here it is the queen who slept symbolically with a freshly-sacrificed stallion, which was later cooked for a communal feast. But does this go back further than that, before horses were status symbols, before the sort of élites we might recognise as kings? Any precedents would involve cattle, rather than horses. Indeed Bronze Age rock art at Bohuslän in Sweden seems to depict just such a copulation with a cow.

While we have ritually-deposited cattle skulls from the Neolithic, we have no indication of the élite symbolically mating with them as part of the ritual. Presumably the élite sacrificed cattle each November. Perhaps these rituals involved wonderful polished axe heads – many of which have little in the way of wear marks – and so visibly anticipate the elaborate maces of modern sovereigns and mayors. If so, are the ditches of the henges to keep cattle in – a herd of all the tribe's wealth gathered together once a year for a ritual hunt? And if I were taking part in such a 'bull fight', having plenty of hefty earth-fast stones to dodge behind might just save me from becoming a human sacrifice to the bull-deity.

A 'grey' horse.

Giraldus refers specifically to a white horse – and country folk to within living memory would always refer to such animals as 'greys', no matter how washing powder white they looked – so maybe in the age of kings an even earlier association with whiteness assimilated with the then new-fangled horse cult. Were these horses in some way associated with other sacred white animals – such as the fabled red-eared snow-white hounds of Annwn?

Was this whiteness an attribute of sovereignty that emerged in the Neolithic or maybe even earlier? And was the white chalk of the Avebury area significant because of this? As with many of my speculations, I will return to them later. Indeed, I will come back to the complex association of ideas which interweave between kingship/sovereignty/queens, kith/ken/kin, cunt and Kennet.

Apis, Isis and Osiris

Horses as 'cult' animals do not significantly predate the Iron Age. Before then the cult animals were cattle, as the finds of numerous ox skulls and cattle bones at British Neolithic monuments attest. But those finds remain mute about the significance and rituals associated with them. The oldest evidence for the myths associated with bull worship are recorded in Egyptian hieroglyphics and 'coffin texts'. The depiction of the ruler of Egypt as a bull goes back to the Predynastic Period (starting around 3,100 BCE) and is presumably older. The bull god, known at that time as Mnevis, was black and a herald of the sun gods Re and Atum.

There are various depictions of an annual ritual in which the ruler led four calves up a staircase and across a threshing floor, later the calves were led to an ithyphallic statue of Amun-Re and, presumably, sacrificed. The oldest known such depiction appears in Old Kingdom times (approximately 2,700 to 2,200 BCE) and, remarkably,

Egyptian women lifting their garments in devotion to the bull Apis at the Memphis temple. Illustration by Winifred Milius Lubell.

continues – although the god changes to various local deities – for the following three thousand years (Mysliwiec 2004: 16).

Later the sacred bull was known as Apis and his cult was associated with fertility – Egyptian women went on pilgrimages to his cult centre at Memphis and lifted their dresses to reveal their genitals and 'womb'. Several clay statuettes have been discovered showing this gesture. Furthermore, when a pharaoh's body was mummified his penis was mummified separately and regarded as the phallus of Apis. This 'scared relic' was essential to ensure the fertility of the ruler, even after death.

The significance of these relics was shared with the cult of Osiris, a god associated with springtime 'resurrection' whose legends recount how his dismembered body was cast into the Nile and, thanks to the efforts of Isis, his body was brought back together – apart from his phallus. This did not stop Isis, in the guise of a falcon, ritually mating with a recumbent Osiris equipped with a suitable replacement. The resulting child of this union was Horus, and the many statues of Isis with the infant Horus were the precursors of the christian iconography of the Virgin Mary with the child Jesus.

In the Late Period Plutarch reports that the Phallus of Osiris was a key aspect of annual ritual processions; these rituals seem to be the precursors to the Greek's Eleusinian Mysteries (Mysliwiec 2004: 60). Such fertility associations have survived the millennia. 'As late as the nineteenth century, archaeologists found that when an object representing a bull was unearthed, Arab women approached so that they might sit on this fertility symbol.' (Mysliwiec 2004: 77)

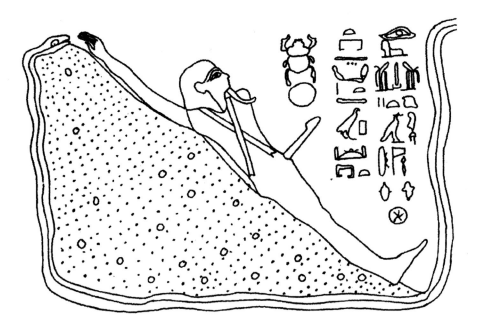

The resurrection of Osiris on the slopes of the hill of Khepri. Drawing of a painting on the Papyrus Hor-Uben B (Twenty-first Dynasty, circa 1000 BCE). After Mysliwiec 1998.

Interestingly the ritual copulation between Osiris and Isis takes place on the slopes of the hill of Khepri, another deity of resurrection. Some depictions of the act (or at least the ithyphallic Osiris without Isis) show him reclined on this slope. And this hill is linked to the legends of primordial creation – the primeval mound at the beginning of time.

While clearly ancient Egyptians are not the precursors to early Neolithic people in Britain, they are branches from the same cultural roots. After all, all the sheep, goats and domesticated cattle in Neolithic Britain are descendants of animals first domesticated in what is now Iraq. Likewise, pottery-making and farming starts in the same area. So, as myths and legends are just as capable of being imported as livestock and 'technologies', are these Egyptian bull – and phallocentric – cults not too far removed from ideas also prevalent in Britain around the same time? I will look at this question again in Chapter Nine.

Where was Kennet?

For the moment I want to look in more detail at what we can say more-or-less for certain about the word Kennet. Kennet enters the historical records not only as the name of the river. It also described a rectangular block of land which was later divided into the parishes of Avebury, Overton, Winterbourne Monkton, Beckhampton, and both East and West Kennett. Much of what was later part of Avebury was probably still known as Kennet(t) in 1086, as were East and West Kennett.

The confluence of the Sambourne (left) and Winterbourne (right) to the west of Avebury henge and village, February 2011.

The Roman road that predates the modern A4 forms the boundary to the south – although at one time it may have continued southwards to the chalk escarpment. The split between Avebury and Overton parishes follows the line of the Ridgeway, although prehistoric field systems are crossed by the route of the Ridgeway so this boundary cannot predate the fields. Modern byways also define the western side and also run close to what may have been the northern boundary. However these routeways presumably came first and the boundaries were drawn up according to these existing landmarks. In the north-west corner of this unit of land sits Windmill Hill, the early Neolithic enclosure (once called 'causeway camps') which is approximately contemporary with West Kennett chambered long barrow and which seems to have been abandoned soon after construction of the henge started.

Although clearly known collectively as the Kennett before the successive splits into modern parishes, what is curious is that – a part from the south-eastern corner where the River Kennet separates Avebury parish from West Kennett – the rivers which largely define this territory are not now known as the Kennet. They are the Winterbourne (once known as the Lambourne), running more or less north to south from Winterbourne Monkton, and the Sambourne, a lesser stream which runs roughly west to east – Windmill Hill stands above the shallow valleys associated with these two seasonal streams. Their confluence is, significantly, just to the west of Avebury village, a few hundred metres away from the henge and close to the line of the lost Beckhampton Avenue. From this confluence the river flows in a narrower valley southwards for about 1.5 kilometres (running close to Silbury) to the spring at

The stepping stones at the source of the River Kennet, March 2011. Water from Swallowhead Spring (just visible through the curved branch of the willow tree) joins with the Winterbourne (flowing from the north) to form the Kennet (flowing eastwards, to the left of this photograph.

Swallowhead, where it turns sharply eastwards and makes its way parallel to the A4 towards Marlborough, Hungerford and Newbury, eventually joining the Thames at Reading.

The Kennet is one of a number of tributaries of the Thames, although the only one flowing from due west. Anyone looking at a modern Ordnance Survey map may well think that the River Thames above its confluence with the Thame at Dorchester-on-Thames was once known as the Isis, as the maps state 'River Thames or Isis'. Indeed, until recently, residents of Oxford used to refer to the stretch of the Thames which runs through the city as the Isis. In the nineteenth century it was widely held that from its source all the way to the confluence with the Thame the Thames was originally known as the Isis, and that Thames is a contraction of 'Thame-Isis'.. However modern scholarship differs, and regards the Latin name for the Thames, Tamesis, as a borrowing from the Brittonic name for the river. Whether or not this name was used all the way to its sources in the Cotswolds is less clear, but any earlier names for the upper stretches have not been recorded.

Windmill Hill from the north, February 2011.

The tributaries of the Thames near its source in the Cotswolds are the Churn, Coln and Leach. While these are clearly important within the Thames basin, we should not allow the convention of calling the river network the Thames to blind us to the significance of the Kennet as one of the more important tributaries, especially as it links the estuary to an area of the West Country quite separate to the Cotswolds sources. And the predominately eastwards flow all the way from Swallowhead to the North Sea makes the Thames-Kennet a unique watercourse in southern Britain.

Getting lost in the woods

At the risk of going further off topic, the Savenake Forest – once a much larger area of woodland straddling the Kennet valley on the Wiltshire/Berkshire border – just might take its name from the pre-Celtic word which comes down to us as 'Severn', presumably once meaning 'river' in that language. In Ireland the river Lee that flows through Cork was formerly known as the Sabrann. The modern Welsh name for the River Severn, Afon Hafren, suggests the earlier form was probably closer to *hafren*. Geoffrey of Monmouth recounts how a princess called Hafren drowned in the river Severn, which was then named after her. This might be the last vestiges of legends about a tutelary river deity called Hafren.

The original extent of the Savernake Forest linked up with the Forest of Chute on the Wiltshire/Hampshire border. Together this made an almost impenetrable border zone around the chalk uplands of the Marlborough Downs and Avebury area. Anyone travelling to Avebury from the east along the Kennet would come up through this extensive 'wild wood' before reaching the Marlborough Downs, distinctive for the vast numbers of sarsen boulders which then all-but covered the ground.

At the centre of the land

The original land unit known as Kennett encompasses all the major prehistoric monuments – Avebury henge, both avenues, Silbury Hill, the Sanctuary, Windmill Hill, Beckhampton and West Kennett chambered long barrow, and several other (but less well-known) long barrows. The henge at Avebury is close to the centre of this Anglo-Saxon land unit. Possibly it is the south-eastern quarter of a much earlier and larger land unit which had Windmill Hill near its centre – but that has to be undiluted speculation (although it mirrors minor folk regions in Anglo-Saxon England with their well-developed 'heartland' surrounded by hunting territory and summer pasture (Hooke 1998).) Whatever the extent of the original land unit, is this the 'kith' – in the sense of 'native country, home' – which my composite sense of Kennet alludes to?

Whoever got together for seasonal feasting at Windmill Hill – and archaeologists agree that it would only have been a seasonal settlement, not a permanent one – were making the transition from hunter-gathering lifestyles to early farming. The vast number of butchered bones in the ditches of Windmill Hill reveal they were rearing early domesticated breeds of cattle, sheep, goats and pigs. But we should think more of 'ranching' these herds in open landscape rather than anything resembling modern farming in fields. After each seasonal get-together the different family groups would set off in different directions, with little expectation of seeing each other until the next periodic gathering. I find it easy to believe that when everyone got together again – perhaps just once a year for a few weeks – there would be a great sense of 'homecoming', a return to the tribe's symbolic centre.

Archaeological evidence suggests that one family at least travelled to and from the Mendips. On that basis the Cotswolds, Vale of Pewsey and the Lambourn valley seem likely territories too. The high ground of these sarsen-strewn downs (the summit of Windmill Hill is 187 metres above sea level – for comparison Stonehenge and Marden henge are about 100 metres above sea-level) would have been on the margins of all these hunting and grazing lands, a logical place for annual or seasonal gatherings.

When Avebury henge took over in the wake of Windmill Hill's steady demise then this focus simply shifted from a hilltop to the more sheltered valley below. The reasons were possibly not simply pragmatic – more probably they were a response to changing religious beliefs and practices that meant being nearer to water.

We know nothing about the rites that would celebrate those born since the last meeting, or how grief was expressed and shared for those who had died in the meantime. But we need only think of modern day seasonal family 'get togethers' (such as birthdays and Christmas) as well as rites of passage which are not seasonal (christenings, weddings and funerals) to get some idea of how emotionally-engaged such gatherings always are. Surely it was these shared experiences at Windmill Hill or the henge which are the 'lived experience' of my composite meaning of Kennet.

Pedantically, the sense of 'kingship' may have been alien to the Windmill Hill people, but the later Neolithic provides evidence for the emergence of an élite, so presumably merges effortlessly into this sense of place. Perhaps the relocation from Windmill Hill to Avebury henge is, at least in part, a result of such social changes.

One thing we can be sure is that this strong sense of identity with the upper Kennet valley and its tributaries would have been enlivened with a rich repertoire of myths and legends. In the final chapter I will speculate even more wildly about the possible nature of these tales.

How big was the Kennet?

For the moment I would just like to consider a counter-argument to this idea of the Kennet being an area of land centred on either Avebury henge or, in a possible earlier version, Windmill Hill. Should we instead be looking along the whole length of the Kennet towards modern-day Reading and regarding this as part of this 'kith' too?

Visitors coming from London or Berkshire are likely to come along almost the same route – the A4 follows the Kennet valley and the M4 meanders along the northern slopes of this valley. But prehistoric visitors to the Kennet 'country' did not come by main roads. They probably didn't even come by land. The easiest way to get here would have been along the river itself. As already discussed in Chapter One, Wiltshire is at the head of rivers flowing east, north-west and south. While the land to the north, west and south of the upper Kennet valley would presumably continue to have been important to Neolithic people, the Kennet valley to the east would have been the most important for its resources and as a trade route.

We know that Bronze Age people made many ritual deposits in rivers. We know this because the bronze objects – often high-status weapons – have survived. For reasons that have yet to be understood, such finds are most common in rivers flowing eastwards. The significance of eastward flow was retained into early christianity as this Anglo-Saxon cure confirms:

> If cysts pain a man at the heart, let a virgin go to a spring which runs straight east, and draw forth one cup full, with [the direction of?] the current, and sing thereon the Creed and Pater noster… do this so you have three [cupfuls]; do this nine days, soon he will be well
>
> (Jolly 1996: 117)

East has remained a sacred direction – with few exceptions churches are orientated so the congregation faces east. Indeed the word 'orientation' is from 'Orient', itself from the Latin *orientem* 'the rising sun, the east'.

Above: *Looking east along the River Kennet from the Swallowhead stepping stones, February 2011. The Winterbourne is flowing into the Kennet from the left; water from Swallowhead Spring can just be seen bottom right.*

Facing page: *Looking east along the River Kennet from a few hundred yards downstream from the photograph above.*

While this preferential interest in rivers lit dramatically by the rising sun may be a Bronze Age innovation, quite possibly it continues an earlier custom for which archaeological evidence is absent. Maybe the remains of the dead were consigned to the flow, in the way the Ganges and other major Indian rivers still carry away the ashes or corpses of Hindus.

Whatever the ultimate age or associations of this custom, the Kennet with its consistently eastward flow to the Thames, and almost direct continuation to the estuary, must have been one of the pre-eminent of such watercourses. And if the eastward flow of the river seemingly had spiritual significance, what was the significance of paddling upstream to its source near Avebury? And why, as I will outline in Chapter Nine, are water birds such as swans so important in myths around the world?

For the moment I am happy to leave open this ambiguity about the extent of the Kennet and the possibilities of complex spiritual symbolism. Indeed, my speculations in the final chapter offer one way of 'resolving' what is perhaps not necessarily a conflicting sense of place and identity.

Chapter 6

By Green Hill to the Broad Ford

I have so far concentrated on just one place-name, Kennet. But clearly everywhere significant has a name – and if somewhere wasn't previously significant enough to other people, we invent 'nicknames' for places. After a time we taken most place-names for granted, and usually take them as just that – names – and forget that most once had literal meanings. Indeed the shift in language since the names originated (usually in the Anglo-Saxon era) often means the literal meaning has been obscured.

While a modern nickname such as 'Spaghetti Junction' might just make a hungry driver think of a plate of pasta, few people who turn off near there for Aston will think of a farmstead notable for its ash trees. Likewise, a curious motorist might wonder if Swindon was once the hill with pigs – indeed it was – but you would have to be both curious and something of an expert in Old English and place-names to recognise Chisledon to the south as not the hill where chisels were once made but, instead, the gravely valley (from *dene*, not *don* 'rounded hill' as current spelling suggests). The Old English word *cisel*. 'gravel or sand' also gives the famously long and pebbly Chesil Beach on the Dorset coast its name.

Many English settlement names end in *–ton, -ham* or *–ingham*. In the former Danelaw area they also end in *–by*. All these endings denote some sort of settlement – probably more of a farmstead, even though Old English *tun* eventually evolves into modern English 'town', and the Scandinavian *–by* retains some of its sense in the word 'bylaws', the regulations specific to a place. *Ham* is the antecedent to the modern word 'home' but meant something more physical and akin to 'house' to the Anglo-Saxons. Many, but by no means all, these endings are compounded with someone's name. Indeed X–*ingham* denotes the home of the people of X. Every English county has numerous examples of these place-names derived from someone's name – if you are not already familiar with some of them in your area then do a little homework with place-name dictionaries.

However my interest in this chapter has little to do with these places which take their name from one-time residents. Instead I want to look at the others – the ones which *describe* the place, such as Swindon, Chisledon or even Spaghetti Junction. Yes, even though Anglo-Saxons were undoubtedly ignorant of pasta, they too used metaphorical references when naming places, as we shall see when we discuss Hoton/Houghton names.

Before I begin a closer examination of Anglo-Saxon descriptive place-names perhaps I should give you some indication of this discussion's destination. I am revisiting a notion briefly expressed in Chapter One – how did we know how to get to far-away places before maps? If you knew that you had to go over the Green Hill (modern Grendon) to the Broad Ford (modern Bradford), then temporarily join another path (Anstey) before branching off to the settlement in the dead-end valley (Compton) and so on, then the journey would be almost as easy as following a printed map. Clearly the longer the journey the greater the difficulty memorising all the names in the correct order. That little problem I consider too in due course.

Pay attention to the detail

Modern development often hides the feature which gave these places their distinctive names. But even before such changes, did people really navigate this way? The honest answer is that we do not know for certain. But the research of place-name experts Margaret Gelling and Ann Cole in recent years have been broadly accepted by their academic counterparts. More work is needed to sort out the finer details but there is a clear association between certain place-names (notably Stretton, Moreton, Drayton, Grafton, Caldecot, Kingston) and known roads, while Eaton names link with waterways (Cole 2007).

Anglo-Saxons had over twenty different names for hill. That's more words than Eskimos reputedly have for snow. Words commonly used by Anglo-Saxons for hills are *hyll, don* and *down, cliff, shelf, ridge, edge, side, ness* (headland), *hoh* (heel-shaped hill), *over/ora, tor, knoll, cop and low*. Less common are *peak, upp, heafod* (head), *bile* (beak), *heap, hat, hlith, hrycg, hyrst* (wooded hill). What is striking about this list is that none of these words are exact synonyms – in other words, a *hyll* is not the same shape as a *don*, and a *cliff* is distinct from both a *shelf* or *ridge*, and so forth (Gelling 1984; Gelling and Cole 2000).

The distinctive shape of hoh *(heel) and* over/oare *place-names.*

An *over* is a long ridge which drops down with the sort of shape of an upturned canoe. Overton Hill to the south-east of Avebury is an excellent example, with the distinct curve descending steeply to the Kennet valley – a path at the side of the Sanctuary allows you to follow exactly down this slope. The word *over* was used mostly in the midlands, Sussex and Somerset. In southern England the Latin loan word *ora* was more common. One such place, Oare, is a few miles to the east of Overton Hill near Avebury, on the main road running south from Marlborough towards Pewsey.

A *hoh* – heel-shaped hill – needs a little explanation. Imagine a giant lying face down, then look at his feet. His heel forms a distinctive shape as it emerges from the ankle and descends to his sole and toes. It's that shape which the 'ho' of Houghton and Hoton place-names describes – as well as places which are not settlements, like Plymouth Ho! If there is more than one *hoh* then the plural is *hohs* – which is how the north Leicestershire village of Hose got its name.

Anglo-Saxons also had several different words for valleys – *dene, dale, coomb* (short, broad, sometimes 'blocked' valleys), *hope* (secluded valley), *glen* (shallow valley), *gil / gryfja* (deep, ravine-like valley), *gnipa* (steep hillside – for example Knipton in Leicestershire), *snoc* (projection), *vale, bottom, clough, chine*. Once more these are not synonyms – rather they are nuanced descriptions which nevertheless would be meaningful to someone new to the area. By paying attention to the detail of the landscape then these place-names would – at least when they were coined – accurately describe their specific location.

Similarly there are about a dozen distinct ways of referring to woodland and clearings: *bearu, denn, graf, holt* (usually a single-species wood), *hyrst, sceaga/shaw, skogr, wald, wudu, frith, lundr.* Similarly *leah, roth* and *thveit* describe different clearings. Watery places and sources of water too have various different names: *bourne/burn, brooke, well, mere, moss, marsh, waesse, fleet, funta/font, pool, pyll* and *seath.*

Furthermore certain types of settlement have specialist functions – these include those already noted as especially prevalent on known roads: Stretton, Moreton, Drayton, Grafton, Caldecot and Kingston. To this list we can add places which are where they are for other reasons but are distinctive, such as Burtons (small 'garrisons' established by King Alfred in the ninth century to defend important towns and river crossings from Viking attacks).

Anywhere called Chester or ending in –*cester* would also have been distinctive, at least in the earlier part of the Anglo-Saxon era, as here the walls and ruins of Roman towns were still standing. Later generations of Anglo-Saxons would rob the stone and subsequent generations would rebuild towns and modern cities over the site. But some of these towns – such as Cunetio near Marlborough, mentioned in the previous two chapters – never did get rebuilt. There the traces of centuries of domestic rubbish – organic matter and ash – made the soil distinctively dark. Some of these places, and Cunetio is no exception, left a record in the field names. The site of Cunetio is known as Black Field. While not all black place-names denote Roman sites (a black

The biggest surviving part of the Roman town of Wroxeter. The –cester ending has been disguised by modern spelling.

hill is more likely to be a former beacon site) this appellation too would have been informative for Anglo-Saxon navigation.

Vegetation can provide landmarks. Roman towns left their traces in the vegetation too – both thistles and nettles grow best in the nitrogen-rich disturbed soils associated with settlements. And both Thistleton (Rutland) and Nettleton (Wilts) are associated with Roman small towns associated with temples. Around the country are several Gartree Hundreds. These are named after either a 'spear-shaped tree' or, more probably, a distinctively damaged tree – the 'goitre tree'. Also Old English are 'shire oaks' (likewise meeting places, this time for the later shires) and variants on 'speech oak' (also meeting places). In post-Reformation times Gospel Oaks would adopt a similar role.

A suitably-distinctive tree in about the right place will become a landmark. But most landmark trees have been deliberately planted at some time – or at least an old tree 'resurrected' by a young sapling nearby which then itself becomes a venerable landmark over the decades.

One species of native tree which has always been distinctive when planted away from its native, northerly habitat is the Scots Pine. It is one of the few native evergreen trees and, even in summer, has a distinctive appearance recognisable at a distance. Nigel Pennick has established that, from at least the eighteenth century, drovers deliberately planted Scots Pines at places where they could stop overnight. Clearly a large herd of cattle or flocks of sheep or geese would be unwelcome to many of the farmers and landowners alongside drovers routes. The sight of a Scots Pine in the distance would provide confirmation that a 'safe' stop for the night was within reach (Pennick 2010; 2011: 22–3). Scots Pines have not left their names on the landscape in the same way as the ashes, oaks and elms of Anglo-Saxon England – but they do confirm that landmarks can take many forms and continued to be important into recent times.

Join me on a journey in east Leicestershire

So far lots of words which reveal the way Anglo-Saxons observed their world in intimate detail . But could they really act as 'maps'? While still living in Leicestershire I took a map of Leicestershire and Rutland and ringed all the village names which were descriptive – several Hoton/Houghtons, a pair of Overtons, and so forth. I also marked Sharnford (the dirty ford) and Thistleton. All parts of these two counties had a sprinkling of names, usually separated by several villages. But the south-east had many more. Curiously this is the one part of the area where there are fewer known Roman roads (although the Gartree Road from Leicester to Medbourne and beyond does run through). If in other parts of the county one could follow the well-rutted former Roman roads, was there a greater need for descriptive place-names in this part?

Whatever the reason, I realised that I could join the dots – so to speak – and make my way from Great Glen (to the south of Leicester), head approximately north around the east of Leicester then turn east and head towards Thistleton near the Lincolnshire boundary on the far side of Rutland. By linking these descriptive names together I could follow this route almost *without any other village names in between.* Grab a road atlas or its online counterpart and join me on this trail.

We will go from Great Glen, (an important Anglo-Saxon Royal estate centre in its shallow glen) through Stretton (the settlement on the Roman road) to Houghton on the Hill (the settlement on the *hoh,* or heel-shaped promontory), past Newton (the new farm), cross over the two fords at Twyford, go past Burrough (the fortified place, actually a dramatically-situated Iron Age hill fort), pause at Pickwell to take a refreshing drink at its eponymous well on the peak, then head to the settlement on the windy and chilly *over* (Cold Overton), through the long settlement (Langham), detouring a little to check out the new settlement where they grow barley (Barleythorpe), then to the well with an ash tree (Ashwell), before heading to the place with old burial mounds or barrows (known just as Barrow to this day), to another overton known as Market Overton (remember *overs* are especially common on routeways so distinguishing prefixes such as 'Cold' and 'Market' are to be expected), and finally to the settlement where a remarkable number of thistles grow.

Whether or not any Anglo-Saxon ever felt the need to get from Great Glen to Thistleton by this route is a moot point – I'll accept that the odds are probably fairly long. But this perambulation along *surviving* village place-names – which ignores minor place-names, such as those for specific hills, and cannot consider names which have changed and been lost – shows that at least some routes can be described in this way.

Do you have a guide to the place-names of your own county and a map with most or all village names on it? If so an evening or two of reading should reveal the extent to which your area could also have once been traversed by following such descriptive names.

Not knots in a hankie

However, as already noted, we would need something more than a few knots in a hankie to remember all these places in the right sequence. For nearly two hundred years most people in Britain have been able to read and write. If we need to remember something we write it down – and then merely have to remember where

Looking towards Birstall and Belgrave from the summit of Castle Hill, Mountsorrel, July 2005,

we put the piece of paper! However, until less than six generations ago most people would have relied on their memories.

Without the 'distraction' of writing the day-to-day reliance on memory means that complex shopping lists and such likes can be recalled accurately – up to and including the words of lengthy epic ballads and the like. Indeed, any actor today must convert complex scripts into infallible memories. People in oral societies develop their skills at such recall as a natural part of their lives. They also use various mnemonics – early Greek orators famously imagined a temple and linked each of the columns with the key words of their speeches. Anglo-Saxon poets used alliteration to aid their recall, and later bards shifted this to the more familiar rhyming endings.

All these tricks help our memories to work better. And they can of course be brought to the aid of recollecting place-names in their rightful sequence. I'm back in Leicestershire, this time about seven miles north of Leicester itself in a place now called Mountsorrel – the sorrel-coloured 'mount' (the attentive will spot that this is a Norman French word rather than the Old English typical of place-names) where there is indeed an inlier of pinkish grano-diorite rock. I want to get to Leicester but I've missed the last bus. I'll need to go through the villages of Rothley, Wanlip, Birstall and Belgrave to get there. Or at least I *think* that's the right order. Certainly someone in about the eighteenth century wanted to remember them in sequence. To help he came up with a bit of a story and some doggerel verse.

Imagine you're an old god called Bel and you're riding an incredibly powerful – magically powerful – sorrel-coloured horse. You make a bet that you can get all the way from Mountsorrel to Leicester – about seven miles, remember – in just five leaps.

So:

> Mountsorrel he mounted at
> Rothley he rode by
> Wanlip he leaped o'er
> At Birstall he burst his gall
> At Belgrave he was buried at.

OK, it will never make any anthologies of great verse. But that little narrative – spurious as it so obviously is – makes the recollection of these five place-names much easier to work out. As I will show later in this chapter, other parts of the country were able to come up with much better stories linking distinctive places together.

Ekstasis in Scottish Travellers' tales and Old English poetry

While it does not prove anything about Anglo-Saxon culture, traditional cultures as far apart as Papua New Guinea, Navaho Indians and the Saami all use place-names as 'narratives' along journeys (Ingold 2007: 89). Closer to home, the Scottish Traveller tradition conveyed by Stanley Robertson (already summarised in Chapter One) also sees the landscape through the eyes of storyteller:

> Ma mither used to say that this particular land [here] between the
> river Dee and the river Don – and they used to say lang ago that
> the Don wis the warlock and the river Dee wis the witch. And this
> land between it wis for her bairns. This land wis oors aa richt
> because there's only twa hooses. But this road has been known
> for many, many supernatural happenings ... there's a lot o
> happiness on this auld road. And every time I ging up it I could
> aye sort o feel the spirits o the past...

(Robertson 1988: 128–9)

At first impression this seems fairly standard folklore. But for Robertson repeatedly-visited places do not simply resound with legends and stories, but they are the 'containers' for the collective memories of his Traveller culture. 'As a child Stanley remembers passing milestones on the road. At these places his father would review a learning principle, asking questions to make sure that he had been understood.' (Reith 2008: 87–8) If Robertson had difficulty remembering a tale, he would imagine himself back at the place where he heard it told.

> First of all I try to remember the actual place where I heard the
> story, maybe Lumphanan or someplace camping. I try to
> remember the setting, everything, even the smells, everything to
> do with the senses.

(cited Reith 2008: 91)

Robertson's way of remembering – and retelling – tales is deeply immersive. As a child of about five or six he and his great aunt passed a dead animal. She asked him to describe the world through the eyes of the skull (Robertson 2009: 107), a 'metaphysical relocation of self' that Robertson later extended to seeing the world from the point of view of landmark trees and other aspects of the landscape. And that fits neatly with the original sense of the Greek word *ekstasis* – 'to stand outside oneself' (although the modern English word ecstatic has a different usage).

Such a sense of *ekstasis* can be recognised among the small amount of Old English poetry that has come down to us. One is a work known as *The Dream of the Rood*, in which the crucifixion of Christ is seen from the point of view of the cross – and this poem may, in part, be a christianised version of a much older myth which sees the world from the perspective of the World Tree (North 1997: 275). The opening verses of *The Dream of the Rood* read like a riddle as the identity of the 'I' is not revealed until line 44. Indeed such first-person viewpoints are used in several surviving Old English riddles, for example:

> I am a wondrous creature: to women a thing of joyful expectation,
> to close-lying companions serviceable. I harm no city-dweller
> excepting my slayer alone. My stem is erect and tall – I stand up
> in bed – and whiskery somewhere down below. Sometimes a
> countryman's quite comely daughter will venture, bumptious girl,
> to get a grip on me. She assaults my red self and seizes my head
> and clenches me in a cramped place. She will soon feel the effect
> of her encounter with me, this curl-locked woman who squeezes
> me. Her eye will be wet.*

With this in mind we can also reinterpret the fragmentary Old English poem known to scholars as *The Wife's Lament*, and conventionally thought to be the autobiographical perspective of an exiled noblewoman. However the text can also be read as the first-person viewpoint of a dead woman in a burial mound. If so, this may be christian euhemerising of legends regarding the goddess Hos sitting on the 'sorrow mound' (Semple 1998: 110–11; 121–2). In other words, the poem is a first-person viewpoint of a pagan deity 'exiled' by the christianisation of late Anglo-Saxon culture.

Consistent with these first-person viewpoints, although perhaps even more strange to modern minds, are the inscriptions on weapons and scabbards written in the first person – the most famous of these is the one on Alfred's Jewel, with reads 'Alfred had me made'. All these examples strongly suggest that Anglo-Saxon culture was familiar with such *ekstasis* relocations of self as looking 'through the eye of the skull', and the singular survival into twentieth century Scottish Traveller culture has much more extensive origins with the British Isles.

But what happens when oral traditions fail to be remembered? What if only fragments of an overall narrative come down to us? And only some of those mininarratives about specific places were brought to the attention of early folklorists? We would be left with something that is a close approximation of the sort of place-

---

* Answer: An onion.

related lore that is typical of county folklore collections and which was subsequently trawled through by the likes of Janet and Colin Bord or Leslie Grinsell (Bord and Bord 1972; Grinsell 1976). The most thorough compilation of such legends, at least for England, which also traces the oldest surviving versions, was published as *The Lore of the Land* (Westwood and Simpson 2005)

When the folk singer Chris Wood was interviewed by Nathaniel Handy in 2010 he had this to say:

> When the songlines thing came out that wound me up! [Chris Wood] fumes. 'People freaking out at this amazing Australian Aboriginal thing where they don't have a map, they just sing a song and then they know where they are. Norfolk fishermen have been doing the same thing for generations. There's a song that tells you all the compass bearings and the landmarks that you would need to navigate from Yarmouth to Newcastle. It's no different, but because the songlines happened in Australia, everyone is into it. The concept of anything so beautiful and rich and wonderful and canny happening here in our own country is just too much for people to get their heads around.

(Handy 2010)

I suspect that someone who has closely studied the repertoire of traditional East Anglian singers such as Sam Larner or Peter Bellamy might establish which song Chris is referring to. Those who know in great detail the songs sung by fishermen in other parts of the British Isles may well come up with additional examples. Indeed it would be perverse if there were not originally many more examples – although no good reason why many should make the notebooks of folksong collectors.

Keep to the right at Anglesey

How far back can we pick up descriptions of journeys? Despite one of the surviving Old English poems being called *The Wanderer* we do not have any explicit descriptions of Anglo-Saxon journeys. Even the legendary accounts of Welsh and Cornish saints which, as previously mentioned, give the impression that their lives were spent on seemingly-endless sacred journeys, do not amount to travel diaries.

But when Middle English emerges out of the oral realm and begins to be written down in the second half of the fourteenth century then three of the greatest works are precursors to road movies. One is Geoffrey Chaucer's *Canterbury Tales*, where the whole framing story is about a pilgrimage. The second is William Langland's *The Vision of Piers Plowman,* inspired by a journey from Shropshire to London. While resting on the Malvern Hills Langland visualised the kingdom as 'a field full of folk'. The third is an alliterative poem, *Sir Gawain and the Green Knight,* written in Cheshire dialect by an author whose name is not known but referred to by scholars as the 'Pearl Poet' after the name of one of his other works. That three of the few surviving works of early Middle English literature feature journeys suggest that there

St Winifred's Well, Holywell, as depicted in 1713. Courtesy of Fortean Picture Library.

was an oral tradition (maintained while Norman French and Latin were the only languages being written) in which journeys were a common trope.

While *Sir Gawain and the Green Knight* is not about a journey, the Pearl Poet starts his poem by describing how Sir Gawain sets off from Camelot 'in the fictional kingdom of Logres, the poetical name for Britain used in much medieval Arthurian literature.' (Twomey 2004) We have to assume that the Pearl Poet believed Camelot to be somewhere in or near Snowdonia as Sir Gawain firstly 'keeps all the isles of Anglesey on his left', then crosses by ford at 'the Holy Head' (this is not Holyhead on Anglesey but maybe either Holywell near Flint or Pulford, site of Poulton Abbey) to the Wirral, to arrive at the liminal time between Christmas and New Year at Bertilak's castle Hautdesert (which might have been where Staffordshire, Derbyshire and Cheshire come together – more liminality – close to the River Dane, an area now known as Swythamley Park).

The Green Chapel which features in the legend is often thought to be Lud's Church near Swythamley, but more probably near Wetton Mill, east of Leek, on land that was either a hermitage or grange of Poulton Abbey. (See Twomey 2004 for a detailed account of visiting all these places, together with translations of the relevant lines of the poem.)

The Pearl Poet's mention of fording at 'The Holy Head' fits well with Holywell, where the decapitated St Winefrid (or Winifred) was, and still is, venerated. She was beheaded by a local chieftain named Caradoc when she spurned a request to satisfy his lust, and then became one of the rather numerous saints who make miraculous journeys with their heads tucked under their arm. Her head was restored to its rightful place by her uncle, St Beuno, but a white scar remained for the rest of her life. Given the prominence which decapitation – or at least its threat – plays in the later stages of the Sir Gawain poem, it would seem a fitting preliminary allusion. And the 'nick' on the neck which Sir Gawain receives from the Green Knight was presumably severe enough to leave a permanent scar, recalling St Winefrid's miraculous recovery. Another parallel is that both St Winefride and Sir Gawain refuse sexual advances from noble persons. Such subtle weaving of ideas is entirely consistent with the Pearl Poet's erudition and style.

Whatever the exact details of this journey, it is a realistic route and not merely poetic licence. His distinctive regional dialect affirms that the Pearl Poet was local to Cheshire and could well have travelled this route into north Wales himself, perhaps on a number of occasions. His skill at transferring his interest in the landscape extends to lively descriptions of such courtly activities as conversation, wooing and hunting. His knowledge of 'technical' hunting terminology suggests this was also from personal experience. But *Sir Gawain* shares with the three other poems attributed to this author a recurrent interest in setting out a 'chivalrous' lifestyle where patience and humility are contrasted with pride, courtesy is a noble virtue, and purity must be paramount. The latter is denoted by pearls, which the poet introduces into each of his works – hence his nickname.

The sleeping knights of Alderley Edge

We must transfer our attention from the anonymous fourteenth century author of *Sir Gawain* to a nameless late eighteenth century storyteller for perhaps the best surviving example of place-names and place-related lore linking together into a journey. The 'Legend of Alderley Edge' was first published in a letter to the *Manchester Mail* in 1805. This was followed by an anonymous poem called 'The Iron Gates: A legend of Alderley' which was published in the February 1839 edition of *Blackwood's Magazine*, and another account by the Hon. Miss Letitia D. Stanley in her book *Alderley Edge and Its Neighbourhood* which appeared in 1843.

The 1805 account is said to be based 'chiefly from the report of a very old man, commonly known among his junior brethren by the familiar appellation of "Old Daddy" and who has spent the major part of his life in the service of T. Stanley, Esq.' Quite who T. Stanley Esq. might have been we can leave open – it is the sort of detail which storytellers introduce to give a sense of veracity to timeless legends. Similarly the author of the 1839 account claims to have first heard the legend when a child from his 'grandame'. The most recently published retelling of this legend is by Alan Garner – yes, the author of such fantasy fiction as *The Weirdstone of Brisingamen*, *The Owl Service*, *The Moon of Gomrath* and *Thursbitch* – who, following this tradition closely, claims to have learnt the tale from his grandfather in the once-liminal space of a smithy, or by flickering firelight:

> My grandfather told me a story. He told it in the dark of his forge,
> and beside his hearth, and in his garden as we pulled rhubarb. It
> was his truth, a part of him, which he passed on.
> (Garner 2010: 5).

Sir Gawain's adversary, the Green Knight. Illustration by Ian Brown.

Alan Garner was born in Congleton, not that far from Alderley Edge, and clearly has a detailed knowledge of the land and its history acquired not only from his grandfather but also by living there for a long time.

However before we look in more detail at Garner's insights, here is my retelling of the legend, drawing upon the previously-published versions. As with *Sir Gawain* the time is a liminal one – this time Hallowe'en. For reasons unknown a farmer living at Mobberley decides to sell a white mare at Macclesfield market. This itself is rather odd as the journey will take him at least twelve miles and the terrain is difficult, including a scarp slope well over a hundred metres high. By waiting a week he could have gone over level ground to Knutsford horse fair, just three miles away. But this is not as odd as Garner thinks – farmers only ever buy from certain markets and only sell at others – and which markets these are follow precedents set by their fathers. Quite how many generations have maintained these traditions is unknown but, given the generally conservative nature of farmers, we should assume that this is a long-established way of avoiding in-bred livestock.

Back to the legend. The Mobberley farmer sets off before daybreak and rides the horse up the steep slope to a place known as Thieves' Hole. This is not a hole in the way you or I think but a 'hollow way' – a linear earthwork that is simultaneously a boundary, a one-time line of defence, and a routeway. Indeed, Alan Garner establishes that Thieves' Hole was once a crossroads (Garner 2010: 14). It took its name because, in Old English, it was where ða ðeofes licgað – where 'the thieves lie'. This is not where they lay in wait. That sense of 'to lie' was still in the future. These thieves lie in the earth, in death, after their execution at such a liminal location. Later generations of thieves would not lie at rest but rather their corpses would be hung in gibbets at just such execution sites.

As if subliminally aware of the preternatural power of the place, the mare locks herself rigid. No matter what oaths the farmer utters, she moves not an inch. Then he too freezes, at least for a moment. A tall old man, not much more to him than a ghost but carrying a hefty staff in his hand, has appeared as if out of nowhere. Without a word of greeting he speaks: 'She is just the mare I am after. How much will you sell her for?'

'I'll not sell to the likes of you,' retorts the farmer, 'I'll get a better price at the market.' 'Be on your way then,' the old man replies, with a harshness to his voice. 'Mark my words, she'll not be sold this day. But when you come back this way tonight, I'll be here waiting for you.'

With that the mare moves forward and continues on her way to Mobberley and they stand at the fair. Despite the farmer being told many times what a fine animal she is, no one offers to buy her. Not one. Far from having some money to celebrate with a few drinks in the local inn, and take some ribbons back for his wife as she asked, he faces a long and difficult journey home in the gathering dark, with no doubt some harsh words from his missus when he does arrive. Not to mention the risk of again meeting that strange old man at Thieves' Hole.

Alderley Edge, December 2000.

He sets off as soon as he can but by the time he arrives at Thieves Hole the sun has just slipped below the horizon.

'Now will you sell her?' the familiar voice challenges. The farmer turns towards where the voice came from. Knowing that the old man knows he has little by way of bargaining power, he can only ask: 'How much are you offering?'

'Enough,' comes the enigmatic reply. 'Follow me.' As if this was already an agreed deal, the old man sets off. As if entranced, the farmer and the mare follow into the growing dark. The route was not direct but zigzagged between some curiously-named local landmarks on the high ground near Alderley Edge. First to Seven Firs, then to Goldenstone, detouring to Stormy Point before climbing up to Saddlebole. On Saddlebole is a massive boulder, not much smaller than the farmer's house. The old man strikes this rock with his staff and, with a clatter, the rock splits open to reveal a pair of iron gates beyond. A slightly more gentle touch from the staff and these too open, and the old man, the farmer and the mare walk through, into a cave in the hillside. Except that, as the farmer's eyes become accustomed to the dark, he sees the cave opens out into a massive cavern and from that cavern other caves lead off.

Fearing that he is being led into the land of faery, a hollow hill from which he may escape, if at all, only a hundred or more years in the future, he cries to the old man

'Let me go! Just keep the horse, I'll take no money from you if you let me leave this place right now!'

'No harm will come to you, if you stay,' reassures the old man. 'Continue to follow me, you'll come to no harm at all.' And when they have crossed the cavern and approach one of the caves beyond he hears the sound of snoring. Not of one man but of many. And as he enters the cave the limited light reveals that each of these snoring men is dressed in armour. How many men he cannot count in the gloom. But each one rests his head against the side of a white horse. Except one... One has no horse.

'This,' announces the old man, 'this is the sleeping army. These knights are resting, and will continue to rest until the day of the world's final battle. When that day comes I must awaken them. But, as you noticed, one is without a horse. Yours is the horse I want. Leave her here and come with me.'

The farmer follows to another cave and is bewildered by the sight of so much gold, silver and other treasure. Some of it is stored neatly and some has spilled onto the floor. Just a handful would make the farmer a rich man. Were he to take his hat off and fill it to the brim he would be rich beyond his wildest dreams.

'Have as much as you can carry,' says the old man. 'That's your rightful payment.' Without so much as a thought of shaking hands to agree the deal, the farmer fills the pockets in his britches with the brightest and shiniest of the golden coins. He indeed takes his hat off and empties a large pot of coins into it, not bothering that a good many spill over onto the floor. More coins he slides between his riding boots and his legs. Yet still there seems to be as much treasure as when he first set eyes in the cave. He takes off his jacket and uses it to wrap around jewellery and other bigger pieces of treasure.

He can barely walk under the weight of what he has taken in exchange for the mare but the old man simply nods and once more says 'Follow me.' They go back out through the iron gates and the rock, which clatters again before shutting with a resounding bang. The night is as dark as if a bag were over the farmer's head.

Eventually he arrives home. He cannot hide his new-found wealth from his friends and they demand to know how he came by it. He tells them the tale of the old man and the circuitous route to the iron gates. They tell their friends the tale too and soon a large number of men make their way up to Saddlebole. But the rock resolutely remains in one piece and neither the iron gates, the sleeping knights or the hidden treasure have ever been seen since.

The power of names

The modern Ordnance Survey map for the Alderley Edge area does not show Thieves' Hole, Seven Firs, Goldenstone, Stormy Point or Saddlebole. But Alan Garner established where they were and also researched the origins of the places' names. I have already included his research into Thieves' Hole as part of my scene-

Alderley Edge, December 2000.

setting. Goldenstone is a landmark on the boundary of Over Alderley and Nether Alderley parishes. It is a sandstone conglomerate which, far from being golden, looks from a distance as grey. But close up a remarkable number of quartz pebbles can be seen, making it distinctive from locally-outcropping rocks.

In place-names not everything called 'gold' is necessarily golden. The Old English word *gylden* can indeed mean 'gold-coloured'. But it also has the broader sense of 'splendid, wealthy, treasure'. It can also mean 'sacrifice'. This is because another layer of meaning is 'tax, tribute'; this evolves into 'geld' (in the sense of money and payment). So the Goldenstone was the place to pay your 'geld', your taxes – yield (another cognate word) your valuables. Sometimes it may well have felt like a sacrifice. Indeed before coins perhaps your 'geld' was your best horse, who was indeed sacrificed...

Stormy Point is near the Devils' Grave and Pikelow, and near these are two of six surviving flat-topped artificial mounds in this area. They are about a metre high and four metres across. Their age or purpose has never been established. Best guess is that there are eighteenth century landscaping, presumably intended to have one or more trees on them. Indeed only one of them has a name and that is Seven Firs, one of the landmarks on the farmer's journey.

The Devil's Grave is perhaps an Otherworldly trench (from Old English *graef*), with the devil appearing in the place-name (but presumably not in person) around the seventeenth or eighteenth centuries (Harte 2010: 26). Pikelow is from the Old

English *piced hlaw*, the pointed ('peaked') burial mound. Pikelow is indeed a landmark – the boundaries of three parish meet there. Stormy Point would, in Old English, have the sense of a 'stormy place'.

Like Pikelow, Saddlebow is a boundary landmark. It is distinctive a spur-like promontory of Stormy Point with a dip in the middle that makes it appear saddle-shaped. In Old English *bol* was a smooth, rounded hill. But Old English *bolla* is our words 'bowl' and 'hollow', with the additional meaning of a smelter's crucible – and copper and lead deposits were extracted from this part of Alderley Edge. Bearing in mind that early metalworkers were regarded as almost Otherworldly – magical 'achemists' who could transform dull ores into shiny metal – then perhaps their workings were considered akin to Otherwordly trenches too.

The rock which opened to reveal the iron gates is now known as Iron Gate. And this name is not a result of the legend. It predates the legend, probably by many centuries. Indeed, the more cold-blooded folklorist will consider the legend to be a 'back-formation' – the adaptation of a well-known tale (and the sleeping knights are indeed known from a great many other places) to 'explain' a curious place-name. Just as gold is not, in place-names, always gold, so too iron isn't to be trusted to be what it seems – although Garner reads rather too much into the Peterborough lapidary of about 1500 which states that 'Iren is a stone'. Gate is from the Scandinavian *gata* for 'road' or 'way'. So Iron Gate implies, at least to Garner, a stone road. And, indeed, archaeological investigation in 1999 revealed just such a structure running on to Stormy Point (Garner 2010: 13).

But maybe there was a gate. With its Otherworld guardian. Although not named in the legends, old documents refer to Avardeshache as being near Iron Gate. Garner derives this from Aelfweardhoec (Garner 2010: 15). In this case we are dealing with the modern sense of the word 'gate' (Old English *hoec*) guarded (Old English *weard* – from which modern 'warden' or 'warder') and the Old English *aelf* which is exactly as it sounds – 'elf'. So 'the elf-guarded gate' or 'the gate of the elf-guard'. Isn't that an excellent description of the old man and the iron gates? Don't worry that the old man is described as being tall – elves were as big as humans until the late medieval era when (at least according to legends since then) they diminished to being rather more wee and twee and generally less bothersome than hitherto. And anyway, in the worldview of Anglo-Saxons, the sleeping knights would also inhabit the world of the elves – they, not the old man, were the *aelf weard*. So perhaps this story is not so much a back-formation of Iron Gate as a derivation and embellishment of a tale associated with Avardeshache?

Even Mobberley deserves more attention – this derives from 'moot mound' so would have been a regional meeting place. And it is during the *return* to Mobberley that the most interesting part of this tale takes place – the outward trek is little more than 'prequel' to the main tale.

And, as Garner so wonderfully realises, why did the sleeping knights need a mare? The weight of their armour meant they rode specially-bred stallions not some farmer's mare. Legend does however tell us why a king needed a white mare – and I have described that already in the previous chapter when discussing the inauguration of medieval kings.

Legends as big as a country

I have recounted and discussed the legend of Alderley in some detail because, thanks to Alan Garner's knowledge and research, it is so far the best-constructed example of how the names and legends of individual places form part of a greater narrative. But, in the final analysis, it is only a construction – not a 'genuine relic'. Garner was told the tale by his grandfather, but his grandfather got to know – directly or otherwise – the tale from the mid-nineteenth century literary versions. And that tale shares too much with Scottish tales of Thomas the Rhymer for it not to be yet another example of a well-known legend which is relocated to a new locality (the proliferation of candidates for King Arthur's Camelot are perhaps the best examples). Despite Garner's pronouncements about Old English place-names, this tale is a back formation – albeit a seductively clever one – that dates back little, if at all, before its first appearance in print (See Harte 2011 for a more extended critique of Garner's account.).

Whatever the age and origins of the expedition around Alderley Edge, Garner shows us how readily specific places in the landscape can be woven into a memorable narrative. His Cheshire mare has much more going for her than the ditty about the supernatural leaps that took the Leicestershire horse, Bel, to his supposed grave.

The authors of both these tales have much in common with A.A. Milne when he transformed the physical landscape of Posingford Wood and the Ashdown Forest into Pooh Corner and invented an expotition – also involving the equine character, Eyore – to somewhere as 'other' as the North Pole. Such expeditions as metaphors for 'otherwordly' journeys involve horses and their ilk to a greater extent than is necessary for functional reasons.

In partial contrast, the poem about *Sir Gawain* is a remarkable work of literature, in which the supernatural aspects – splendid as they are – are secondary to setting expectations of chivalrous conduct. That Sir Gawain was travelling by horse is implicit for someone of his social status – it would be remarkable only if he were not. The place-related lore in *Sir Gawain*, although of specific interest to me, is just another level of meaning within the author's complex interweaving of ideas.

But there is one other work which weaves its hero into the landscape, and which seemingly dates to before the era when horses were inevitable companions. In this case the landscape is as big as a kingdom – at least the north Wales kingdom of Gwynedd at its greatest extent. And its hero is not merely supernatural but god-like – although some would say that his shape-shifting skills were as much shamanic as divine. To do justice to the complexities of Taliesin's mythical travels would, however, be difficult to summarise within a few pages. It needs a whole book to itself. Thankfully Michael Dames has already done just that, as I have already mentioned briefly in Chapter Three.

Dames' *Taliesin's Travels: A demi-god at large* is a complex work that draws together

both evidence and ideas from different time-spans to show how, at least from a modern perspective, key stages in Taliesin's life are intimately linked to specific places in the north Wales landscape. His approach succeeds in bringing the landscape back to life, mythologically speaking, even though the surviving sources for the tales of Taliesin have lost such intimate links with places.

Thirty years before publishing *Taliesin's Travels* Dames had established himself as a writer with two books which similarly re-mythologise the Avebury landscape (Dames 1976, 1977). These books have influenced how a great many people have thought about the prehistoric monuments of the upper Kennet valley since, and indeed influence later chapters of this book.

Legends as big as a galaxy

Myths did not only provide ways of memorising the landmarks for terrestrial journeys. We still find our way around the night sky by giving mythic names to the constellations; most of our Greek and Roman myths can be 'decoded' as originally starting out as narratives that 'explained' the relative position of these star formations. Behind the surviving myths are fragments of the myths of earlier societies and their star lore. I will touch upon some specific constellations later in this book but leave you to consider the way myths once provided celestial 'songlines'. And those myths must have their antecedents in the culture that built such monuments as Stonehenge and other astronomically-aligned henges.

But before I venture again back to the Neolithic, I want to follow up some of the many references to Anglo-Saxon words and ideas in this chapter by looking more closely at what we know about that era, especially the transition from paganism to christianity.

Facing page: Llyn Geirionydd, the place of Talisin's magical transformation, July 2006. Michael Dames wrote in Taliesin's Travels *that:*

> Whenever the demi-god Taliesin arrives at Llyn Geirionydd, he sits by the shore and listens to what the *llyn* has to say. On windless occasions, when not the faintest lapping sounds come to his ears, he is puzzled by the lake's silence, thinking: 'Have I come all this way, and endured so much, for no response? Lake Disappointment, you are cruel!' Sulkily he stares at the glass-smooth surface and sees his image, floating there. His inverted self lies captured by the lake in a companionable quiescence. Geirionydd is sharing a pause, as she mimes the positive value of absolute stillness and calm. So, at the core of his febrile travels Taliesin discovers a sublime repose lying beyond words. After that, the faintest ripples appear on the lake, as if from a submerged oracle, whispering the coalescence of every possible sound, making the chord that may underlie all languages, but audible only to itself. Putting an ear to the water, Taliesin hopes to catch something of that proto-Esperanto, but hears nothing.

Chapter 7

Anglo-Saxon Sacred Places

While we know nothing for certain about the beliefs or myths of the people who constructed the Neolithic monuments of Avebury and the upper Kennet valley we can, as I have already started to show, deduce some possibilities from the monuments themselves and their relationship to the landscape. We can also make the assumption that some of the more widespread pre-christian practices and beliefs have a long tradition, one which stretches back towards the Neolithic. Exactly which pre-christian practices and beliefs have this long pedigree is a very contentious point (see Hutton 1996 for the best assessment of the British evidence). And, even if there has been some sort of continuity, there will have been changes – not least to the meaning and significance bestowed on 'timeless traditions'.

The slaves who lived apart

We have a partial, and decidedly one-sided, view of the last era of paganism in Britain through the writings of the Anglo-Saxon clerics between about 500 and 1000 CE. These writings both shed light and cast confusing shadows over the complexity of Anglo-Saxon culture in this time of radical religious and social change. But to understand Anglo-Saxon culture we need first to understand who the Anglo-Saxon people were. Yes, they were from Anglia, Saxony, Jutland and Frisia on the North Sea coast. But they did not land in an empty country. There were still people living in the wake of the collapse of the Roman economy and way of life, the Roman-British, speaking a version of Celtic scholars now call British or Brittonic, closely related to Welsh and Cornish.

Archaeologists may debate the extent to which the Brittonic-speaking locals were 'displaced' (a term which euphemistically embraces either being moved on, murdered or enslaved) by Anglo-Saxon settlers. But the linguistic evidence is fairly harsh – the Anglo-Saxons referred to the locals as *walh*, a word which evolves into the modern word 'Welsh' but used then in the sense of 'Celtic-speaking slave'. The many Walton place-names in England reveal where, at one time, the enslaved indigenous people had their townships. The usage of 'townships' here is not

The south-west sector of Avebury henge, November 2007. The medieval church tower is just visible; this was earlier the site of an Anglo-Saxon minster.

frivolous. Everything about the Anglo-Saxons and the Brittonic-speaking natives smacks of apartheid. Linguistically there are close parallels with the colonisation of South Africa and Australia. This is in contrast to India, where many English words entered into the local languages (so-called 'Hobson-Jobson') and a substantial number of Indian words have become part of everyday English (spread across all types of linguistic usages, such as bungalow, cashmere, cheetah, chit, curry, cushy, dekko, gymkhana, jungle, karma, khaki, mongoose, pariah, polo, pukka, pundit, pyjamas, sadhu, sari, sitar, swami, swastika, thug, yoga, yogi). The linguistic evidence fits the facts – the British and Indian empires 'collided' in ways which enriched at least some sectors of both societies. In contrast, very few Aborigine words have entered English (and the exceptions are boomerang, budgerigar, didgeridoo, dingo, kangaroo, koala, wallaby, wombat – species of animals and artefacts for which there are no parallels in Britain). Similarly, Afrikaans has few borrowings from Zulu or Shona.

Likewise Old English borrows almost no words from Brittonic. There are only four definite exceptions. Firstly, *binn* in the sense of 'manger'. Secondly, *brocc*, the badger. The third is *torr* for 'outcrop, peak'. And finally, *cumb*, the modern word 'coombe' which describes a blocked valley, as this topography is rarely found in northern Europe. There are some other questionable contenders and scholarly debate regarding a small number of place-names which Anglo-Saxons took over from Brittonic settlement names (see Coates 2004 for a thorough discussion). There would have been little need for new words or borrowings because the invaders would have been familiar with most of the flora and fauna of Britain, and local cultural customs would have been similar.

Indeed Old English evolved from its continental origins with few external influences until Scandinavian settlement brought both new words and synonyms (wapentakes for hundreds comes first to mind). A similar process of borrowing specialist terminology entered into English with the Norman conquest – especially terms relating to Norman courtly life for which there was no English precedent.

English became 'invisible' – or, rather, unrecorded – for several centuries during the heyday of the Normans until emerging, much transformed, as the Middle English of Chaucer and the Pearl Poet. So too Brittonic becomes invisible, and most certainly unrecorded, from early in the Anglo-Saxon settlement era – and never makes a comeback.

Old English is not a creole of Germanic and Brittonic, as is normal when cultures come into contact in a 'natural' manner – each gives a bit, with plenty of synonyms. Middle English, with its borrowings from French and Latin, is an example, another is modern day Spanglish of bilingual Hispanic cultures in America. As Old English is not by any stretch of the imagination a creole, we are compelled to conclude that British natives and Anglo-Saxon settlers did not come into contact in a 'natural' manner. This is all-but conclusive evidence that Britons ever would be slaves, at least in the eyes of their Germanic-speaking colonisers. How similar this was to apartheid South Africa is an open question but they certainly lived apart, as the recurrent place-name Walton attests.

We have to ask, too, just what sort of lifestyle these Brittonic-speaking immediate successors to Roman Britain were living. At Wroxeter and a few other places on the Western borders where Roman influence had been brokered through local warlords, these dynasties were able to sustain some resemblance of a Roman life-style for several generations. But there is no comparable evidence from most of England. The collapse of the economy presumably meant that any number of small-time bandits fought for local power, quite likely with plenty of 'collateral damage' to the crops, homes and lives of the population. Add to that one or more successive years of poor harvests – the climate was getting colder and wetter than hitherto – which would cause widespread death directly and from famine-induced illnesses, and the impact on society would be profound. In a society where all aspects of its culture, including religious belief, were passed on by oral traditions, then people who 'knew the old ways' simply may not have lived long enough to pass on enough to keep these old ways alive. Conceivably, the Anglo-Saxons coming to England found both a near-vacuum of political power and a near-absence of anything they recognised as culture too.

Under such circumstances how much of the indigenous British religious beliefs might be expected to survive? And of that which survived, how much was absorbed into pagan Anglo-Saxon practice? Given that the Old English word for 'druid', *dry*, is borrowed from Old Irish and not from Brittonic, my suspicion is that the answer to both these questions is 'Not a lot'. We simply cannot assume that the evidence which has reached us for paganism in Britain before christianity predates the Anglo-Saxons. Nevertheless, there are some tantalising exceptions which I will look at later in this chapter. But before we get to those most arcane layers of this metaphorical onion, first we need to establish what can be said about the 'outer layers' of Anglo-Saxon paganism.

Pagans and christians

The evidence we have for paganism in Britain was written down between 500 to 1000 CE by christian clerics who were, on the one hand, proscribing pagan practices and, on the other, recording healing charms that, in a somewhat complex manner, reflect the christianisation of indigenous culture. But the process was not one-way. Despite the self-evident emphasis on beliefs originating in the eastern Mediterranean, British chistianity has never been an exact match for the eastern 'orthodox' churches. The eastern thinking quickly became 'westernised' – more specifically, popular christianity mix-and-matched what the priest was preaching with beliefs and practices deeply rooted in Germanic culture. Indeed, since a pioneering study by James Russell published in 1994, scholars have adopted the phrase 'the Germanization of early medieval christianity' to describe this two-way mixing. Russell's approach was developed in greater detail by Karen Jolly in her study of popular religion in late Anglo-Saxon England, published soon after in 1996.

Much has been made by historians of the repeated edicts against worshipping 'earth-fast stones' and the like – clearly just being told not to do it once was not enough to stop such deep-rooted practices. At the synod of 747 held at Clofeshoh (most probably Croft Hill in Leicestershire) there was just such prohibition of pagan practices 'that is divinations, fortune telling by casting lots, from the flight of birds, from watching birds, amulets, incantations, all the filth of the ungodly and errors of the heathen.' (Wilson 1192: 38) But, as with most of such decrees, the main emphasis is on divinatory practices not religious worship as such.

The reasons for naming four of the days of the week after pagan deities (*Tiwesdaeg, Wodensdaeg, Thunresdaeg* and *Frigdaeg*) have less to do with maintaining pagan practices as with 'translating' Classical traditions – inherited from the formative period of christianity in the Mediterranean – into local counterparts. This is confirmed by the remaining three days being named after the sun, moon and Saturn – all deified in Classical paganism. Tiw, Woden, Thunor and Frig were regarded as the indigenous parallels to Classical gods.

Pagan places

Our most comprehensive evidence for Anglo-Saxon comes from the place-names which contain the names of deities such as Woden, Thor, and Frig, or which contain words known to refer to pagan shrines. There are not a great many of these and, while some are undisputed, at least some offer more certain evidence of pre-christian belief or activity.

Thor. Illustration by Ian Brown.

The curiously-named Roseberry Topping was originally Othins bjarg *('Odin's rock or crag'). Photograph by Ian Brown.*

The first well-publicised evaluation of pagan place-name elements was by Frank Stenton in 1943. His work is still widely quoted although as long ago as 1961 Margaret Gelling published a paper re-evaluating all of Stenton's fifty-or-so examples and reducing the number to about forty without adding any of her own. Subsequently the number has been added to by Brian Branston (1980) and Kenneth Cameron (1988) and the whole lot reconsidered by Gelling (1988) and David Wilson (1992). Does all this matter? Only that a number of more recent writers have taken some of the early sources – often Branston – uncritically. Don't believe everything you read...

The nature of such debates has shifted to the Internet and the Wikipedia page for 'List of places named after Woden' has a substantial number of entries for both Britain and Continental countries (plus 'exported' examples in Texas, Baffin Island and Australia). Many of the British examples are in southern counties, although a notable exception is the dramatic-looking Roseberry Topping near Teesside – the modern name is a corruption of *Othins bjarg* ('Odin's rock or crag', with the dialect 'topping' added more recently). Indeed hills are the place to meet Odin and Woden, such as Wednesbury (West Midlands). Or he may be encountered by his nickname 'Grimr' ('the masked one') – although this was also a personal names so Grimstons and Grimsbys are presumed to derive from real people not gods.

Thor place-names are more difficult to unravel because the Thor was commonly used in personal names. In Leicestershire alone Thringstone, Thrussington, Thurcaston, Thurlaston and Thurmaston all derive from men called Thor-something.

Adam's Grave – earlier Woden's beorg *– near the Wansdyke, Wiltshire, in May 2009.*

However Thundersley in Essex is either 'Thunor's grove' (*leah*) or 'Thunor's mound' (*hlaw*). Near Bexhill was another, now-lost, Thunorslege ('Thunor's grove). And Thurstable, also in Essex, is 'Thors' pillar' (*stapol*).

Woden and Thunor are typically linked words for open spaces, *feld* and *leah*. This suggests that Tislea and Tuesley (Surrey) are groves of Tiw. Tysoe (Tiw's *hoh* or heel-shaped hill) in Warwickshire is famous for the now-lost image of a red horse on the hill-side (the local soils are red) but whether this is evidence for a pagan horse cult is debatable.

The goddess Frig would seem to be present in the various 'Friday' place-names but caution is needed. Before the Reformation Friday was a day of fasting so the name probably indicates poor farming land. Bear in mind that people have always had a sense of irony – Honey Street denotes muddy routes, Klondike Lane signifies remoteness, and so forth. And some 'Fri-' place-names, such as Frisby, are most likely to refer to people from Frisia. So far as I can tell there are no English place-names which undisputedly refer to Frigg, Freyr or Freyja.

The belt of trees running across the photograph in the mid-distance marks the course of the Wansdyke. The gap in the middle is a road running in a valley once known as Woden's dene. Photograph taken from near Knap Hill Neolithic causewayed camp, August 2009. Adam's Grave is about half-a-mile from the left of the Wansdyke.

Woden in the middle of Wiltshire

Woden was present – at least in place-names – to the south of Avebury. The valley which leads from Lockeridge towards Knap Hill was once Woden's *dene* ('valley'). And Adam's Grave, the Neolithic chamber tomb which overlooks the Knap Hill causewayed enclosure, was Woden's *beorg* ('barrow') when in 592 CE two warriors, Coel and Caewlin, fought there.

Woden's *beorg* probably takes its names from the Wansdyke (Woden's ditch) which cuts across the valley between Lockeridge and Knap Hill, overlooked from the chamber tomb. Some place-name scholars suggest that, rather than the ditch being attributed to the work of Woden, the name is a corruption of a phrase that meant 'the ditch near Woden's valley'. In other words the whole length of the Anglo-Saxon defensive earthwork has become known as the Wansdyke although initially only a part of the defences were so-called. However, as the Wansdyke may, in part, overlay a smaller Bronze Age boundary earthwork which plausibly might have been attributed to Woden, then nothing is in the least certain about how, why or when the name Wansdyke arose.

Harrow Hill, Wychford, Warwickshire, July 2008. A good example of the dramtic 'beached whale' shaped hills that some – although not all – heargs occupy.

'Temples' and shrines

Overall, certain references to pagan deities in place-names are relatively rare. But the names of places where they were venerated survive more frequently. The main examples are *hearg* and *weoh*. These usually enter modern spelling as 'Harrow' and 'Wy-' or 'Wee-'. Most of the harrows are on hill tops – Harrow on the Hill (Middlesex) is the most obvious.

Depending on how you interpret Bede and other early accounts, harrows were surrounded by a hedge and/or ditch enclosure and had altars and images of the gods. At least two of the later harrows – Yeavering and Godmanchester – had wooden temple buildings but this may have been a case of 'keeping up with the Joneses' by emulating early christian churches and does not necessarily reflect traditional pagan practices.

Interestingly, Harrow place-names do not form compound words with names of any of the deities. Presumably they were places where there were different shrines to the major and local deities, or where each group of people 'did their own thing'. Sarah Semple's thorough re-evaluation of the archaeological discoveries at some of the *hearg* sites counters the previous thinking that they were pagan 'temples' (Semple 2007, critiquing Blair 1995 and North 1997: 97–103). Instead harrows were tens of

This unprepossessing area of tree planting at Six Hills in north Leicestershire is on the site of a probable hearg *that may have been the 'Especially Sacred Grove' which gave the nearby Roman small town of Vernemetum its name.*

hectares in size, with evidence of ritual activity from the Anglo-Saxon, Roman and Iron Age eras. Consistently conspicuous by its absence was any evidence for occupation within the area of a *hearg*.

No matter what might have survived in the way of Roman shrines and such like, Anglo-Saxons presumably did not have an accurate idea that these sites had been continuously used for around 1,500 years previously. But, while we do not know exactly what Anglo-Saxons were referring to with the word *hearg*, clearly this was a name they gave to well-established sacred places.

Likewise the word *weoh* has a specific usage and is not a synonym for *hearg*. *Weoh* means both 'shrine' and 'graven image' or 'idol'. There is no contradiction here – think of Roman Catholic Mediterranean countries where a wayside image of a saint or the Virgin Mary is referred to as a 'shrine'. Without the icon there would be no shrine, but the presence of the icon (usually in a protective 'niche') *de facto* makes a shrine. Just as such wayside shrines are commonplace in Catholic countries so too *woehs* were once encountered on routes (indeed such christian statues might be considered as an example of the 'Germanisation' of christianity). So Weeford (Staffordshire) and Wyfordby (Leicestershire) are self-evidently on routes. Others are in clearings (presumably sacred groves) such as Weoley (Worcestershire), Willey

Waden Hill seen from West Kennett Avenue, October 2010.

(Surrey and Warwickshire) and Whiligh (Sussex). There are also *weohs* on hills as the Weedons in Northamptonshire and Buckinghamshire suggest.

Perhaps the most interestingly-located *weoh* – at least from the perspective of this book – is the one overlooking the Avebury monuments. The summit of Waden Hill, which runs alongside the West Kennett Avenue, offers panoramic views of Silbury, the henge, West Kennett chambered tomb, with Windmill Hill to the north. Some sources state that it derives from 'Woden's hill' but the early spellings make it clear it was *weoh don*, 'shrine hill'. Ploughed-out Bronze Age barrows on the summit (near where a small covered reservoir has been constructed) would have been clearly visible in the Anglo-Saxon era. Indeed they were probably re-used for burials by the Anglo-Saxons; sadly there was no archaeological investigation prior to their destruction by farming. If, as is likely, there were Anglo-Saxon burials on this part of Waden Hill then they would have become *weoh munds* – 'shrine mounds', presumably with a simple 'idol' on top of each one re-used for burials. We even have the name of someone perhaps buried in such a manner at Patchway in Sussex; the name derives from the personal name Paccel and *weoh*.

What did one of these 'idols' look like? Frankly we don't know but the lack of any surviving carvings indicates that they were carved from wood. Just possibly it was such idols that were in Aldhelm's mind around 680 when he wrote, in Latin, to Heathfrith about *ermula cruda* being venerated. The expression translates as 'crude little herms', with the world 'herm' being a reference to Classical Greek and Roman sculptures with a head on the top of a square-section column on which male genitals appeared at the appropriate height. Exactly what Aldhelm meant has intrigued

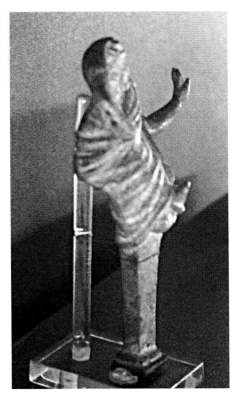
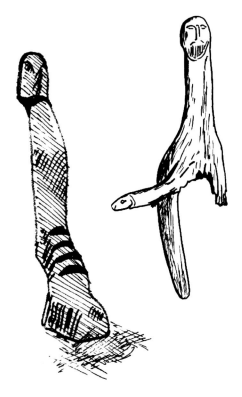

Left: *A first-century CE Roman miniature Herm, cast bronze.*
Centre and right: *Two wooden 'idols' of uncertain age recovered from Danish bogs.*

scholars. Maybe these were some sort of 'totem poles' with an animal or man's head at the top. But Aldhelm would have been aware that there was an Old English word for these, *stapol*. Were the *ermula cruda* re-used Roman altars – but in which case why not use the Latin word *aras*? And if they were idols then the word *idola* was known to Bede so why not to Aldhelm? The best guess – although it is only a guess – is that Aldhelm was attempting to refer to prehistoric standing stones, or more-or-less uncarved wooden posts which had a similarly phallic appearance.

One piece of place-name evidence seems to support this – the early forms of Wigston Parva in Leicestershire suggest *wig* (or *weoh*) *stan*, meaning 'idol stone' (however Wigston Magna, also in Leicestershire, derives from different early forms.)

Aldhelm is clearly seeing, through the eyes of a christian cleric, the local evidence of a cult which continued much longer in Scandinavia. There are a surprising number of standing stones and wooden idols which have survived in Denmark and Sweden and these suggest a complex range of 'idols' were part of religious practice which Alexandra Sanmark has written about in detail (Sanmark 2002: Ch.4). The one type of idol which might be expected – portrayals of deities – is the one which is absent, although crude 'phallic' figures have been presumed by researchers to be associated with the veneration of Frey.

Bede twice states that shrines were fenced or hedged. Archaeologists have found square ditched enclosures at many Anglo-Saxon inhumation cemeteries, sometimes over prehistoric burial mounds. This suggests that in the Anglo-Saxon mind shrines and ancestors went together – just as christian churches would become the focus of a community's religion and the place of burial.

If all barrows were regarded similarly to the one in *Beowulf* – with the restless dead and a 'grave light' – then perhaps the enclosure was to dissuade fidgety ancestors from wandering away. And, if so, what did the Anglo-Saxons make of the much more massive enclosure around the stones of the henge? What sort of gigantic fidgety entities was a ditch that size intended to constrain?

Stapols and *beams*

Some of these cemetery enclosures reveal evidence for a central timber post. Presumably this would have been carved or painted and known as a *stapol* or *beam*. *Stapol* is found in such place-names as Stapleford (and the Leicestershire village is still pronounced 'stapulfud' by locals, and the Nottinghamshire one was until the 1970s when the influx of people moving into a large housing estate changed the pronunciation to follow the written form). Dunstable was the *stapol* on the 'dune' or heath as before the twelfth century there was no town at this crossing of two important Roman roads. Thurstable, 'Thor's *stapol*' in Essex I have already mentioned. Many long-since gone *stapols* are referred to as boundary markers in Anglo-Saxon charters.

If these *stapols* typically had a real or carved animal's head at the top then they may have given their name to such places as Shepshed, Leicestershire ('sheep's head'), Gateshead, Tyneside ('goat's head'), Broxted, Essex and Broxhead, Hampshire ('badger's head'), Eversheds, Surrey ('boar's head') and Swineshead, Bedfordshire and Swinesherd, Worcestershire.

A hundred in Bedfordshire is known as Manshead and one in Cumbria was Thiefside (thief's head). The probable moot site for the Selkely Hundred in Wiltshire – which included Avebury – is Manshead near Ogbourne St George (Pollard and Reynolds 2002: 223–4). One may assume that the various hundreds named after 'marked' (or 'goitred') trees – the Gartree Hundreds – are only one step removed from carved posts. And we can only speculate as to how these gartrees and stapols with men's heads overlapped with gallows sites and similar. And carved depictions of a judicial execution on a tree were to take off big time with the christian era – although these depictions seem to have been called either a rood or *beam* (from which the modern word for a worked timber derives, but originally meaning 'tree' and later 'post' or 'pillar' or 'cross'). Bladbean in Kent is from 'blood beam'; there is also an Anglo-Saxon charter referring even more specifically to a *cristelmaelbeam* ('crucifix-beam').

The lost place of *Bemblowe* in Gloucestershire presumably took its name from a *hlaew* (burial mound) with a *beam* on top. This fits what archaeologists describe when they excavate a burial mound with a central post hole. Did such *beam hlaew* once make the top of *weoh don* at Avebury – still Waleditch at the time – distinctive?

Montisfont's funta, *June 2008.*

And would the double row of standing stones running along the side of this *weoh don* be thought of, had Aldhelm visited, as *ermula cruda*?

Pagan sites were never holy

One thing we can be sure of is that neither Aldhelm nor any other christian cleric would have described them as *halig* – 'holy'. This is a word which is only used to describe places or objects of christian sanctity. So people looking for pre-christian 'holy wells' will not find them by following up early references to *halig wella* (Harte 2008). There is however just one example of a *weoh wella* which gives us Wyville in the Lincolnshire parish of Saltby (other place-names containing Wyville derive from Norman lords of that name).

Indeed, as Jeremy Harte succinctly points out:

> In Iceland, though paganism survived until much later, sacred springs were identified as something distinctively Christian. When Bishop Guthmund Arason toured Iceland in the late twelfth century, he asserted the rights of the Church by performing miracles and consecrating springs. Many took a dim view of these blessings and counterattacked by pissing in springs which the Bishop had just dedicated. This would have been self-defeating if they had been converted heathen sacred places.

(Harte 2008: 114)

Where pre-christian sacred wells may have been is where the Anglo-Saxons borrowed the Brittonic word *funta* (itself borrowed from the Latin *fontana*) and gave us place-names such as Mottisfont (Hampshire) and Urchfont and the Teffonts (all in Wiltshire).

The *land wights*

Perhaps Guthmund should have paid more attention to the *elfen* inhabitants of Iceland. If place-names and even personal names offer any sort of census then there were lots of them. But scholars struggle to find a consensus of what the word meant. In *Beowulf* the *ylfe* is one of the creatures descended from Cain, along with *eotenas, orcneas* and *gigantas*. *Elf* appears in old manuscripts as a gloss for the Latin *nymphae* and other mythological beings, and appears compounded in words related to ailments, female beauty or deceit. Scholars have long puzzled over the distinction in the *Prose Edda* between light elves, dark elves and dwarves; J.R.R. Tolkien's well-known take on these has hardly helped clear up the confusion. (See Hall 2007, especially chapters 3 and 9, for an extended discussion of *aelfe* names.)

Early Anglo-Saxons – and maybe their ancestors too – 'may have thought of *elf* as otherworldly non-monstrous, good-natured, beautiful, human-like beings' (Martinez 2010).

> Some of the compounds with that word implied womanly beauty or deceit, like *aelfsciene* or *aelfscinu*, related to the verb *scinan* ('to shine'), and translated as 'beautiful like an elf', but also comparable to the noun *scin* ('a deceptive appearance, phantom'), present in words as *scin-craeft* ('magic art'), *scin-lac* ('necromancy, sorcery'), scinna ('spectre'), etc. [...]

> Thus, in the late Anglo-Saxon period *aelfe* belonged to an unclear class of perilous *wights*, and in that class they could be mixed with other native creatures like *dweorgas, entas, eotenas, niceras, byrsas,* or *wuduwasan*, as well as with creatures of Classic and other foreign mythologies.

> (Martinez 2010)

So, to be *elf* was, in modern parlance, to be 'paranormal', 'Otherworldly' or 'enchanted'. The reason we have a problem understanding it is in part because when the Normans arrived they brought with them a French word which, until the nineteenth century, had a similar sense. That word was 'fairy'. Indeed it is still the sense of the phrase 'fairy tales', as not all such tales feature fairies, but they are tales of enchantment. And remember that fairies once had 'glamour' – meaning the ability to change their appearance at will, recalling the Old English *aelfscinu*. Originally the world 'fascinating' had the same sense. Fairies changed greatly once Shakepeare got hold of them, and were transformed out of all recognition by Victorian nursery tales writers. Their twee namesakes who abound in modern popular literature and on the Internet have little resemblance to their elven origins.

Breedon on the Hill – are these puca *with the* aelfscinu *to appear as* pocca?

Elves not only became fairies but they were demonised. Literally. In Latin they were *daimones,* which gives us the modern word 'demons'. In Classical Roman times *daimones* were neutral spirits, intermediate between gods and humans. They were capable of serving either good or evil purposes. However, in the christian world view, as for most Jews, they were angels who had turned against their creator and turned wholly to evil (Kieckhefer 1990: 38). The survived into remoter parts of seventeenth century Britain as 'spirit helpers' who may be good or evil; although, according to the understandably scant records, women 'only' asked for good from their spirit helpers (Wilby 2005: 50–2).

As Helios de Rosario Martinez states, elves were among a broad class of *land wights,* which were akin to the *genii loci* of Roman and Romano-British paganism, which we will encounter again in Chapter Nine. Elves and giants (*thyrs* – such as Grendel in *Beowulf*) were the main types of *wights* but there were others, including *scucca* (giving us place-names such as Shugboough, Staffordshire and the Norfolk dialect name for phantom black dogs, 'Black Shuck') and *puca* (usually translated as 'goblins'). *Puca* becomes the Puck of medieval and early modern folklore, the indigenous British trickster. While Coyote, Anasai and the tricksters of other places' traditional cultures are beloved by modern storytellers, they ignore our very own Puck (see Trubshaw 2002 Ch. 7 for a more detailed critique of modern storytelling).

Puca seems to be the origin of place-names such as Pucks Hill, the inspiration for Rudyard Kipling. However more recent place-name scholarship suggests that puck-place-names may be where fallow deer (*pocca*) were to be seen, not *puca*. Or was the ambiguity always there? Were the man-headed animals depicted by the Anglo-Saxon mason working at Breedon on the Hill, Leicestershire (yes, 'hill hill on the hill') in about 800 CE a visual pun on such *puca* with the *aelfscinu* to appear as *pocca*? A herd of Minotaurs does not seem to be the intended interpretation… We think now of fauns as two-legged rather than on four feet, but otherwise the fawn-like

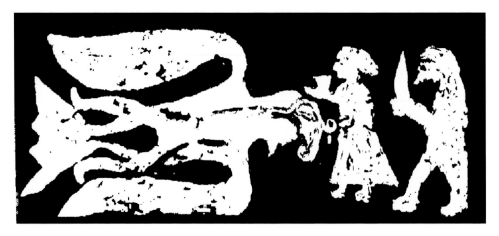

Odin wearing a flying cloak as depicted on a picture stone from Lärbro Stora Hammars on Gotland.

appearance suggests Otherworldly fauns (to use two words that would *not* have been known to the sculptor!)

Anglo-Saxon shamanism

The converse of these carvings – men with stag's heads – go back to the Mesolithic deer head-dress found at Star Carr and a Eurasian Paleolithic stag cult. Stags remained a cult creature well into the medieval period – and indeed might still be considered so within Highland Scottish culture. Aspects of *Beowulf* attest to such cultic status (see Nicholson 1988). So does the use of red deer antlers as picks to construct Neolithic monuments such as Avebury henge and Silbury Hill – with used or broken picks being deposited in a ritual manner. And there is evidence of red deer antler being used as tools in Mesolithic Scottish islands, suggesting that these magnificent creatures have been honoured in the British Isles since people returned after the last ice age.

Whether we can think of stags, or even other animals, as 'totemic' animals in the more shamanic sense within Anglo-Saxon culture is debatable. Stephen Glosecki has made a strong case for an 'implicit' shamanic initiation legend forming the structure of *Beowulf*; he even argues that in the Old English poem *The Dream of the Rood* the crucifixion of Christ is written as if it is a parody of a shamanic rebirth. He specifically looks at the importance of flying and shape-shifting in the legends of Woden, suggesting that these have a long shamanic ancestry. He also discusses various 'mighty women', such as valkyries and Norns, again arguing for roots in more overtly shamanic traditions. (Glosecki 1989)

While such better-known works about Anglo-Saxon shamanism as Brian Bates' *The Way of Wyrd* (1983) are now considered to lack scholarly rigour, the broader ideas of Glosecki's study of Anglo-Saxons shamanism have held up to the scrutiny of later scholarship. Indeed, Emma Wilby has looked at evidence for shamanic practices surviving in seventeenth century Scotland (Wilby 2010).

Reading Karen Jolly's study of Old English charms gives some indication of how such world-views survived, at least in terms of healing animals and people who were 'elf-shot'. Invocations to deities came three-fold, as Shakespeare's Weird Sisters would later affirm to Macbeth with the words

> Thrice to thine and thrice to mine
> And thrice again, to make up nine.
> Peace! the charm's wound up.

Apart from specific healing charms, we also have from the Anglo-Saxon era a charm comprised of 'nonce' wording, sounding rather like Latin but not making sense in either Latin, Old English or Brittonic. Is this the degraded survival of words that generations of shamanic valkyries once uttered on someone's *weoh hlaew* at a *hearg*, seeking either to placate the restless dead or communicate with them for divination? Try it out in the right place and time… just remember to be careful what you wish for!

> Tigath, tigath, tigath. Calicet aclu cluel sedes adclocles acre earce
> arnem nonabiuth aer aernum nithren arcum cunath. Arcum
> cunath arcum arctua fligara uflen binchi cutern nicuparam raf afth
> egal uflen. Arta, arta, arta trancula trancula.

Chapter 8

The Hills are Alive...

One of the wonderful advantages of walking is that we can fully experience where we are. Most Western people are so dominated by their visual experiences that they rarely fully engage their other senses. Yet even with the limited sensitivity of the human nose a walk through woodland on a damp autumn day can offer a feast of olfactory experiences. Even when in the countryside few actively listen to the sounds around them. Only the most striking of bird songs or burbling brooks consciously register. The changes in the sounds of our footfalls as we pass from grassland to the dry soil of an arable field, over a timber footbridge, on to a gravel path, splash through a puddle, kick up some dead leaves, then swish past some undergrowth rarely break through our cognitive filtering processes into conscious awareness. We generally walk through our surroundings with the soundtrack turned off.

Vision is the dominant perception of modern culture. When we say 'I see what you mean' we do not necessarily mean this literally. Yet the dominant aim of rationalism and science is to make things visible – from graphs and flow diagrams through to telescopes, microscopes, X-rays, nuclear magnetic resonance, chromatographs and much, much else. It is as if the ultimate dream of rationalism is to see all human knowledge laid out, arranged in order – just as a landscape painting presents the scene from an idealised viewpoint (and this is not a casual comparison but reveals how the visually-dominated metaphor of 'seeing = understanding' is *causal* in our culture).

Despite the dominance of vision, our hearing is nevertheless essential to develop a 'sense of place'. Sounds fill our surroundings (whether natural or built) and give places a specific character or 'presence'. However, unlike vision, we cannot readily map sounds. Neither do we customarily record sounds in the same way photographs or drawings quite commonly 'freeze' our vision. This means that sound is typically experienced directly. And, equally importantly, if we notice sounds at all we tend to 'experience the moment' more intensely than with visual stimuli. And, unlike vision, our sense of hearing is not diminished in the darkness (indeed, in the absence of distracting visual stimulation, our hearing may appear more acute in low light).

Before the invention of writing all verbal communication was part of our sound world rather than an aspect of our visual experiences (see Ong 1982 for the classic study of this). Because we cannot 'close our ears' in the same way as we can close our eyes and because our hearing is omni-directional we always hear our complete acoustic environment, even though our cognitive processes have devised sophisticated ways of filtering out non-threatening and 'background' sounds.

Hearing is believing

Sound is different to vision in three profound ways. We do not need an equivalent of light to hear – our ears work just as well after dark. We do not need a direct 'light of sight' to hear, at least for moderately loud sounds. And we do not have to be facing the direction of a sound to hear it.

The Inuit, who need to hunt in the dark, use the sounds of places to denote landmarks and resources, in the same way we would refer to a fence or hedge. Similarly people who live in dense jungle cannot visualise the space around them. Whereas Westerners might think 'I thought I heard a monkey – Ah, yes! I can see it over there', Amazonians would only believe there was a monkey if they *heard* the monkey, and would regard a sighting in the same way a Westerner would respond to the sound alone. For the Amazonians 'hearing is believing', in contrast to the Western 'seeing is believing' (Thorn 1997). The Suya of Brazil use the expression 'it is in my ear' where we would say 'I see what you mean'. Keen hearing is the mark of a 'fully socialised individual' and sight is considered by Suya people to be anti-social, cultivated only by witches (Classen 1993: 9). For the Songhai in central West Africa vision is often less important than taste, smell and hearing. In the Songhai language one tastes kinship, smells witches, and hears the ancestors (Stoller 1989 :5).

In such societies aural landscapes share with visual ones the concepts of landmarks and boundaries. For the Umeda of Papua New Guinea the auditory horizon is a tall ridge around the knoll where their village stands. The words used to encode these features and the traversing of the jungle create an auditory map which can only be understood dynamically, as movement (Gell 1995).

Hearing is fundamental to knowledge for Australian Aborigines in a subtly different way. According to Bruce Chatwin, they only believe the country exists when they could both see it and *sing it* by chanting the relevant 'Dreaming track' or so-called 'song line' (already discussed in the Preface). There must be a mental concept – the words of the song – before the landscape can be said to exist.

Indeed before writing was used by everyone, everything anyone 'knew' had come to them *aurally*. Knowledge was acquired by hearing – or at least best understood that way. Which is why accountants today 'audit' accounts – for many years these who wanted to know if the books balanced asked their book-keepers to read the accounts out loud, as this way they made more sense that seeing the written record.

There is much more that could be said about the 'anthropology' of sound and vision constructing our sense of place. Indeed Tim Ingold has already written a remarkable book on just this topic (Ingold 2000, esp. Ch.14). For the moment I want to look less at the anthropology of sound and instead at its archaeology.

Immersive experiences

The Hal Saflieni hypogeum on Malta, constructed in several phases between 3600 and 2500 BCE, has numerous examples of anomalous 'sound effects'. For example, a voice speaking into a certain recess resonates throughout the vaults, perhaps awing the faithful with disembodied voices capable of a full range of tones from thunderous to whispered. But there was much more to this manmade rock-cut multi-level tomb complex than acoustic oddities. All the senses would have been engaged, as Robin Skeates describes:

> Some things would have been illuminated and seen clearly, but others would have been controlled and concealed, with the vision of the spectators often intentionally obstructed. The visitors would have kept an eye on each other, their bodies communicating through blurred facial expressions, gestures, postures, and proximities. Like non-sighted persons, any impoverishment of their sense of sight would have been compensated for by an enhancement of their other senses and their visual imaginations. They would have felt their way through the gloom, some with confidence, others holding hands, their bodies occasionally bumping into obstacles and each other, as they tripped or fell. They would have felt contrasts, between roughly carved walls and smoothed or drilled surfaces of... limestone, between the damp ceilings and dry walls, between the living and the dead, and between flesh and bones. They would have carried things ranging from heavy corpses to hand-held tools, and would have handled, even caressed, some highly tactile sacred objects. They would have sensed the size and shape of the different chambers that they entered and the strange airless humidity of the underground environment, surrounded by living rock. They would have made and heard sounds that reverberated through those underground spaces, communicating in the dark with the sound of their breathing, footsteps, whispers, announcements, chants, and ceremonial instruments. They might have tasted some of the food that they offered as gifts to the dead. They may also have been conscious of the smell of the invisible odour of decomposing human bodies that characterized this inadequately ventilated space, as well as the familiar smell of close kin and friends... The visitors might have sensed the haunting presence of spirits of the dead and supernatural forces, announced by flashes of light or conspicuous sounds or smells in these fantastic dream-spaces. These senses would have triggered a range of emotions...

(Skeates 2008)

I have not been to the Hal Saflieni hypogeum. Nevertheless Skeates' portrayal fits well with my responses to the much smaller spaces of early Neolithic chamber tombs, such as West Kennett.

Skeates' multi-sensory approach to Hal Saflieni is so far something of an exception. Most researchers, if they step beyond the visual and spatial aspects, only venture into the acoustic aspects. Even more of an exception are prehistorians who consider the effects of synaesthesia – where the brain 'blends' the senses, an effect some people encounter as part of normal experience but is mostly encountered while 'stoned' on psychoactive plants or drugs (see Gyrus 1999 for one of the few exceptions).

While I would like you to bear in mind such overall 'immersive experiences', this chapter is mostly concerned with just the sound worlds of the past.

Acoustics and our ancestors

Early examples of the use of sound to enhance the sacredness of a place have been recognised in the caves at Ariege beneath the French Pyrénées. These contain extensive Palaeolithic wall paintings. At certain places close to significant motifs anyone singing or whistling at the correct pitch will set up dramatic resonances. This is not an isolated example; in later periods temples were designed to amplify sound as part of the ritual procedures.

American rock art consistently occupies places which provide abnormally strong echoes or where sounds such as clapping re-echo as the sound of running animals. Similar examples have been found in Australia. (Waller 1993a, 1993b).

In the mid-1990s more scientific investigation of the acoustic properties of prehistoric sites began (Jahn 1995; Jahn *et al* 1996; Devereux and Jahn 1996; Watson and Keating 1999, 2000) and this continues in the research of Rupert Till (see soundsofstonehenge.wordpress.com). Paul Devereux has provided an accessible introduction to this pioneering research (Devereux 2001) and a more up-to-date overview (Devereux 2008). Three broad acoustic responses at prehistoric sites were investigated. The first reveals that carved or painted rock art, whether in caves or 'rock shelters', is cited at spots where the echoes are more pronounced. So chanting, singing, clapping or drumming calls forth sounds that seemingly emanate from the decorated rock surface – as if the spirits of the image are talking back.

The nearest I have come to a personal experience of such eerie effects is when a group of pagans were drumming in the nave of a high-roofed Victorian church (with the consent of a very ecumenical vicar!). The multiple echoes formed complex sound patterns quite unrelated to the rhythm and pitch of the drums, for all the world sounding like the roof space was filled with Otherworldly spirits fluttering and chattering. The resonant space also created what are known as 'standing waves', meaning the sounds had no clear source and walking slowly around made the sound louder and quieter with every few steps. Had there been even less light, or other factors had created more of an altered state of consciousness, then the illusion of 'angels' would have been entirely real.

The two surviving stones of the Cove, Avebury, looking north-east to one of the stones of the north circle, dawn November 2007.

The second effect discovered so far is anomalous sound reflections at stone circles, especially the Scottish ones with so-called 'recumbent' stones, where the recumbent megalith acts as a 'sounding board' to help project the voice of someone standing in front. Such 'sound reinforcement' works only within the ring of stones, except for some really curious instances where the sound is also remarkably clear at a nearby prehistoric site, even though all-but inaudible *between* the two. The same effect has been observed between Camster Round and Camster Long tombs in Caithness (Watson and Keating 1999: 330) – drumming in one can be heard in the other 190 metres away – but not in between. In this context we should think of the trilithon 'ring' at Stonehenge, which clearly all-but blocks sound going out from the centre – and the later bluestone horseshoe with its parabolic shape which directs sound in one direction (north-east) to the exclusion of audibility in other directions (see soundsofstonehenge.wordpress.com for details). So perhaps it is not coincidence that when the Cove in the Avebury henge still had a third large stone that too would have directed sound very effectively in the same north-easterly direction.

The third aspect of the acoustic research shows that Neolithic chambered tombs have a natural resonant frequency that falls within the range of the male voice. Experiments with setting up 'standing waves' in, say, Newgrange have resulted in decidedly odd experiences. Paul Devereux reports being inside a chamber tomb when such a standing wave was created by researchers. Moving away from the sound source the chamber would first fall silent (at the 'troughs' in the standing wave, where the 'echo' cancels out the source) then increase in loudness (at the 'crests', where the echo augments the source). 'To a people who did not understand sound in terms of waves, this would seem very mysterious indeed.' (Devereux 2002: 29) If someone else moves within the chamber this can cause dramatic alterations in the 'distribution' of the sound and its loudness at a particular place. Other effects include 'ventriloquism', that is the sound source seems to be in an improbable place. When a standing wave is set up speech is distorted with extraordinary harmonics.

These are all wonderfully impressive 'special effects' for ritual activities – as if the interior of a chamber tomb (especially while it still contained the bones of one's ancestors and other sacred objects) was not already a powerful setting for ritual activities. Mike Williams is among the most recent of many authors to write from first-hand experience of the trance-inducing effects of drumming (Williams 2010; 33). Peter Knight devotes part of his recent book about West Kennett chambered long barrow to just this sort of 'experiential' engagement with the monument (Knight 2011: 118–28).

Soundtrack for the supernatural

Standing waves can be set up by chanting, singing or drumming. They can also arise if the wind blows across the entrance to such chambers, creating a lower-frequency version of the eerie sound created by blowing across an empty bottle. Thomas Hardy wrote in *Tess of the D'Urbervilles* of the wind blowing at Stonehenge and creating 'a booming tone, like the note of some gigantic one-stringed harp' (cited in Dickinson 2001: 98). David Toop also notes Hardy's writing about Stonehenge and also the sound of wind etc in Thomas de Quincey's writing (Toop 2010: 174) as well as evocatively drawing attention to 'preternatural sound' in James Fenimore Cooper's *The Last of the Mohicans* (Toop 2010: viii).

In recent decades first 'alternative archaeology' and then academic archaeologists have recognised that Neolithic and Bronze Age monuments incorporate complex alignments, astronomical orientations, shadow paths, and such like (see Trubshaw 2005: Ch.5). Predictably, modern minds are more likely to recognise such *visual* complexity. However, as prehistoric people probably used all their senses more equally, quite plausibly our ancestors intentionally incorporated equally sophisticated *acoustic* complexity in their monuments.

If you're singing and making rhythmic noises then – especially if you're getting a bit 'spacey' too – then fairly inevitably you will start dancing too. As Aubrey Burl put it:

> Legends of impious girls who danced on the Sabbath being transformed into a circle of stones are too many to be coincidental. As early as the twelfth century Geoffrey of Monmouth referred to Stonehenge as Chorea Gigantum, the Giants' Dance. As far away as the Shetlands a circle was called Haltadans, 'the limping dance' and three cairns nearby are known as the Fiddlers' Crus (enclosures). At Stanton Drew, close to Avebury, the three circles are nicknamed the Weddings with

particular stones identified as the Fiddlers, the Maids and the
Bride and Bridegroom. Whether at Land's End or on Bodmin Moor
or in Wicklow there are the same stories that people danced in
the stone rings whose every shape and size encourages this
belief... Near Peshawur in Pakistan, the natives knew nothing of a
concentric circle of tall stones except that 'a wedding party,
passing over the plain, were turned into stone by some powerful
magician'.

(Burl 1979: 210)

'Avebury need be no different,' noted Burl, 'with lines of face-painted men and
women circling the sarsens, drums beating, torches burning in the blackness of the
night.' Since those pioneering thoughts in the 1970s much consideration has been
given to sound in prehistory. Investigations into 'archaeo-acoustics' reported at a
conference in June 2003 by about twenty researchers includes studying echoes in
Palaeolithic painted caves (including the then recently-discovered paintings at
Cresswell Crags in Derbyshire) and Swedish rock art sites (see Tilley 2008 for some
wonderful first-hand accounts). Various Neolithic chamber tombs were also found to
resonate at 100 Hz, an audio frequency which significantly affects the pre-frontal
and temporal cortex of the human brain (Mortimer 2003).

At a complex rock art site created by the Algonkian Indians of the Ontario region of
Canada between 600 and 1,100 years ago the main group of carvings are on a
deeply-fissured outcrop of marble. At certain times of the year water can be heard
issuing from the fissure – and it sounds like a babble of voices. Presumably the
Indians venerated the site because they thought these were the voices of *manitous* or
spirits. (Devereux 2004). Other rock art sites in the Ontario region were associated
with anomalous echoes. Indeed one set of carvings is in a park known as Bon Echo.
'Had the Indians, like the ancient Greeks, believed echoes to be the sound of spirits
calling, mimicking human-made noises to do so?' asks Devereux.

Sacred resonances

Interesting acoustic effects are not restricted to prehistoric sites. The acoustics of
Classical Greek and Roman theatres reveal an exceptional ability to make the voices
of the actors heard by a large number of people. Graeme Lawson has reported on
remarkable acoustic discoveries at Wells Cathedral (Lawson 2003). Bob Dickinson
has provided overviews of 'sacred resonances' in caves, mosques and even English
cathedrals, such as Lincoln (Dickinson 1990a&b, 1998, 2001).

Almost certainly Anglo-Saxon plainchant could generate spectacular standing wave
effects in the small cave-like stone-built churches of the time, although to my
knowledge no one has attempted to replicate this experience – and there is no way
of knowing if such effects were intentionally sought by early christians. Later
'polyphonic' plainchant of the medieval era resounding through a cathedral built at
the time such music was composed is a wonderful experience although modern
singers typically do not attempt to pitch their voices according to the natural
resonances of the building (I have been informed of a solo singer at St Ouen in

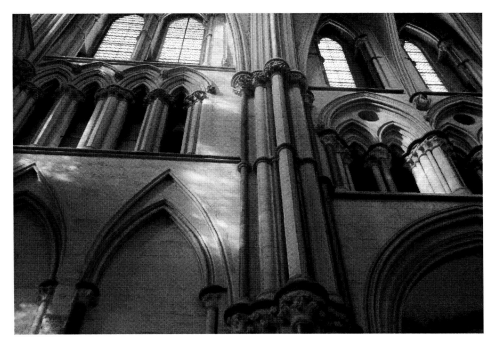

Columns in Lincoln Cathedral.

Rouen who sang close to the columns; his voice caused the columns to resonate resulting in a strangely disembodied sound that had no clear place or origin).

If this sounds a little far-fetched then consider the clusters of musical stone pillars in the Nellaiyappar temple dedicated to Shiva, the Hindu 'Lord of the Dance'. Gently tapping the columns produces the seven notes of the scale used in Indian classical music. According to the temple's own chronicle these pillars were erected in the seventh century. There is a total of 161 tuned pillars, arranged in clusters with up to 48 smaller columns around a larger pillar. Each cluster is hewn out of a single piece of rock. No other temple has such an elaborate arrangement, although eight other temples in the south of India with musical pillars are known. Such musical pillars are clearly counterparts to the many Indian temples where the columns are decorated with depictions of musicians or dancers (Venkatesh 2004). Elsewhere in southern India, at Hiregudda Hill, are gong-like musical boulders associated with rock art which dates back from recent times to the Neolithic (Bolvin 2004). Other ringing rocks are known from the Karnataka (dated to around 3,000 BCE), Kupgal and Deccan districts of India, and also from South Africa (Rifkin 2009).

Such effects may have also been known in the British Isles (Fagg 1957). In the Presceli district of south-west Wales (where the 'blue stones' at Stonehenge came from) there is a hamlet called Maenclochog which translates as 'ringing rocks'. The rock type is dolerite similar to that at Hiregudda Hill which makes a ringing sound when struck. The ringing rocks at Maenclochog are thought to have been destroyed by quarrying in the late eighteenth century. However it raises the possibility that the Stonehenge 'blue stones' were originally significant as 'ringing rocks', before being silenced by being stood up in the ground.

If you think hitting rocks would produce a rather limited range of sounds then seek out some recordings of the traditional Basque *txalaparta*. This comprises two or more long beams of wood, set out on trestles, and struck with two round wooden shafts. In the hands of virtuosi *txalapartaris* these generate a wealth of 'trancy' sounds. A suitable 'rock xylophone' would have been a less portable version.

But maybe the ringing rocks of Presceli needed no virtuoso. Paul Devereux also reports that in 1983 a woman was waiting for the sunrise at Stonehenge. Just before dawn 'she suddenly heard a "ringing" sound issuing from a stone close to her' (Devereux 1990: 144), although it is not clear if the stone was a bluestone or a sarsen.

Bring back the roaring bull

Despite the evidence of modern paganism, drumming or playing a didjeridoo is not the only way to connect with the spirits of place – although they may be effective. There is a more evocative way to 'summon the spirits' – using a flattish piece of wood whirled around the head on a thin rope. Not to be attempted near other people, please note!

The sound is decidedly Otherwordly, more so in the dark, and it is easy to see why it was thought to be the voices of ancestors, or spirits, or even deities. As it whirls around the pitch rises and falls as the instrument approaches and recedes from the listener (we now know it as the Doppler effect). By twisting the cord before starting to whirl the wood, a 'roaring' vibrato can be induced. Changing the speed of whirling changes the pitch. Increasing the length of the cord – or extending the arm holding it – also affects the sound. The complex sound which results from this simple device has a low frequency component which carries surprisingly far, especially downwind.

Quite why they are commonly known in English as bullroarers I have not established; the word may not predate the nineteenth century. They were still being made for use as toys in Britain less than a hundred years ago. But they are indeed archaic. What seems to be a bullroarer from 17,000 BCE was found in the Ukraine. They were one of the sacred instruments used in the Greek Dionysian Mysteries. They are used for ritual purposes throughout the world – they were part of native American religious rites and continue to be used in male initiation rites by Australian Aboriginal tribes. The altogether rather wonderful Pitt Rivers Museum in Oxford has a number of different examples from around the world.

Interestingly, Steve Marshall has found that Neolithic ritual deposits sometimes include a distinctive style of worked flint with no signs of use. Archaeologists term them 'plano-convex knives' but Marshall discovered a replica made a very effective bullroarer. He tested it out in the Avebury henge, near the Cove stones (Marshall 2010).

Riding the sound wave to the Otherworld

Bullroarers are used to evoke the Otherworld. Bells, gongs, rattles, whistles, fireworks, drums, shouts, foot stamping, chants, mantras and hymns are used world-wide to banish Otherworldy demons and entities. The early christian saints carried hand bells for use at key moments in the Mass, although they seem to be a continuation of pre-christian practices for banishing unwanted otherworldly entities, as the 'bell, book and candle' of christian exorcism clearly confirms. The larger bells of church towers were until recent times widely credited with the ability to frighten away the Devil.

And the Devil certainly had a way with words. Or at least those accused of being in league with the Lord of Darkness did. The power of witches was as much in what they said as what they did. In the Bocage area of rural France witchcraft was still a hidden but very influential aspect of community life during the 1970s. Jeanne Favret-Saad was able to 'infiltrate' the communities sufficiently to understand what was happening. She discovered that it worked like 'rumours' – and everyone, herself included, became part of this process. Innuendo rather than curses is what created the fear (Favret-Saad 1981).

We consider witchcraft to be distinct from healing magic but the reality is that there is no real distinction between cursing and curing. Karen Jolly's study of Anglo-Saxon charms reveals that what was said was at least as important as what was done (Jolly 1996). As already noted in Chapter Four, the priest with his 'patter' held real power. It didn't matter that only the priest – and perhaps not always him – understood the meaning. As Jolly states:

> Latin hymns by the laity ignorant of Latin on the grounds that the sounds of praise were just as significant. Charms containing garbled, untranslatable foreign language words relied on the sound of the words – their mystery and assonance-to achieve some connection with spiritual powers. Also, they were ennobled by their vague association with the venerable classical languages, Latin and Greek. Consequently the Latin prayers used with these garbled foreign charms would sound equally mysterious and powerful to an illiterate Anglo-Saxon ear.

(Jolly 1996: 118)

Buddhists too make much of mantras and other sacred chants. This is shared with the other dharmic religions such as hinduism – where the sacred word *aum* or *om* has especial significance. Does this help us understand the enigmatic symbolic 'opening of the mouth' ceremony in the mummification rituals of ancient Egyptians? If, to an ancient Egyptian, it was obvious that you need to chant your way to the Otherworld, or at least chant to be able to closely encounter the deities when you arrive there, then clearly having your mouth closed off by the fabric and resins used for mummification would be a major hindrance.

The symbol for om *or* aum.

Chanting, drumming, clapping and beating together sticks are all time-honoured aids to entering trance. A reductionist approach will see this as certain biological effects 'kicking in' (see Winkelman 2008). A more experiential account would note that there is considerable subtlety to the effects. Indeed researchers who have closely studied Australian chanting, stick-beating and didjeridoo playing recognise that this creates 'a multi-layered system of finesse and intricacy of performance that Westerners can scarcely comprehend' (Hume 2007: 52 summarising the work of Catherine Ellis).

Indeed modern Westerners are distinctive because of their inability to hear what people in a wide variety of traditional societies readily perceive. The Nigerian Songhay sorcerer who Paul Stoller was apprenticed to for several years reportedly said that '... you must learn how to hear, or you will learn little about our ways.' (Stoller and Olkes 1987: 560) While I make no claims to be a sorcerer's apprentice, still less a master of such mysteries, reading that passage put me in mind of my own experiences in recent weeks while walking alone around the upper Kennet landscape. 'Learning how to listen' does indeed open up a whole new way of interacting with the landscape – and its *land wights* or *genni loci* or fair folk or whatever other name seems to suit.

The unnamed Songhay sorcerer might have had as his apprentice a more able student if Stoller had been brought up a Muslim, as the beauty and perfection of the divine message of the *Qur'an* needs to be appreciated through listening, not reading. And this is only right because, over the course of twenty-three years, the prophet Mohammad received the word of Allah via the angel Gabriel – which is why it is the *Qur'an* or 'recitation'. A Muslim – as indeed those of any faith – needs to open not only their heart but their ears to god (Erlmann 2004: 12).

Lawrence Sullivan has brought together considerable research into the 'enchanting powers' of music in the world's religions (Sullivan 1997). Sound is an essential part of the immersive experience of religious experiences, from whirling sufi dervishes through to the most shamanic of contemporary christian religious practice, pentecostalism – and much else, of course. How far back can we take this? The gut reaction is 'all the way to the Paleolithic caves', but can this be substantiated?

In a previous incarnation the Songhay sorcerer might also have got well with Marsilo Ficino, the Florentine humanist who lived between 1433 and 1499. Ficino, being aware of well-established tradition, thought that 'all realities emit vibrating rays which together compose the harmonious chorus of the universe.' These were ideas which echo all the way back two thousand years to Pythagoras.

And all the way across to Tibet. In a discussion which corrects numerous errors by Western scholars, Lama Anagaraika Govinda provides a detailed insight into how mantras function in the Tibetan buddhist world-view. The whole book offers an insight into how profoundly different this world-view is from popular understanding of oriental religion. But here I will concentrate on the section where he describes how mantras form 'the key to the riddles of creation and of creativeness'. He states:

> ... the power and effect of a mantra depend on the spiritual attitude, the knowledge and responsiveness of the individual. The *sabda* or sound of the mantra is not a physical sound (although it may be accompanied by such a one) but a spiritual one. It cannot be heard by the ears but only by the heart, and it cannot be uttered by the mouth but only by the mind. The mantra has power and meaning only for the initiated, i.e., for one who has gone through a particular kind of experience connected with the mantra.

> (Govinda 1960: 27)

This experience 'can only be acquired under the guidance of a competent Guru' and requires 'self-discipline, concentration, inner experience and insight'.

In quite a different realm of writing, the adventurer Ian Baker describes his expedition into the Tsangpo Gorge, Pemako, Tibet (Baker 2004). This inaccessible gorge is traditionally seen as the body of goddess Dorje Pagmo, with different parts corresponding to the five chakras. The entire gorge is the gathering place of dakas and dakinis – 'When observed in their essential nature, all the mountains, rocks, trees, and rivers [here] appear as magical realms or deities' wrote Lelung Shepe Dorje in *The Delightful True Stories of the Supreme Land of Pemako* published in 1729.

No one can go to the Tsangpo Gorge without being accompanied by a lama. Baker 'by chance' encounters a lama with several monks who just happen to want to travel this fearsomely difficult route. He describes how they continually chanted mantras and laughed their way through the various vicissitudes that made the journey physically and mentally exhausting. While Baker does not seem to recognise the 'therapeutic' value of their company, I for one doubt that he would have overcome the physical obstacles without the inspiration of the indomitable resolve of the lama and his monks, for whom their continual chanting was self-evidently a key part of their tenacity.

Put yourself in these monks' shoes, in their world-view. The journey may be physically demanding but they were walking on the body of a powerful goddess. While they were not one of the shamans who travel to a certain small lake 'on the August full moon to draw power from the clear black waters' (Baker 2004: 27) they would know the places of spiritual power in this fearsomely dramatic landscape. If their world-view of a remote gorge as the manifestation of a goddess and the empowerment of the August full moon seen reflected in water seems somewhat exotic, then think again about Michael Dames' 1970s interpretation of the Avebury monuments, and the way the August full moon reflected in the then-watery moat around Silbury Hill. His world-views may not have become part of Tibetan buddhism but in other respects the parallels are close. I will return to something like the Tibetan world-view of sacred river courses in the final chapter.

(The opening pages of this chapter are a revised version of Trubshaw 2005: 45–9; however a number of examples of prehistoric locations described in Devereux 2008 have not been added. The middle section benefited from Lynn Hume's overview of sound as 'portals' to Otherworldly experiences (Hume 2008 Ch.3).)

Chapter 9

Swans and their Celestial Songs

If, as we can reasonably assume, Mesolithic and Neolithic people were more aware of the sounds of the landscape than we normally are, then what did they make of the loud honking of large birds which migrated mostly by night? On moonlit nights their distinctive white plumage would make them all-but ghostly presences in the night sky. The sight of a swan serenely swimming on a river or the lake of a municipal park is fairly commonplace but nevertheless inspiring. Seeing them flying is more so. But today we rarely encounter these birds when they do most of their flying, after dark. Indeed this flying is largely seasonal, as most species of swan (such as the whooper and trumpeter) are more migratory than mute swans (who are much less migratory in Britain than in other parts of their range).

In Greek myths swans are sacred birds, especially associated with both Apollo and Aphrodite. But the significance of swans predates Greek myths by many millennia. Andrew Collins, when researching his book *The Cygnus Mystery* (Collins 2008 [2006]), has attempted to identify the long history of swans in myths and early art. Much of the information in this chapter takes Collins' published research as a starting-point for my own follow-up explorations and interpretations. However my interpretations do not necessarily agree with his.

The oldest cave art in Britain, deep inside Church Hole at Creswell Crags in Derbyshire, was created around 10,000 BCE. A long way down one of the more inaccessible passageways is the beautifully stylised head of either a swan or an ibis. Nearby is the depiction of an ibex. As neither ibis nor ibex were native to Britain then – indeed at that time Creswell Crags would have been near the edges of retreating glaciers from the last Ice Age – the people who came to Creswell must have travelled far and wide.

Stylised flying swan pendants made from mammoth ivory were also discovered in two locations in the Siberian Angara valley. These have been dated to around 13,000 BCE. This may help to explain why ethnographers researching Tungus Siberian shamans have photographed depictions of the world tree made from a bare tree

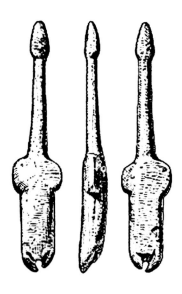

Left: *Bronze* tintinabulum *(wind chime) with a lion-legged winged phallus; Roman first century CE.*
Above: *Mammoth ivory pendants carved as stylised swans, from the Angara valley.*

trunk surmounted by a large wooden carving of a flying swan (see Collins 2008: 54). These bird totems helped the shaman ascend the world tree to the sky world during trances known as 'soul flights'.

While in more recent times such shamans think of their drum as a 'spirit horse' clearly such associations only post-date the domestication of horses in around 3,000 years ago. Before that other animals must have been ridden by the shaman to travel to the spirit worlds. While bear cults have long been part of Siberian shamanism, the idea of riding a real-world bear seems incongruous – and neither does bear-riding feature in any myths or legends. However riding swans, new-born babies being delivered by swans or storks, and other legends about geese are all part of 'fairy tales'. This does not prove that the swan carvings photographed on top of world trees are successors to a cult going back to pre-horse times, but they do add to the probability of their being most archaic.

A pure hunch but could these ivory pendants be wearable versions of larger wooden artefacts that have not survived? These would not be pendants but bullroarers, as discussed in the previous chapter. And another aside: the Angara pendants have been described as a rather phallic shape. Indeed they seem to be more associated with male graves – although one was also found in the grave of a child of unknown-

Bird-headed ithyphallic man, bird on pole and bison. Lascaux.

sex. Are they in some sense the Paleolithic precursors to Ted Hughes' 'blind swan of insemination'? More lurid imaginations than have mine have suggested that these are the distant ancestors of the winged phallus pendants and graffiti well-known in the Roman empire. This Classical winged phallus (or *tintinabulum* as they originally had small bells attached by chains) mutates into the modern image of a heart penetrated by an arrow – except the original anatomy was not a heart but somewhere the shape resembles more accurately. I leave it for you to work that one out – and then to reconsider an alternative reading of all the bumper stickers and T-shirts which proclaim 'I-heart-something'. And for that matter look again at the winged phallus and ask yourself what the 1960s interior design cliché of three diminishing ducks reminds you of…

Perhaps we should see the ithyphallic man next to a bird on pole in the Lascaux cave painting as a shaman with his world tree. This painting is in the more inaccessible part of the cave and a couple of millennia older than the probable age of the Angara valley pendants.

Undated prehistoric rock art, probably Neolithic, from around Lake Onega in Russia includes a large number of depictions of swans – including a giant over four metres long. These swans 'are often stylised to long-necked unearthly creatures merging into crevices' (Poikalainen 1999: 63). Lake Onega is fairly close to the Finnish border and this whole region was once the territory of Saami reindeer herders. According to their beliefs, Saami shamans rode on the back of swans to take them to the Otherworld.

Although rarely picked up by people who have popularised shamanism in recent decades, swans seem to have a deep relationship with all the circumpolar shamanic traditions. Siberian shamans from the Altai mountains believed that the world came into existence when a swan dived down into the primordial ocean and fetched up silt to create land. This myth is so old it travelled over the one-time land bridge into the Americas where the 'diver bird' (rarely a swan however) is a frequent creation myth among New World cultures. Swans also appear in the creation myths of the Ainu of Japan, who predate the now-dominant Mongoloid population.

The kitsch counterparts to stellar swan lore? Or well-disguised flying phalli?

Valkyries and swan maidens

Like women in many societies, Ainu women wail loudly as part of funeral rites. But the Ainu women do it to mimic the cry of swans. Now, as I will discuss later in the chapter, the sounds of swans are indeed distinctive, why is it a 'death cry'? We have Aesop to thank for the answer – according to his fable (although it is only a fable) swans that remain silent all their lives let out a fearful cry at the time of their death. Others hear it as a beautiful song. Or we could look to more recent Germanic myths of the 'swan maidens' who are indistinguishable from the valkyries, most renowned for bringing the souls of the dead to the afterlife at Valhalla. Indeed their name means literally 'chooser of the slain'. We might think of valkeries as beautiful maidens on swan-white horses. But for the Anglo-Saxons they were *waelcyrge* – a word also used to gloss the Classical Furies, who are wrathful killers rather than benignly 'tidying up' stray souls.

In Scandinavian sagas the *waelcyrge* were real people. Hild, Brynhild, Sigrdrifa, Svafa and Sigrun are all flesh-and-blood women, albeit legendary. At the beginning of the eleventh century, the Anglo-Saxon Archbishop Wulfstan wrote about 'witches and valkyries' as real ills to be banished from the christian world. Tacitus, Caeser, Plutarch and Saxo do not name valkyries but all describe battle magic that seems to fall well within the remit of such women. Such magic is described in some detail as part of the account of the twelfth-century struggles between Hereward and the Norman 'yoke', the *Gesta Herewardi*. The description closely matches the descriptions of *seithr* trances recorded in Scandinavian sagas. The valkyries were living women who could enter the Otherworlds – they quite literally walked on the boundaries between our reality and the reality we know now only from legends. They were themselves both real and 'legendary' (Ewing 2008: 98–102).

Were these flesh-and-blood valkyries the same women who, according to widespread Scandinavian folk traditions, wore swans' plumage and 'swan-dresses' (Kauffman 1903: 56)? Were such women also known for their divinatory skills, explaining why in Germany today to say 'swan's feathers are growing on me' denotes suddenly developing prophecy powers? And to what extent did these swan

Swans in flight. Illustration by Ian Brown.

legends overlap with the accounts of Freya's flying cloak? The sagas explicitly state this is made from falcon's feathers, not from swans, however. It is the same cloak borrowed by Odin when needs must for a shamanic-style flight. Both Freya and Odin engage in shape-shifting too, in other adventurous deeds. And much ink has flowed regarding the widespread folk belief that medieval witches could fly – whether by broomstick or flying lotions – and shift into the shape of cats, hares, and the like (though seemingly not swans, at least in British accounts).

Were these swan-dressed maidens and associated legends the inspiration for widespread later European legends which tell how legendary women shape-shifted between swan and human forms – and, falling foul of some prohibition, permanently back? These are fairy tales in the literal sense and once more show the transcending of the boundaries between the mundane world and the Otherworld.

While we have romantic associations with the word 'maiden', these swan maidens were not necessarily young or beautiful. Spinsters they would have literally have been, but this word did not yet apply only to unmarried older women. The origins of the term 'maiden' denoted all ages of unmarried women – and implied all the dangers of 'women without a master', as later law codes would deem them. These original 'Swan Vestas' were perhaps more than a match for any man...

Swans as psychopomps

Another still-current German expression translates literally as 'it swans me' and is used for those circumstances when the English would say 'someone has walked over my grave'. Americans are more likely to say 'a ghost has walked over my grave'. But this is just a corruption of 'a goose has just walked over my grave'. Perhaps this is a back-formation from the goose-bumps which go with such a suggestion – but equally probably the goose-bumps and the goose walking are the origins of the later forms.

There is even British folklore which speaks of people's souls being embodied in swans (Armstrong 1959: 48). One of the more comprehensive accounts of these beliefs comes from the Scottish Western Isles where people seeing either whooper swans or greylag geese migrating north to their Icelandic breeding grounds thought they were carrying the souls of the dead to heaven which lay 'north beyond the north wind' (Collins 2008: 100; based on personal communication with Eileen Buchanan in 2004).

Ceaser says that the Gaulish Celts believed that they are descendants of Dis Pater, the god of the dead.

> It seems likely that Donn is the Irish equivalent of Dis Pater so that
> when the Celts die they return to their great Ancestor, to their
> fathers. In the *Metrical Dindsenchas* the 9th century poet Mael
> Muru tells us that Donn himself asserted: *Chughamsa do mo
> theach, tiocfaifh sibh uile ndiaidh bhur mbais* (To me, to my
> house, you will all come after your death).
>
> (Meyer 1919: 538, cited in O Duinn 2008: 216).

In numerous local traditions it is unlucky to injure or kill a swan. Mute swans were special in English law, being the only birds owned by default by the Crown (and the exceptions are those on the River Thames which form the focus of the annual swan-upping ceremony every July). As it was illegal to kill a swan without the monarch's permission they became a 'taboo' food. St John's College, Cambridge had a special royal licence to have an annual swan supper – a right it still maintains, even though recent laws, such as the Wildlife and Countryside Act 1981, protect all wild swans and their eggs from being hunted or harassed anywhere in the UK.

I share with Collins the sense that swans were once widely thought of as carrying the souls of the dead to their resting place in the north. The presence of swans in Palaeolithic art – in contexts which fit with funereal or shamanic activities – suggests that these beliefs are widespread because of their great age. Collins uses archaeoastronomy to confirm that these traditions go back to about 13,000 BCE – I will summarise details of his arguments shortly. But first I want to consider how this movement of souls was not simply northwards.

Spirits of the unborn

The valkyries merge into the Norns, the weavers of fate according to Snorri's version of *Gylfaginning*. Some of these Norns cut short a person's life. Other Norns 'come to everyone when they are born to shape their lives'. Other sagas also reveal close associations between the Norns and birth (Ewing 2008: 103). While the Norns are not linked directly with swans in any of the surviving accounts, these accounts do not make firm distinctions between Norns and valkyries, who do overlap with swan maidens. As if by confirmation, in the Baltic region the mythopoetic role in procreation given to storks in Britain (where storks are not found!) is attributed to swans. And, with the Siberian shamans' swan-topped world tree back in mind, what should we make of Mircea Eliade's remark:

> The Goldi, the Dolgan, and the Tungus say that, before birth, the souls of children perch like little birds on the branches of the Cosmic Tree and the shamans go there to find them. This mythical motif is not confined to Central and North Asia; it is attested, for example, in Africa and Indonesia.

> (Elaide 1964: 272–3)

There is more to swans than conveyors of the dead – they also seem to be associated with the 'recycling' of souls. To my knowledge no one has yet discovered evidence for when people first began to believe in reincarnation. It is widespread (although not world-wide) and does seem to many people a satisfying world-view.

In the next section I will show that the journey the souls of the deceased took on the back of swans went 'north beyond the north wind' into the branches of the world tree itself. And, wherever this was thought to be – and the Avebury landscape is one such place – was also where the souls of the as-yet unborn awaited.

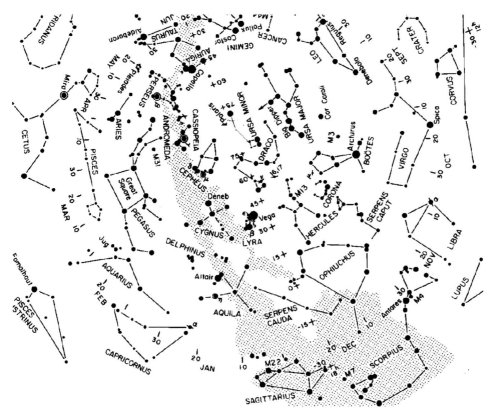

The Milky Way (shown shaded grey) with the constellation Cygnus near the centre.

The Way of the Birds

The English phrase 'Milky Way' describes the distinctively white belt of stars spanning the celestial sphere from horizon to horizon (although not visible where there is light pollution in urban areas). It is, we now know, the combined light from the billions of stars which make up our galaxy, seen 'edge on' so to speak. As with most European languages Milky Way is a translation from the Latin *Via Lactea,* itself as translation of the Greek *Galaxias Kyklos,* or 'Milky Circle' as, in Greek myths, the Milky Way was formed from milk spilt by Hera when suckling Heracles.

But there are other mythic explanations. The Mayan see the Milky Way in the night sky as the World Tree. In Ancient Egypt the Milky Way was the goddess Nut, stretched out as a sky goddess. Indeed she is normally depicted either naked or clad in a long gown covered with innumerable stars. In Oriental cultures the Milky Way is called the River (or Road) to the Otherworld. Indeed its whiteness means that it was closely associated with death in these cultures (which, unlike the West, link whiteness rather than black with death). Blackfoot Indians call it the 'Wolf Trial' – seen as a sacred path taking the spirits of the dead to the afterlife. Most other Amerindian tribes from California to Canada called it the 'Ghost Road' or something similar. And in Lithuanian, Estonian and Finnish it is 'The Birds' Path' or 'Way of the Birds' – strongly echoing the psychopompic role for swans already outlined.

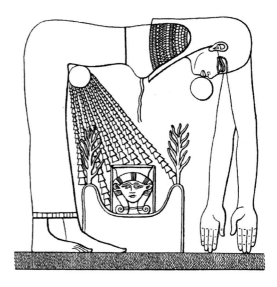

Nut depicted as a sky goddess who swallows the sun in the evening and gives birth to it again in the morning. After a Ptolomaic-Roman period ((300 BCE to 300 CE) relief in the temple of Hathor at Dendera (after Myeliwiec 2004).

The Milky Way does not have a constant width – it 'ripples' like a river. Indeed towards the north it forks – this is known to astronomers as the Great Rift. The Ancient Egyptian depictions of the goddess Nut as the Milky Way make the Great Rift her crotch, and legends tell how each year at midwinter she lays an egg which descends to Earth. Interestingly, Nut is sometimes depicted with a goose at her feet. Is she the original Mother Goose? She is certainly the precursor to Leda who, after being raped by the Greek sky god Zeus in the form of a swan, bears two eggs, said to be the stars Castor and Pollux. The Greek legend of Leda and the swan seems to be a degraded descendant of star-lore where the story has taken on a life of its own and lost the original significance.

Interestingly, bearing in mind the discussion of cattle and sacred bulls in Chapter Five, Nut was also depicted as a celestial cow. Most commonly she is depicted as a sky goddess who swallows the sun in the evening and gives birth to it again in the morning.

Back on the Nile

In Chapter Five I briefly described the bull cults associated with deities such as Osiris and Amun-Re. Earlier versions of the ritual where the king led four calves across the threshing floor seem to be associated with the veneration of Min. In a separate annual harvest ritual associated with Min, four doves or geese are released to each of the four directions by priests wearing feather headdresses, a ritual act that had religio-political significance (Mysliwiec 2004: 15). However its antecedents presumably lie in Egyptian primordial creation myths, which include two birds flying off in opposite directions and the primordial mound being created where their flight crosses. So the Min harvest ritual seems to be defining the idea of a 'central place' or omphalos, while the flight of the four birds symbolise the king ruling over the four quarters of the (Egyptian) world.

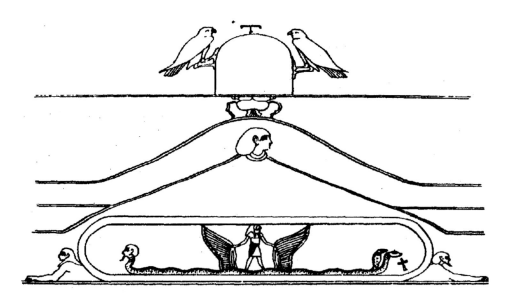

On of many Ancient Egyptian depictions of two birds either side of the omphalos mound.

In other versions of the creation myth, an egg floated in the primeval ocean. From this cosmic egg came either a falcon – the sky god – or a goose, known as the Great Gaggler whose voice first broke the silence (Mysliwiec 2004: 39–40). In later times the shells of ibis were kept in temples as relics of this cosmogony. Bearing in mind the ambiguous swan-ibis carving in the caves at Cresswell Crags in Derbyshire, dated to around 10,000 BCE, perhaps this ibis-goose-swan hybrid was also thought of a primordial Great Gaggler?

At the time of creation the souls, or *ka*, of millions of creatures and humans came into being. The word *ka* is also used to refer to the souls of the dead as well as the unborn. In later iconography these *ka* were depicted by a winged Isis. Is this too an idea which has its origins 12,000 or more years ago, and is as deeply rooted in British culture as it was in ancient Egypt and elsewhere? I have already noted in Chapter Five that Neolithic culture is a 'package' of domesticated animals (sheep, goats, cows) and technologies (pottery-making, farming) which spreads out into Europe from its origins in modern-day Iraq. So shared origins for myths and beliefs seem probable – even if we mostly only encounter the branches that develop from the common roots, and not necessarily cultures which shared close contacts.

In this seemingly-shared mythology we can recognise primordial mounds, bulls, geese, ibis, swans, souls of he dead and unborn, and phallocentric regeneration myths. Should we be seeing the Avebury landscape in such terms? There were numerous phallic-shaped mounds: the chambered long barrows (such as West Kennett) and the earthen long barrows (such as Beckhampton and the now-lost examples at South Street and Horslip). Windmill Hill causewayed enclosure just

Wakah Chan, the Mayan World Tree, which represents the Milky Way. The constellation Scorpio is at the base of the tree and the constellation Cygnus at the top, where the cosmic bird is perched.

might have been thought of as a primordial mound – it almost certainly functioned as a sacred centre for the people who met there and created it. Later will come the biggest man-made 'primordial mound' in Europe – Silbury – with its slopes remarkably similar to the hill of Khepri on which the ithyphallic Osiris was 'resurrected' by Isis, and from the top of which geese or swans could be ritually released to the four directions (see illustration on page 56).

At this stage it all seems rather speculative. More evidence is needed. And that evidence comes from the stars – or, more specifically, the star-lore that seems to go back before the Neolithic.

Stellar swan lore

In Mayan myths the Great Rift of the Milky Way is seen as a 'uterus' – and Yucatan folklore includes a tale which curiously echoes the Mother Goose legend but with strong links to Central American mythology and cosmology. In Chapter Two I have already noted that bull's heads were possibly seen as visual metaphors for the uterus, and noted in the previous chapter that so-called 'bull roarers' are archaic sacred instruments. Furthermore the constellation associated with the Great Rift is Cygnus. Indeed, the Great Rift is often called the Cygnus Rift. It is a bird in other cultures' star-lore too – indeed the principal star, Deneb (one of the brightest stars in the sky), takes its name from a contraction of the Arabic *Al Dhanab al Dajajah* 'the Hen's Tail'. In early Vedic Indian astronomy, the swan-goose god Hamsa seemingly was associated with this constellation (Collins 2008: 190). In Mayan myth the Milky Way, their World Tree, has *Itzam-ye*, the Celestial Bird, sitting on top. The version of Leda and

Zeus-as-swan myth which comes down to us presumably derives from a 'dreamtime' legend in which a sky goddess (the Milky Way) is impregnated by a sky god (the constellation Cygnus) situated at her crotch (the Great Rift).

However there is something even more interesting about the constellation Cygnus. Long before the Pole Star or Polaris was, well, the pole star, the celestial pole had been in the constellation Draco. And before that, Cygnus marked the unsetting centre of the celestial sphere, the place around which all the other stars came and went in their nightly procession. And if you think of where Cygnus is within the Milky Way, this meant that the whole Milky Way went directly overhead, not at about sixty degrees as it does now. This is much closer to how the Ancient Egyptians depicted Nut spread over the sky. Only there is a problem – when these depictions of Nut were drawn, the Milky Way was no longer overhead, and Cygnus was no longer the pole star.

Cygnus was the polar marker not during pharaonic Egypt but between 15,000 to 13,000 BCE. This predates the Paleolithic depiction of a swan/ibis at Cresswell Crags and the many swan pendants at Angara, mentioned earlier in this chapter. Andrew Collins devotes the main parts of his book *The Cygnus Mystery* (Collins 2006) to detailed arguments as to how and why such a long-standing mythological association between the Great Rift of the Milky Way and swans do plausibly date back so far. Even if we doubt his arguments – although I see no reason not to accept the broad sweep of his work – the Cygnus constellation is still interesting. Two meteor showers appear to emanate from the constellation. The 'October Cygnids' is visible between 26 September and 10 October. Cygnus is low in the northern sky at this time of year – but would once have been higher. This shower is now sparse and irregular, but would not necessarily always have been so modest. The 'Kappa Cygnids' peak in early August. Within modern times this used to be a concentrated shower but is now less intense. And, somewhere between 3,000 and 6,000 BCE, according to the estimates of astronomers, there was supernova in Cygus which would have been brighter that the full moon at its peak.

In Korean star lore the constellation Cygnus is known as the Ferry of the Sky; in Chinese star lore (which often tends to be derived from Korean precedents) it is the Ford. These have the connotations of Egyptian myths of the 'final ferryman' and Classical Greek and Roman successors. So, following Collins' suggestions, should we see the annual northerly migration of swans as taking souls not merely 'north beyond the north wind' but into the doorway to the Otherworld – the Great Rift marked by the asterism Cygnus? And did these souls get reborn by the sky goddess as a 'goose egg'? And when the circumpolar shaman chant and drum to ascend their World Tree are they embarking on a journey which once took these souls along this Ghost Way, or Way of the Birds? Are the valkyries and swan maidens of Germanic myth also echoes of this same 'swan song'?

So many questions. But the available evidence indicates that the answers should be 'yes'. But I have one further question: does any of this have anything to do with Avebury?

The Winterbourne to the west of Avebury, looking south to Silbury Hill, April 2011. Swallowhead Spring is out of sight, just beyond Silbury Hill. The confluence of the Sambourne and Winterbourne is to the north, about one hundred yards behind where this photograph was taken.

Avebury as a microcosm of world tree

If we think of the Milky Way, as Asians do, as the 'River to the Otherworld', then the Great Rift is a confluence. And a suggestion that there were pre-Greek myths which made the links between Cygnus and celestial journeys come from the most commonly-repeated account of how the constellation Cygnus came about. These myths recall how Phaeton, the mortal son of the sun-god Helios, was recklessly allowed by his father to drive the sun-chariot, which then went out of control. Thinking the world was threatened, Zeus struck Phaeton down. His body fell into the River Eridanus, whereupon his devoted friend Cygnus, after a struggle, recovered it from the water. Zeus, taking pity on Cygnus, transformed him into a celestial swan. OK, so it's day not night but in other respects the myth describes the Way of the Birds, the Milky Way, across the heavens. This is probably a later version of the Babylonian *Epic of Gilgamesh* which has a similar story of the Bull of Heaven devastating the rivers and land, in retribution for Gilgamesh's rebuttal of Ishtar.

Anyway, back to confluences and comparatively firm ground. The River Kennet officially starts where the south-flowing Winterbourne reaches Swallowhead Springs and turns east. But the Winterbourne has its own confluence – where the Sambourne flows into it, just to the west of Avebury henge (see photograph on page 57). As already noted, Windmill Hill – the Neolithic precursor to the henge – sits above the valleys of these two streams, somewhat as Cygnus sits in the 'door to the Otherworld', the Milky Way's Great Rift.

Oh well, you say, all that's just my mind running off on one. The relevant sections of John North's nothing if not comprehensive study of Neolithic astronomy suggest otherwise (North 1996). He identified several alignments at Stonehenge and other Wiltshire which mark where Deneb (one of the brightest stars in the sky, remember) would have risen in the Neolithic. And Collins has noted that one of these is the main axis of the north and south circles of the Avebury henge – which in turn points towards Windmill Hill. I would stress that although the henge alignment does fit the rising of Deneb, the continuation to Windmill Hill does not appear to be an *exact* marker for the rising of either Deneb or other stars in Cygnus. But there certainly seems to be a symbolic relationship between the axis of the henge and Windmill Hill.

Andrew Collins has observed that the same alignment exists at Marden mega-henge, ten miles to the south of the slightly smaller Avebury henge (pers. comm.). However that alignment is only a modern hedgerow – albeit a hedge through a significant part of the prehistoric monument – and there is no evidence that the hedge follows a prehistoric feature. While little is known about the Marden henge, significantly it is situated near the source of the River Avon running south past Stonehenge to the Solent at Christchurch. Souls heading north past the north wind from settlements on the south coast would, like swans on their annual migration, fly up the Avon valley to Stonehenge or Marden. The souls and swans would arrive further north at Avebury, either after rising over the escarpment with the still-impressive remains of the early Neolithic enclosure at Knap Hill (a close cousin to the less well-preserved one at Windmill Hill), or by keeping to the dry valley below the Rybury Neolithic enclosure (and later Iron Age hill fort) to the north of All Cannings and turning to pick up the line of the Beckhampton Avenue,

Ride a white swan

If – and maybe I am going off on one here – for the moment we think of Neolithic people believing that the souls of their loved ones travelled on the backs of swans and then entered a realm where they stayed until reborn then could that 'place of the souls' have been envisaged initially as Windmill Hill (with its symbolic relationship to the confluence which forms the Kennet) and then, after a shift in cultural practices, to the henge at Avebury? Did the causeways of Windmill Hill, Knap Hill and other such early hill-top enclosures once exist to dissuade the souls of the ancestors from wandering? Did the vastly deep ditches of Avebury henge serve a similar purpose? After all they are *inside* the bank so intended to keep something in rather than out.

While Iron Age practices tell us nothing for certain about earlier times, archaeologists have noted that Iron Age pottery and artefacts are conspicuous only by their almost total absence from the Avebury henge and surrounding monuments. Odd, because they had impressive hill forts at Barbury Castle to the north-east, Oldbury (above Cherhill) not far away to the west, and Rybury to the south. Given the amount of archaeological activity in and around Avebury it is reasonable to expect that more Iron Age evidence would have turned up, if only by chance. So, for once, the absence of evidence can be interpreted as evidence of absence.

A winged St Michael defeating Leviathan. A twelfth century tympanum at Hallaton, Leicestershire.

Presumably in the Iron Age the Avebury landscape was the subject of myths and stories which rendered it taboo to people. Was it an area where the gods roamed or where the ancestors strolled? As it seems to fit poorly with the much more watery and boggy places where Iron Age people made offerings to their deities – and no such finds have been discovered anywhere near Avebury – maybe its location as the source of an east-flowing river enhanced its Otherworldly status. But, given that the Bronze Age people had built numerous barrows overlooking the Avebury area – including the now-gone ones on the summit of Waden Hill – my money is on the dead rather than the deities putting the frighteners on the people of this era.

Could Avebury's megalithic stones – with their distinctive faces revealed by the new-born sun – be where the souls 'rested'? And that these souls were closely associated with swans? There are ethnographic parallels for spirits taking on the form of stones (Roe and Taki 1999: 418–9). If it seems I'm going off on one then so it seems is the Gaelic language too. The word for 'swan' (*eala, eal* or *ai*), sounds all-but the same as for a pillar of stone or cemetery (*elad* or *ealagh*) (Collins 2008: 116–17).

And indeed could the whole of christianity be off on the same one? The constellation Cygnus is cross-shaped – exactly the same cross-shape as adopted by early christians as the 'world tree' on which Jesus was crucified prior to his resurrection (whereas in reality Roman crucifixions used a T-shaped 'cross'). We know that christianity brought together a variety of earlier beliefs – could the New Testament ideas of death and rebirth be the reworking of myths which went back to when Cygnus was in the apex of the night sky, where the door to the Otherworld opened? And just where does that put the medieval images of angels – white-coloured theriomorphs of humans with swan-like wings? In any other culture ethnographers would be deeming them evidence for shamanic religion...

A rather posh spiritus. Examples of these can be found on the wall monuments in many English parish churches. This one is in the church at Avebury.

They are closely linked in the Romanesque era with winged saints – and with an iconography which has since died out, winged depictions of Christ. Saints, especially St Michael, have tended to keep their wings. But in doing so they look rather like Gabriel or other biblical angels. As a result of a revival of interest in Reginald Scot's seventeenth century *Discoverie of Witchcraft* in the 1870s, the concept of the Holy Guardian Angel become established in British occult orders such as the Golden Dawn, and in recent decades the idea of a personal 'guardian angel' become almost commonplace. In another time – but not necessarily another place – they might have been called an *aelf weard*, the Old English phrase we encountered up on Alderley Edge.

The angelic – or dove-like – human *spiritus* was also popular about three hundred years ago when it became a key part of Enlightenment iconography. Numerous eighteenth century wall monuments to departed nobility depict the soul of the deceased as a cherubic head with a pair of wings – known as the 'spiritus'. The head, as back in the early Neolithic in Britian and the Middle East, is seen as the dwelling place of the spirit – in contrast, these more secular days which just think of our 'consciousness' as being inside our heads, but the difference is slight. This winged head motif also enters lower social strata around the 1730s when slate-like Charnwood rocks (often referred to as Swithland Slate) began to be used for grave markers; some of these have similar but more stylised faces known (incorrectly) as 'Belvoir angels'. However they are not angels but the same spiritus – the soul of the deceased. They are akin to ancient Egyptian *ka*, mentioned above, represented by a winged Isis.

Furthermore, in christianity a white dove has become the most prevalent image of the Holy Spirit – even though in the New Testament it is also described as tongues of

A so-called 'Belvoir angel' on an early eighteenth century gravestone in Nether Broughton churchyard, Leicestershire. However they are not angels but the same spiritus – the soul of the deceased. The name 'Belvoir' (pronounced 'beaver') is from their origin near the Vale of Belvoir on the Leicestershire/ Nottinghamshire border, although they can be found throughout both those counties and as far south as Northampton, and the adjoining parts of Lincolnshire and Derbyshire.

fire, water or – most commonly – as breath or wind. The dove symbolism derives from Luke 3:22 where the Holy Spirit descends in the form of a *yonah* at Christ's baptism. *Yonah* is either a dove or pigeon, and the word appears in the Old Testament many times as the typical bird to sacrifice at temples. Baptism is of course a key christian 'rite of passage' when the new spiritual life commences – the person is 'born again'. This parallels the beliefs associated with Brahminical baptism, although this is not the place to write a book on the many parallels between pre-Pauline christianity and contemporary Indian worship (see Saher 1969 for such a book).

The Holy Spirit makes an appearance earlier in Luke's gospel when it 'overshadows' Mary at the time of Christ's conception. However we need to be careful how we gender this trick of the light! The Holy Spirit was initially a feminine procreative or regenerative principle. It is the same spirit of god which 'moved on the face of the waters' at the time of primordial creation (Genesis 1:2) that was, in several pre-judaic religions, seen as a dove or pigeon.

The chanting cygnets of the Kennet

Elsewhere in the Bible, at the start of John's gospel, we are told that 'in the beginning was the Logos.' Logos is usually translated as 'word' and implies that words – especially perhaps songs and chants – brought the world into existence. While neither jews or christians re-enact primordial creation, many other religions do. Presumably in all such rituals singing and chanting would be a major aspect.

As indicated in the previous chapter, singing and chanting would not have been incidental to Neolithic worship, in the same way it is not an optional extra in all other major religions (only the Quakers come to mind as an exception, as they are to many other expectations of religious practice). So what about the sounds of swans? Firstly the English word 'swan' is one of a group of Germanic words for this bird, all having their origin with the Proto-Indo-European root *swon-* or *swen-*, meaning 'to sing, make sound'. Significantly, one species of swan is known as the 'whooper' in Britain and 'trumpeter' in America, while another species (the one most commonly encountered in Britain) is distinctive because it is 'mute'. Their 'songs' were once as distinctive as their all-white appearance. Secondly, two of the oldest musical instruments so far found (in the Ach Valley, south-west Germany) were whistles made from the bones of a whooper swan; they have been dated to over 30,000 BCE.

However the Latin name for this genus of birds in *Cygnus*. While the word 'cygnet' is used in English only to denote young swans (hence the diminutive 'et' ending), among modern European languages variants of this word are used for adult swans as well. The Latin *cygnus* in turn is from the Greek *kyknos* which is perhaps from the Proto-Indo-European verb *keuk* meaning 'to be white'. Note that Greek and Proto-Indo-European words have a hard 'k' rather than the soft 'c' of cygnet. So a literal translation of the phrase 'swan song' into early Greek would be pronounced something like 'kyknos kanos' ('cygnets chanting'). Etymologically, the literal meaning of 'swan song' would be 'the song of the singing birds' while 'cygnets chanting' would be 'the singing of those who are white'. (Remember too that ancient Egyptians thought the primordial silence was broken by the sound of a goose, the Great Gaggler, as discussed in Chapter Five.)

The onomatopoeic 'honking' of swans could, to my way of hearing, also be rendered phonetically as 'konking'. Or should the verb form of 'konk' be 'to konket' – a further near-homophone of Kennet? Or did swans once 'keen' the dead, as the Old Irish word (only imported into English as recently as the early nineteenth century) also suggestively sounds? Was there once a verb synonymous with 'to lament' which sounded like 'to keenet'?

I will answer that question with another. Does a flock of swans honk in concerto? 'Concerto' is a fairly recent adaptation of 'concert' which originates with the Latin *concentare,* 'to sing together' (con- + *cantare* 'to sing'). *Cantare* is from the Proto-Indo-European root word *kan,* with the sense of 'to sing'. It gives us 'chant' and many similar words in other European languages. Given the shifts in sounds that words undergo over the millennia, 'chant' is as close to the proposed word 'keenet' as is necessary. I cannot prove that such a word ever existed, but linguistically it is entirely plausible.

Chanting is deeply religious. Few people, no matter how secular their lives, are unmoved by Gregorian chant or recordings of the rituals of Tibetan monks. In other cultures chanting was used to invoke deities. And yes I do mean invoke and not evoke – these practices require the 'participant' to become as one with a deity, not merely worship from afar or give the god a 'shopping list' of instructions. The shaman became in all senses 'enchanted'. (For an interesting 'reconstruction' of invoking deities by chanting see Johnson and Wallis 2005 Ch. 5.)

The phrase 'swan song' is still redolent with emotion. This originates with a widespread myth known as far back as classical mythology (when swans were sacred to Apollo and Venus) and alluded to by Chaucer that swans sing to foretell a death. Different versions of the legend say that otherwise silent swans emit a long drawn-out wail as their own death approaches. This tradition reaches a somewhat paradoxical apotheosis in Tchaikovsky's ballet score for *Swan Lake*. Based on a combination of Russian folktales, in outline the plot concerns a princess, Odette, who is transformed into a swan by an evil sorcerer's curse and then, after suitably romantic subplots, Odette drowns herself. Although the conventions of classical ballet require the dancers to remain silent, the choreographer of the original production, Julius Reisinger, ended the ballet with a long drawn-out death scene for Odette, famously scored by Tchaikovsky as ever-slower music. This long silent 'scream' mimes the death wail legendarily attributed to swans.

Although Kennet is not cognate with either *keuk* or *kan*, I would like to think that at least some Neolithic people who – with no knowledge of Proto-Indo-European etymology – on seeing and hearing swans on the waters of the Kennet near Avebury, also shared some of my fascination with near-homophones and alliteration and thought that the river's name was linked with the Otherworldly birds who lived on it.

White on white

Swans are distinctive for their whiteness. The Milky Way was the 'Ghost Way', the Road of the Dead presumably because, at one time, white was either the colour of death or more generally the colour of the 'Otherworld'. In relatively recent Welsh myth and lore, the hounds of Annwn (*Cwn Annwn*) were the spectral hounds of the otherworldly paradise, Annwn. As noted in Chapter Five, they were white with red ears – presumably albino. In the legends of the *Cwn Annwn* they are regarded as escorting souls as they travel to the Otherworld realms ruled by Gwyn ap Nudd. The *Cwn Annwn* are said to have hunted in various parts of Wales, including Cadair Idris, where anyone hearing their howling would soon die. Welsh folklore linked these hounds, not with swans, but with geese – however the reason is interchangeable with swans as the nocturnal honking of migrating geese reminded people of barking dogs.

Similar spectral hounds are found are found in the Isle of Man (the Yell hounds) and in England (the Gabriel hounds or the Wisht hounds of Dartmoor) and seem to be the inspiration for Herne the Hunter's hounds, as associated with Windsor Park in a loop of the River Thames. These canine apparitions could also have influenced the tales of shape-shifting paranormal phenomena that folklorists 'fixed' as phantom black dogs (see contributors to Trubshaw 2005b).

However, when we think of spectres and Otherworldly presences we do not normally first think of dogs, geese or swans. The archetypal ghost is either a white lady or a monk in a dark-coloured cowl. Before the Reformation people in this country also reported seeing visions of the Virgin Mary – and carried on doing so in Catholic Continental countries where there was no incentive to secularise the experience as an anonymous white female. But how were such spectres construed in pre-christian times?

Firstly we should consider that the legendary Guinevere takes her name from the Welsh Gwenhwyfar, meaning 'white phantom or shadow', which in Irish is exactly cognate with Finnabhair, the daughter of Medb. However in Ireland this white lady was most associated with the deity Brigit (also spelt Brigid, Brighid, Brid or Brig), who is the better-known counterpart to the British Brigantia, the Roman's Minerva and the Greek's Athena. All these goddesses were linked with 'elevated states', whether physical or psychological – partly recalling the pagan Scandinavian *seithr* rituals where the seeress sat on a specially-constructed high tower or platform. So high hills and poetic excellence are among the many attributes these deities 'patronise'.

White on high

There has been much debate about whether Brigid's name is cognate with the Celtic word *bree*, itself from an earlier root word meaning 'high, mighty'. Bree- is a common place-name element, usually in such forms as Breedon which combines the Celtic and Old English words for 'hill', indicating that whatever Anglo-Saxons understood by the word 'bree' it was not simply 'hill'. The temptation is to see the avowed deity of hill places as closely associated with places known as 'bree' – or to push the association back to the early Neolithic enclosures, such as Windmill Hill. After all, medieval Irish legends tell us that a different goddess of the land, Temair, gave her name to the Hill of Tara, the traditional seat of Irish kingship.

High hills and mountains were sacred the world over. In many societies mountains are seen not only as the cosmic axis, but also the places where Earth comes closest to the deities. When Yahweh asked Moses to take down a bit of dictation, he needed to take his tablets of stone to the top of Mount Sinai. The Japanese national icon is the snow-capped peak of Mount Fuji; furthermore many other mountains in Japan are also sacred. Mount Olympus was the abode of the gods for the ancient Greeks. The Maoris regard the volcanoes at the heart of the Tongariro National Park as so sacred that no humans can venture on its slopes. A volcanic peak in Wyoming venerated by various Great Plains tribes was also the site selected by Steven Spielberg for the arrival of the aliens in the *Close Encounters of the Third Kind.*

Moses, Jesus and Mohammed all felt, heard or saw a presence, saw lights or felt fear when they were on mountains. The same phenomena is experienced by contemporary mountaineers as these are first symptoms of altitude sickness. Bear in mind that Mount Olympus, at 2,911 metres, is no mere hill, and the summit of Mount Sinai is 2,285 metres. You wouldn't have to even get near the top to risk the onset of altitude sickness. Even if you didn't experience this yourself, there would be plenty of tales about people who had.

Mountains and lesser hills are almost always in the marginal land that divides the more resource-rich valleys. Their sacred associations, as the home of the gods, become extended to include the home of other spirits and Otherworldly entities, and – in some, but not all, societies – they are where the dead are buried and therefore also become the realm of the spirits of the ancestors. Such sacred sites between territories become the seasonal meeting places where people must gather to trade or exchange livestock and to meet marriage partners. In Britain we see the record as early Neolithic enclosures, and the much later Bronze Age and Iron Age so-called 'hill forts' (and a number of these become early christian minster sites, associated with annual fairs and weekly markets).

White and bright

So Brigit's association with high places has plenty of parallels. She is also associated with brightness and flames, linking her to the Roman goddess Vesta – whose vestal virgins maintained a never-dying fire, just as her christianised successor (St Brigid) had a cult centre at Kildare where a never-dying fire was attended by nuns until the Reformation. Few scholars doubt that this was the continuation of a pre-christian custom, so presumably Brigid had been the 'sovereign' of Leinster. St Brigid's feast day is celebrated on 1st February, also known as Candlemas, a date attributed as the time of the pre-christian Imbolc by modern pagans (see Torma 2002; Wright 2009).

The pagan Brigid – bright and possibly white – has some other curious links to the ideas in this book. According to the Cath Maige Tuireadh, when Brigit (or Bríg as she appears in this work) lost her son in a battle, she invented keening. In the same section of the myth she also invents a whistle used in some manner to help travelling at night. Closer connections with the attributes of swans would be harder to find.

Simply because in Robert Graves' overly-fervent imagination – and the imaginations of rather too many modern pagans influenced by his ideas – this 'white goddess' became something much more than she could ever have been does not mean that she did not once exist at all.

White – and hooded ?

But – according to some versions of the Irish myths – Brigid was not flawless. While one side of her face was very attractive, the other side was ugly. Is this perhaps a fading memory of the time when she was a bringer of both life and death? Or should

Genii cucullati *from Housesteads.*

we think again about the apparitions of black monks? But why the assumption that white ghosts are female and dark ones are male? Such apparitions are often too amorphous to be clearly described, let alone 'sexed'. While few real-life men dress in white, women dressed in dark colours as much as light ones. Despite their attribution as male should we see them as the white goddess in her darker manifestation? Or the genderless dark and light elves of the Anglo-Saxon and Scandinavian world-view?

Going back in time before christian monks dressed in shapeless dark habits, what did these shadow-like ghosts resemble? They summon memories of the three-fold hooded spirits of place, the *genii cucullati* known from Romano-British carvings excavated in various places in Gloucestershire, along Hadrian's Wall, and elsewhere. These 'spirits' (*genii*) take their name from the *culcullus*, a full-length hooded woollen. robe. Indeed the distinctive attire of medieval monks may well have borrowed more-or-less directly from this pragmatic attire. *Cucullati* seem to be the male counterparts to the three-fold *Matronae*, and all are seemingly related to the cult of the Greco–Roman (but perhaps originally Germanic) deity Telesphorus, also depicted cloaked. Telesphorus was the child of Asklepios, the healer deity, and his powers were in the realms of sleep and dreams; he was also the protector of children and a fertility deity, and may have shared his father's attributes as a healer.

On the Continent some *cucullati* are depicted with the *cucullus* open to expose the penis. Others are depicted with eggs or moneybags – both overtly sexual symbols at the time. The shape of a *cucullati* figure is inevitably phallic. Small carved cucullati are found as grave goods, suggesting they were protective after death. Were *cucullati* seen as life-long protectors, from conception to death – and beyond?

Every morning when I wake up and open the bedroom curtains I see several of these *cucallati* on the skyline to the south. The surviving stones at the henge end of Avebury Avenue have the distinctive shape of dark, hooded figures when seen from the henge – even though these stones are very much wider when seen face-on. Given the prevalence of simulacra faces on other stones, I do not think that my impression is entirely frivolous. Rather, when looking along its length, the Avenue acts as a double row of hooded 'mourners' to honour the dead – or maybe just their

The West Kennett Avenue in its aspect as a double row of hooded figures. A misty morning, March 2011.

souls – on their final journey; a double row of psychopomps offering eternal advice the newly-deceased spirits, silently chanting a 'swan song' to guide them through their nocturnal journey. Indeed there is no reason to suppose that the Avenue marked out a processional way for humans – just as conceivably it defined a taboo zone the dead could pass along unhindered.

Anyone who follows the Avenue towards the henge will be surprised that the stone circle – the largest surviving in Europe – cannot be seen until almost at the end of the Avenue. The Avenue also twists a little before the ridge where the henge becomes visible, meaning that the alignment is *not* towards to the henge at the place where it becomes visible. It is instead directed to Windmill Hill, as if the people constructing the Avenue felt the need to 'reference' a monument already over a millennia old by this time.

And if we follow this through then the early Neolithic precursor to Brigid would feel at home on the hill ridge where West Kennett chambered long barrow is located, with the original whiteness of the mound making her feel even more as if she belonged. And, given that the small number of people whose remains were inside that tomb include one with a deformed skull, two with spina bifeda and three with the lesser condition of spina bifeda occulta, could it be that we are dealing with a group of people (quite possibly related) who were Otherworldly because they were physically 'other'?

Contrary to earlier archaeologists' assumptions that these were in some way 'high status' people, maybe they received special status because they were feared or loathed. After all some exceptionally expensive 'homes' today house people we do not think of as 'high status' but as violent prisoners. Could it be that West Kennett's original 'inhabitants' had been 'walled up' in death? Or, just maybe, alive?

Another view of the same stones, August 2008.

Whether reviled or revered, they were in some respect 'other' to most of their contemporaries. 'Otherness' could of course be in ways which are not associated with skeletal traits – as would be the case for albinos, who are still regarded with great trepidation in many African countries and are at risk of being ritually murdered. If you were born albino in the early Neolithic – or even earlier – were you thought of as a soul who had failed to find a 'proper' body? Would your half-in-this-world and half-in-the-Otherworld appearance mean you were fated to become a shaman helping the swans to shuttle immortal souls to their destinations?

The hilltop location and Otherworldly whiteness of the West Kennett mound would be shared with the ditches of Windmill Hill and other enclosures. Later the whiteness would be the most distinctive aspect of Avebury's henge ditch and bank, and later of the steadily-growing Silbury mound and its associated ditch. Whether it was here that forerunners of the later 'swan maidens' and valkyries, perhaps accompanied by white-coloured dogs, officiated at rites of a goddess named something like Brigid is, however, entirely in the realms of speculation.

Chapter 10

The Rivers of Life and Cauldrons of Creation

T.S. Eliot famously thought 'that the river is a strong brown god' (Eliot 1943). He was, presumably, thinking of the Thames as it flows through London rather than its tributary, the Kennet, as it flows through east Wiltshire into Berkshire. But the smaller, clear-flowing rivers of the Wiltshire chalk seem also to have once been deified.

Since the Mesolithic rivers have been important sources of food and other resources. Until widespread clearance of the natural woodland then it was also easier to move along rivers than overland, as I have already discussed in Chapter One. This makes the high ground and watersheds between rivers 'marginal' – seasonal hunting grounds, and later summer pastures. And as places for burial, homes of the ancestors and of spirits. Integral to such places on the margins, near the watersheds, were the various springs which gave birth to the rivers.

For a moment, ignore modern thinking which attributes the sources of the Thames to a variety of streams in the Cotswolds. Instead think of the Swallowhead Springs, the source of the Kennet, as the source of the Thames. This gives us the most consistently eastwards-flowing river in Britain – surely significant to our prehistoric ancestors. And that source was in one of the most magical topographical relationships to the landscape possible. Add to that the seasonal Winterbourne flowing in from the north, from the lower slopes of Windmill Hill and a minor confluence to the west of Avebury henge, and that magic is further intensified.

As I established in Chapter One, people during the Mesolithic and Neolithic would have pottered along in small boats rather than tried to walk substantial distances. Early Neolithic enclosures – once called 'causewayed camps' – are always on hill tops so intimately linked to the valleys and watersheds which 'define' the hills. Later henges are more specifically situated near small rivers, with Avebury and Marden near the presumed limits of navigation for even small watercraft.

The water from Swallowhead Spring flowing into the Winterbourne at the start of the River Kennet, March 2011.

All such routes would have acquired place-related legends. Indeed, if we pay more attention to the Aboriginal 'Dreamtime tracks' than Bruce Chatwin seemingly did, we note that they follow watercourses in the Outback – routes which, between the occasional rains, are often arid (Tilley 1994). These place-specific legends inevitably were situated in the broad sweep of myths which defined a culture. Myths create – almost invisibly for those within the culture – metaphorical relationships with places, deities, spirits, and everything which makes up human life.

Rivers are a metaphor for life, as already noted. The Indus and Ganges rivers are key to understanding Indian religious world-views, as was the now-dry Sarasvati River in former times. This world-view extends to the heavens in those Asian countries, including India, where the Milky Way is called the River of Heaven. And, for reasons I want to explore, there is every reason to think that rivers were key to the world-views of early Neolithic people too.

World-views by their very nature 'create' the reality of a society. They define the expected relationships between life and afterlife, gods and mortals, kings and their subjects, men and women, and much else. To anyone outside the society they are profoundly metaphysical – and probably quite 'unbelievable'. That is the way Western researchers have looked upon traditional cultures – and the way that non-Western cultures look back at the assorted madnesses which make up our world-view.

Many of the presumptions which underpin the madnesses of the Western world-view derive from early Greek philosophers such as Socrates and Plato. One of their assumptions, which has only been questioned in recent decades, is that the world is inherently rational. This world-view was created – and sustained – by attempting to ignore all that is deemed irrational. Eric Dodds was the first writer to recognise this back in 1951; see also Tambiah 1990.

Until the twentieth century Western philosophers also maintained the Platonic tradition that language accurately mirrors or maps the structure of 'reality'. This gives a world-view where 'reality' was made up of things and events (nouns and verbs), while the verb 'to be' is synonymous with Plato's concept of 'essences' (the 'higher *being*' of a specific class of objects). Some of the weaknesses in the Platonic worldview were addressed by Heidegger, who considered that *Dasein* (usually translated as 'Being') is the ultimate manifestation of reality because it erased object:subject dualisms. But not until Ludwig Wittgenstein's *Tractatus Logico-Philosophicus* of 1921 were these linguistically-led assumptions fundamentally questioned in the West.

However a fuller understanding of the problem was not achieved in Wittgenstein's lifetime. That fuller understanding arrived in the 1970s when Derridean deconstruction dismantled all the linguistic biases underlying philosophical issues to the extent that every founding assumption of Western philosophy was undermined. The iconoclasm was completed by Richard Rorty's early 1980s books which extensively argue that any philosophical system can only be an expression of *prior* assumptions and not – as so many philosophers have claimed – an attempt to access the 'reality' behind our assumptions. For Rorty the problem of how we know something is fundamental:

> Perhaps a new form of systematic philosophy will be found which
> has nothing whatever to do with epistemology but which
> nevertheless makes normal philosophical inquiry possible.

(Rorty cited Lucas 1989: vi)

Rorty's post-epistemological philosophy has however yet to make itself known.

This dismantling of the very basis for philosophical enquiry was however part of the early Greek thinking thrown out by Socrates. A whole school of pioneering philosophers, known as the Eliatics, had argued that the world was not inherently rational. In a book revised in the same year that Rorty first unleashed his radical opinions, a noted scholar of pre-Socratic philosophy defended the status quo unequivocally:

> If the Eliatics are right, scientists may as well give up their
> activities: *a priori* ratiocination reveals that the phenomena which
> science attempts to understand and explain are figments of our
> deceptive sense: the scientist has little or nothing to investigate –
> let him turn to poetry or gardening.

(Barnes 1982: 305)

Mr Heraclitus, about to step into the river.

Which means the rest of this chapter should, in Barnes's view, be filed under poetry or gardening... What is it that Barnes' study of pre-Socratic philosophers missed? Socrates – at least according to the versions of his ideas written down by Plato and Xenophanes – dismissed the ideas of previous early Greek philosophers. In his view the world was made of objects to which things happened. Curiously this is exactly the way the Greek language, and all other Western languages, are structured. Well, of course, language is there to describe the world so it helps if the language 'mirrors' the world.

Well, actually, there's no 'of course' about it. Our languages *structure* how we see the world – and a great deal of ethnographic, linguistic and philosophical effort has been expended establishing that this is indeed the case (key works are Lakoff 1987, Lakoff and Johnson 1980, 1999). We think that objects and events are the way the world 'is' *because* our languages are based around nouns and verbs. In languages – such as Chinese – where the distinction between nouns and verbs is more fluid, the world view is instead of 'processes'. So the Chinese word for 'cup' translates as 'cupping'. Indeed a cup is indeed clay which is currently cupping, pending its eventual transformation into shards.

Perhaps a cup is not the best example. Think instead of a whirlpool or a candle. There is no 'thing' that is a whirlpool – you can't take a whirlpool home in a big bucket any more than a breeze can be put in a bag – there is only water that is whirlpooling. Likewise there is no 'thing' that is a candle flame, only a constantly renewing stream of incandescent particles. Our nouns 'whirlpool' and 'candle flame' are convenient metaphysical fictions.

Mr Heraclitus, please step into the river

What evidence is there for the pre-Socratic view of the world being much more 'process-like'? Step forward Heraclitus, whose enigmatic philosophical writings were composed about 500 BCE (he was born about 535 and died in 475). Not for nothing was he known as 'the obscure' and 'the riddler'. He is famous for supposedly expressing the notion that no man can enter the same river twice. His own words seem to have been: 'We both step and do not step in the same rivers. We are and are

Whirlpools a plenty. But not to take home in a bucket...
Waterfalls on the River Black Water, Scotland, May 1993.

not.' However later Greek thinkers considered that the sense of his ideas was 'No man ever steps in the same river twice, for it is not the same river and he is not the same man.' Whether this is an accurate interpretation of Heraclitus's own intentions or simply reflects later rethinking can be left as an unknown for present purposes.

Heraclitus's key concern is how opposites mutually create each other in a process of constant change. So 'By cosmic rule, as day yields night, so winter summer, war peace, plenty famine. All things change.' And 'Men do not know how that which is drawn in different directions harmonises with itself. The harmonious structure of the world depends upon opposite tension like that of the bow and the lyre.' Another of his aphorisms is 'Nothing is permanent but change'.

When I read these surviving fragments of once-longer texts two things came to mind. Firstly, if the ancient Greeks had a word corresponding to our 'dialectics' – the process by which two concepts mutually construct each other – then Heraclitus's writing would be less obscure and riddling. And secondly, I've read all this somewhere else. And it wasn't by someone who read Heraclitus and came up with his own version. It is the surviving writing of someone who was a close-contemporary of Heraclitus but would never have met him. Not without a very long journey from central China.

I am thinking of Lao Tsu, the author of the *Tao te Ching*. (I am aware that romanisation of Chinese now favours Laozi and *Daode jing* over Lao Tsu and *Tao te Ching*, but readers are likely to be more familiar with the older usage, even though it gives a misleading indication of how the words are pronounced in Chinese.) Lao Tsu also sees the world created from a dialectical 'union of opposites' as these examples from *Tao te Ching* illustrate:

> Having and not having arise together.
> Difficult and easy complement each other.
> Long and short contrast each other.
> High and low rest upon each other.
> Voice and sound harmonise each other.
> Front and back follow one another.

(*Tao te Ching* chapter 2)

> Is there a difference between yes and no?
> Is there a difference between good and evil?
> Must I fear what others fear? What nonsense!

(*Tao te Ching* chapter 20)

(All my translations of the *Tao te Ching* are taken or adapted from Gia-Fu Feng and Jane English's 1973 translation.)

These early taoist dualisms might be best thought of inseparable 'polarities' such as the north and south poles of a magnet, the positive and negative potential of electricity, or the cyclical variations that make up a wave. They may be opposites but they are not in opposition and mostly not in conflict. Later Chinese thinking formalised this dialectical process as *yin* and *yang*, but those terms are not used by Lao Tsu. The root meanings of *yang* and *yin* denote the sunny and shady sides of a hill, although these words are more usually glossed as masculine/feminine, firm/yielding, strong/weak, light/dark, rising/falling or heaven/earth. Neither polarity can be eliminated any more than cutting a magnet in half will produce two halves with only a north and south pole each; likewise *yin* and *yang* arise mutually. Taoism is about the balance between opposites, just as when spicy food needs to be balanced with something more bland, such as rice.

Heraclitus's dialectical rhetoric is remarkably similar. Unlike other Greek thinkers, his ideas develop through internal contradictions, embodying his belief in the universality of change. This can be seen in the statement already quoted:

> By cosmic rule, as day yields night, so winter summer, war peace,
> plenty famine. All things change.

And more clearly in this longer quotation:

> This universe, which is the same for all, has not been made by
> any god or man, but it always has been, is, and will be an ever-

> living fire, kindling itself by regular measures and going out by
> regular measures.

Does this mean that Heraclitus and Lao Tsu stepped into the same river of philosophical speculation? Perhaps so if we compare Heraclitus's lyre and bow metaphor:

> Men do not know how that which is drawn in different directions
> harmonises with itself. The harmonious structure of the world
> depends upon opposite tension like that of the bow and the lyre.

with Lao Tsu's:

> The tao of heaven is like the bending of a bow.
> The high is lowered and the low raised.
> If the string is too long, it is shortened.
> If there is not enough, it is made longer.
> The tao of heaven is to take from those who have too much
>   and give to those who do not have enough.

> (*Tao te Ching* chapter 77)

Heraclitus is best known for his quote about rivers. His ideas seem consistent with Chapter 25 of the *Tao te Ching*, which attempts a definition of the 'unnameable' principle of change, the tao:

> I do not know its name.
> Call it tao.
> For lack of a better word, I call it great.
> Being great, it flows.

Chapter 25 also states that the tao 'flows' and 'follows'. This is repeated in Chapter 35:

> 'The great tao flows everywhere... '

The sense of 'flow' and 'process' is also implicit in many of the other chapters of the *Tao te Ching*, reinforcing the sense that whatever the 'tao' may or may not be, the sense of a 'way' or 'process' is fundamental. Note that I am concerned only with how *early* taoists seemingly used the term 'tao'. Over the centuries there have been many alternative ideas; for example the 'Dark Learning' school of about 220–50 CE invented the interpretation of the tao as 'non-being' (Hall 1982: 60; 162).

Although scholarship contests the details (see Kohn 1992: 40–5 for a well-informed overview), the *Tao te Ching* was probably not the work of a single author and, instead, Lao Tsu (which is a nickname translating as 'Old Boy' or, more respectfully, 'Old Master') is perhaps the collective identity of later followers. There are Western parallels for attributing such collective works in this way because the ideas attributed to Pythagoras – approximately a contemporary of the supposed Lao Tsu – are largely the ideas of Pythagoras's followers, although some ideas (such as geometry) are developed from pre-Pythagorian thinking. (Yes, despite the myth inculcated in every Western schoolchild for centuries, Pythagoras's own writings reveal no interest in geometry at all – see Barnes 1987 Ch. 5.)

The Miletian melting pot

Bear in mind that Heraclitus lived in a part of the Greek empire that is now in Turkey. He was born to an aristocratic family in Ephesus (present-day Efes) which, around 500 BCE, was a major trading port. Just along the coast was an even more important port, Miletus, which is where Greek philosophy originated, as it was home to several generations of thinkers immediately before Heraclitus – Thales, Anaximander and Anaximines. The trade routes from the modern Turkish coast extended along what we now think of as the Silk Roads into China. And, while the evidence is often elusive, ideas travel along trade routes every bit as much as produce.

In the Greek era, Miletus was the 'melting pot' where ideas came together, much as Constantinople (later Byzantium, later Istanbul) would become the focus of medieval Arabic culture revitalising the 'dark ages' of medieval christian Europe. In sixth century BC Miletus the ideas that were invigorating Greek society included Zoroastrianism and those of the Persian Magi – after all Persian armies were repeatedly attacking the area around Ephesus in Heraclitus's lifetime. We know, for example, that early Greek astronomy 'borrowed' from earlier eras (Devereux 2009: 79–80).

In Martin West's detailed study of the oriental influences on early Greek philosophers he devotes a chapter to the possible links with Persian religions (West 1971 Ch.6). After a scholarly close-examination of the evidence he concludes that if Persian soldiers were all-but outside the gates of Ephesus then there is every probability that Heraclitus would have known 'a more learned class' of Persian. But rather than see Heraclitus as a Greek-speaking follower of Auramazda and other Zoroastrian beliefs, he argues – convincingly – that the closest parallels to Heraclitus's thinking are in the *Upanishads*. This is his closing remark:

> It is a long walk from Ephesus to India. But the distribution of the human race proves that people, and what they carry with them, have travelled a good deal further in the course of years. In Heraclitus' time, Ephesus and India were linked by the Persian empire. Indians came to mainland Greece with Xerxes' army. The connections between Heraclitus' thought and Persian religion (as we know it from the literature of Zoroastrian orthodoxy) are proportionately strong.

(West 1971: 202)

Bear in mind also that another close contemporary of Lao Tsu and Heraclitus was the historical Buddha, Gautama. He considered that the cause of ubiquitous personal suffering was desire, and that one of the more insidious desires – and a doomed desire – was to stop inevitable changes in oneself, other people, relationships and even the material world. Whether or not we agree that desiring to avoid change is a cause of profound suffering, clearly Gautama also had a worldview in which change was a key component.

While neither Persian magi, Indian brahmins nor early buddhists are Taoist 'old masters', the eastern Mediterranean 2,500 years ago was clearly anything but a cultural backwater. This was a place of real innovation in thinking.

So why are these Milesian philosophers not better known? Largely because a bunch of smart talkers in Samos and Athens – the usual suspects: Pythagoras, Plato, Socrates, plus all their acolytes – came up with a different way of thinking and dismissed the work of their predecessors. Strictly this is only partially true – the fact that any quotes from Heraclitus and his Milesian predecessors have come down to us at all is because for the next millennium writers valued them and quoted them. But they were already 'other' to the dominant Western world-view based around Socrates and his successors.

We're not in Kennet anymore

OK, I can hear the Dorothys among you observing that we not in Kennet any more. But are we closer than such doubters might recognise? If these dialectical ideas of 'everything is change' were known in Greece and China around 500 BCE, how much older would any shared origin be? Frankly the question has no sensible answers. But bear in mind that the origins of taoism lie, in part, with Bon (or Bon-po) religions that also provide Tibetan buddhism with the distinctly shamanic foundations over which the *dhama* of hindu-derived buddhism was overlain.

Instead let's look at the metaphors that go with this Greek and Chinese world-view. They share a sense that 'all is change', making rivers the best metaphor for life itself. Heraclitus's most quoted quote was the one about the river and Lao Tsu saw the 'great ultimate' – the Tao – as flowing everywhere.

What other metaphysical metaphors are seemingly shared? Heraclitus thought that fire was the primary creative energy. However it seems most unlikely that he was the first person to think that fire is the underlying principle of creation. Neither was he the first to link fire with flow and water. Chinese shamans and immortals were regarded as masters over water and fire. (Kahn 1992: 91) The age-less Indian deity of fire and lightning, Agni, also manifests as Apam Napat, 'the child of the waters'. Agni is thought of as a radiant being who dwells in water.

A web of Indo-European myths link Agni to the Irish Nechtan and the Roman Neptunus, both of who are 'radiant' beings associated with water – and, in the Irish tradition, with the 'creative inspiration' of poets. This web of Indo-European myths is described by Alby Stone (Stone 1997: 83) but, for the purposes of this chapter, I simply want to draw attention to these geographically-widespread links between fire, water and creativity.

The universe is a bowl of soup – but sexier

What about the origins of the universe, and the primordial material? Early taoist creation myths are concerned with 'differentiating' and rationally ordering the component parts of the undifferentiated primordial chaos; the same notion is conveyed by the Sanskrit word *rupa*.

For taoists the primordial chaos was not homogenous in the sense of being everywhere the same. Rather it was *hsüan*, which means 'deep, dark and mysterious' as well as 'the chaos preceding order' (Hall 1982; Girardot 1983; Kohn 1992). Taoists refer to the pre-creation 'chaos' metaphorically as wonton soup. Like minestrone soup, wonton soup comprises a variety of ingredients each in small pieces. Such soup can be seen as just that – undifferentiated soup – or it can be 'differentiated' into component parts. And such differentiation is the act of naming things. It is in the context of such a metaphor we should read such cosmogonic expressions as:

> Naming is the origin of heaven and earth
> Naming is the mother of all things

> (*Tao te Ching* chapter 1)

In early Chinese cosmogonies the primordial chaos was created by the initial separation of heaven and earth (Hall 1982: 55–6). In the *Tao te Ching* chapter 5 we are informed:

> The space between heaven and earth is like a bellows.
> The shape changes but not the form.

Chapter 25 of the *Tao te Ching* is usually translated as

> Man follows the Earth
> Earth follows heaven
> Heaven follows the tao
> Tao follows what is natural

A more 'cause-and-effect' paraphrase would read: the tao comes from what is natural; heaven comes from the tao, Earth comes from heaven, and humans come from (or even 'are born from') the Earth. Seemingly sharing the same scriptwriter, *Enuma elish* has Tiamat divide the sky and earth, while in Genesis Yahweh divides heaven from earth. The gap between is, initially at least, 'chaos'. (Hall 1982: 55)

The separation of heaven and earth is the primordial act of creation so can also be read as one of sexual creation, just as all Chinese dualisms are expressions of the all-encompassing *yin/yang* dialectic, of which the female/male associations are a key part. Although woefully anachronistic, the sexual connotations of the initial separation of heaven and earth in early creation myths puts me in mind of the Japanese haiku which translates as 'I am so horny even the crack of dawn had better watch out!' (appropriated by Tom Waits for his song *Nighthawks at the diner*).

The crack of dawn at Avebury. The south entrance, November 2007.

This is not simply back-projecting modern thinking. The earliest Greek poets described how Zeus married Earth and produced the world of nature. Hesiod makes much of the union of earth (female principle) and sky/heaven (male principle). Aristophanes considers that love seeks a unity to overcome the separation or gap (*khaos*) that emerged with the creation of the sexes. In *The Birds*, Aristophanes' version of the Orphic cosmogony, Eros is given the role of creating the order of things:

> Then all things commingling together in love,
> there arose the fair Earth and Sky.

And Chang Tsu, writing a few decades after Lao Tsu, few confirms that Aristophanes was not the first to have such libidinous thoughts:

> The passionate union of *yin* and *yang* and the copulation of
> husband and wife is the eternal pattern of the universe. If heaven
> and earth did not mingle, whence would everything receive life?
> (Watts 1976: 26)

Modern English 'beginning' has its roots in Old Norse *gína* and Old English *gínan*, both of which mean 'to gape' or 'to yawn' and resonate clearly in the north European creation myths where the world originates in Ginnungagap, literally 'the beguiling or bewildering gap'.

The Greeks were onto the same idea. They called it *khaos*, which they thought of as an abyss, gaping wide open over vast emptiness. Contrary to modern conceptions of the word 'chaos' as somehow 'chaotic', both Greek and Chinese thought of chaos as the thus-far undifferentiated 'raw material' of the cosmos. Perhaps James Joyce in *Finnegans Wake* got the closest to a concise expression when he contrived 'Chaosmos' – a word which has gained wider currency after being borrowed by Peter Carroll and other self-styled 'chaos magicians'.

Making a distinction makes the world

'Naming is the mother of all things' reminds me of the Biblical 'In the beginning was the word.' And this process of 'making a distinction' – creating words to name things – is what 'creates' the manifest world. Chapter 42 of the *Tao te Ching* puts it thus:

> The Tao begat one.
> One begat two.
> Two begat three.
> And three begot the ten thousand things.
> (The phrase 'ten thousand things' has the sense of 'everything'.)

The 'act of separation' or 'making a distinction' ('One begat two' as the *Tao te Ching* put it) also forms the basis of G. Spencer Brown's fully self-contained model of mathematics, *The Laws of Form* (Brown 1972). This starts from the entirely theoretical first principle of 'making a distinction' and builds up to a way of describing all mathematical processes. But this is not pure theory as Brown applied his ideas to develop a safe way of interlocking signalling and points systems for British Rail. And the same process of 'making a distinction' at its most uncomplicated is of course the binary code of every digital device.

The human brain naturally differentiates the 'chaosmos' of sensory perceptions as the ongoing part of our cognitive processes. This was first recognised by the Gestalt school of psychologists in the 1930s but research in the last fifteen-or-so years has greatly extended our understanding (see the contributors to Noë 2002 for a useful summary). Interestingly this same research leads to models of consciousness as a complex 'process', so 2,500 years after dialectical processes were suggested as the underlying principle of matter, now an analogous concept is being presented as the underlying principle of how we think we think.

The cauldrons of inspiration

This rather rapid dash through early Greek, Chinese and other cultures' creation myths and metaphysics has aimed to show that quite 'deep' ideas about the nature of existence are shared over a wide geographical area and, seemingly, predate the sixth century BCE – although by how much it is hard to say. On the basis of this overview

Ceridwen's cauldron. Illustration by Ian Brown.

Detail of decoration on a Neolithic pottery vessel.

Did crocks like these precede the cauldrons and possets of later legends?

are parallels between the finer details of Greek, Germanic and Celtic myths also a result of quite ancient shared origins rather than the result of comparatively recent borrowings, or parallel inventiveness?

We can ask the same questions about the origins of alchemy, where ideas about transformation seem to have their origins in both China and the Middle East. Both of these esoteric traditions may be the oldest-surviving evidence for ideas originating elsewhere, or they may be evidence for the sharing of ideas over several millennia. Indeed, the underlying metaphysics of alchemy – the continuing process of changes which make up the alchemists' Great Work – are, understandably, shared with the metaphysics of early taoism. And, less predictably, Heroclitus. I am not alone in such thinking. A modern day alchemical expert, Charles Nicholl, is of the opinion that alchemy is essentially a process:

> There are two directions in which alchemical Mercury leads us. On the one hand, it is a complex elaboration of chemical substance, its various qualities referring back to the properties of quicksilver, or 'common mercury'... But there is another direction entirely, away from chemical matter. Mercury is not, finally, a substance, or even many substances: *it is a process*... All these [alchemical writings] point to one crucial idea: that transformation is something intrinsic and contained inside matter... Each stage of

this self-devouring, self-generating process bears the name 'Mercury'. Mercury, in short, is alchemy itself.

(Nicholl 1980, cited in Gilchrist 2007: 50–1; emphasis added.)

From an alchemical rather than shamanic perspective, the centre is the alembic where the four elements react and transformation takes place. 'Here and now' is the *locus* of ever-changing mercury, of the processes of change – the tao if you like – that animates the sentient aspects of the universe. If for a moment we replace the alchmists' archetypal alembic with what would have been its predecessor, a cauldron, then this process of creation acquires a great many more kin among world-wide myths.

I mentioned the significance of *wonton* soup to early Chinese world-views. While there is no evidence that such soup was used as part of early taoist rituals, with *wanton* soup in mind, think about of the mixture which made up the sacred drink used at the climax of the Eleusinian mysteries. This was called *kykeon*, a word meaning 'to mix or stir'. While its ingredients were part of the secrets of the mystery cult, it contained barley and a variety of other plants. Was one of the secrets of the mysteries an elucidation of this mixed up 'soup' as manifesting the *khaos* of primordial creation?

Could these drinks also be related to the contents of the seething cauldron called Hvergelmir which was under the roots of the Scandinavian World Tree, Yggdrassill? Hvergelmir contained *ond*, the vital animating power of all creation (corresponding to *ch'i* in Chinese thinking). *Ond* was regarded as a chaotic energy, yet to 'take shape' as manifest reality. It is all potential and emergence.

With this in mind think of the Ceridwen's cauldron of inspiration in the tales of Taliesin. In some versions the contents are described as *awen*, also thought of as creativity and associated concepts. And, whatever creativity may or may not be, it is characterised as an 'emergent' process (see Pope 2005: 5, 17, 78, 89). We are back with Agni, Nechtan and Neptunus – the water deities we met earlier in the chapter who, at least in the Irish tradition, are linked to the inspiration of poets. As too are Brigid and her close relatives who we met in the previous chapter.

With all such seething cauldrons and their mixed-up contents in mind, think again about John Aubrey's recounting of the local seventeenth century lore relating to Silbury Hill – 'the hill was raised while a posset of milk was seething'. While a posset is a bowl not a cauldron, and milk is neither *wonton* soup or *kykeon*, consider this traditional recipe for pearl barley pudding:

> Take half a pound of pearl barley, cree it in soft water, and shift it once or twice in the boiling till it be soft; take five eggs, put to them a pint of good cream, and half a pound of powder sugar, grate in half a nutmeg, a little salt, a spoonful or two of rose-water, and half a pound of clarified butter; when your barley is cold mix them altogether, so bake it with a puff-paste round your dish-edge.

Well perhaps puff pastry is rather too *nouvelle cuisine* for the Neolithic – but seething in a posset would do nicely. While pearl barley pudding is not now everyday fare, most people reading this book will have eaten rice pudding, which is hardly a distant relative.

So was one of the wonderful pottery vessels which characterise the Neolithic filled with milk and other ingredients and brought to a boil as part of a ritual re-enacting the primordial creation, a re-enactment which also included vast amounts of chalky-white soil being piled up to create Silbury as we now know it? Was some of the chalky water associated with this construction – as near to naturally occurring 'milk' as it is possible to get – added to this 'posset'? Did, by some stroke of luck, a fragmentary folk memory of this reach Aubrey's ears?

You don't have to be called Sigmund to see the associations between milky or chalky fluids and that other key requirement for creation, semen. So, to compress several millennia of creation myths, was the posset of *wonton*-like milky mixture seething at the 'crack of dawn' as the heavens separated from the earth to create a *khaos*-filled Ginnungagap? And were the angel-like swans bearing the *spiritus* of the yet-to-be-reborn nesting at Swallowhead Springs or along the banks of the Kennet and Winterbourne?

Next time you see someone warming up a tin of rice pudding on a primus stove in their camper van parked in the lay-by between Silbury and Swallowhead ask if they know the answers... I prefer rice pudding with nutmeg on top, by the way.

Chapter 11

Towards a Kennet Dreaming

> '... landscape is the work of the mind. Its scenery is built as much from strata of memory as from layers of rock.'
>
> (Schama 1995: 6–7)

Each chapter so far in this book has explored a specific theme. There are of course points of contact and overlap between the themes, but I have tried fairly hard to stop these overlaps taking over. So far. This chapter and the next are where these themes are allowed to weave together. In this more creative way of writing I am not trying to establish any sort of 'truths' about the past. Instead my aim is to illustrate how orally-transmitted traditions may have multiple levels of meaning, rather than describing a single set of historic events. But such traditions, once the process of transmission has been broken and they are no longer sustained by individual and collective memory, can never be brought back. I am simply inventing myths for the upper Kennet landscape, not attempting to re-discover them. Or you may wish to think of this as a way of re-enchanting this special locality.

In the rest of this book I will cease to regard legends and myths as some sort of 'maps' to spiritual and otherworldly realities. In these realities we have little by the way of maps. Rather, the narratives *are* the territory. These are realms where, contrary to modern preconceptions, humans are subservient to more important agencies. Robert Thomas Rundle Clark was drawing on hieroglyphic records when he wrote about the Ancient Egyptians:

> The community was not merely composed of the living but of the Ancestors as well…. The Ancestors, the custodians of the source of life, were the reservoir of power and vitality, the source whence flowed all forces of vigour, sustenance and growth. Hence, they were not only departed souls but still active, the keepers of life and fortune… The sprouting of the corn, the increase of the herds, potency in men, success in hunting or war, were all

> manifestations of their power and approval. Hence the place
> where the Ancestors dwelt was the most holy spot in the world.
> From whence flowed the well-being of the group. Without the
> tomb, or the cemetery, life on earth would be miserable, perhaps
> impossible.

(Rundle Clark 1959: 119 cited in O Duinn 2008: 218–19)

However his remarks fit what we know of ancient Britons; indeed Sean O Duinn sees close parallels to the surviving myths and legends of the landscape around Loch Gur in the same terms. Even with christian beliefs such a worldview persists – it is not many generations since people expected to be buried, if not in the parish church, at least in the churchyard. Christianity may have moved the 'potency' from the ancestors to the godhead, but in practice the association between ancestors and sanctity remained unchanged.

Christianity, like shamanic cultures the word over, does not regard humans as the 'prime mover' in the universe. If we described the spiritual experiences and associated behaviours of christian cultures only in terms of kinship, warfare and status we would miss the true motivation behind this world-view. Similarly, attempts by ethnologists to explain shamanic cultures in terms of the human realm of kinship, warfare and prestige, miss the motivations behind their actions (Walens 1981: 3). As Geo Athena Trevarthen observes, 'The outward social form is based upon myth and visionary experience, not the other way around' (Trevarthen 2008a: 3)

This quotation is a very good way of thinking about the annual resurrection myths of Osiris and Isis which were re-enacted in annual rituals by the Ancient Egyptians, already described in Chapters Five and Nine. It also explains why numerous hand-shaped castanet-like clappers known as the 'hand of Atem' or the 'hand of god' were to be found in Egyptian temples the length of the Nile; these commemorated the hand used by Atem in an auto-chthonic act to create the first beings by masturbating into his own mouth.

In contrast, the legacy of Victorian and Edwardian prudery still drives a wedge between the sacred and sexuality. But, as Geo Athena Trevarthen writes:

> Experiencing union with the sacred as a divine romance –
> whether that sacred is perceived as a spirit or a deity or God – is
> to join with the sacred in one of the most intimate and emotional
> ways possible. […]

> Psychologically, an indigenous shaman married to a spirit may
> have as powerful an experience as a Christian nun who feels
> herself married to Christ. Mystics like St Gertrude (1256–1302)
> speak of marriage to Christ as the most perfect and transformative
> union…

> (Trevarthen 2008b: 224–5)

Walkabout by Ian Brown.

The upper Kennet valley in the 'dreamtime'

With such thoughts of divine ecstasy and primordial 'Big Bangs' in mind I am about to draw on many of the ideas in the previous chapters to re-enchant the upper Kennet valley landscape. Right at the start of the Prologue I introduced young Kenna and her Grandma travelling up the Kennet in the early Neolithic; the next chapter rejoins them a year later.

However I have imposed some limits on my imagination according to current archaeological evidence for about 3,600 BCE. In many ways it is a 'dream time' – a 'once upon a time' that is not quite then but most certainly not now either. 'It was and it was not', as all Persian fairy tales start.

At this time the enclosures on Windmill Hill (referred to simply as the 'Headland' at the end of the chapter) had been constructed and West Kennett chambered long barrow was already a place of their ancestors.

The Kennet would mostly not have been as narrow or deep as it is now. The watercourses which now exist are the result of many centuries of human interference to deepen channels and create banks. The distribution of sands and gravels (shown on geological maps) confirms that during the Neolithic they would have been wider and shallower, bordered by wide swathes of rushes and other semi-aquatic plants and trees. Where bridges now exist would have once been wide and shallow areas easier to ford, usually with fairly firm chalk or gravel on the bed. Seasonal flooding would have been less constrained than now, but drained away quickly.

Plants growing in the river bed would include watercress and the white, five-petalled flowers of water crowfoot (known locally in recent times as clench). Roasted or boiled bull rush rhyzomes would have been an important source of carbohydrate, although grain was beginning to become more significant.

Since the Mesolithic, people would have cleared a route through reed beds, fallen trees and other obstructions to enable small craft to paddle or punt their way along. We have the archaeological evidence for dug-out log boats although it is reasonable to assume that hide-covered 'coracles' or bark-covered 'canoes' were also used. Maybe also bundles of reeds were tied together to create simple rafts. But in the upper reaches of the rivers then log boats or canoes may have been the only craft narrow enough to negotiate natural obstacles.

The Savernake Forest, through which the Kennet flows, would have been almost impenetrable by foot on this time, and the home to bears, wolves, wild boars and formidable wild cattle standing nearly two metres high at the withers and with horns of similar length. These would have migrated from winter grazing around the tidal zone of the Thames to upland woodland, such as Savernake, in the summer. None of these creatures would welcome encounters with humans.

The next chapter envisages Kenna and her Grandma on a journey from the tidal estuary of the Thames – modern London – up to the confluence with the Kennet at modern-day Reading, then coming through the Savernake Forest. Their final camp is where the Kennet runs past the end of Overton Hill to the south of the Sanctuary, where the palisaded enclosures were excavated. However the Sanctuary and the palisades are still in the future for Kenna and her kin.

The other tribes met by Kenna and her Grandma have either travelled up the Christchurch Avon then followed the dry valley through what is now All Cannings, Bishops Cannings and Beckhampton or from what we know as Somerset, then climbed up the scarp slope from the lower ground around what is now Calne and Wootton Bassett. People from all three regions, but especially those from the Avon valley and the Kennet-Thames valley, would have traded pottery and polished hand axes with people who followed the south coast from the Lizard peninsula.

The 'dream time' in which I have situated Kenna is, I hope, a plausible one. However early Neolithic thinking was probably quite different! The myths, stories and customs of that era were probably far richer than we could ever envisage. Quite conceivably there was a ritual procession – perhaps taking many days – which linked the various sites of the Avebury area. I would like to think that such a pilgrimage had something of the erotic intensity associated with the groves of Braj, the setting for Krishna's seduction of Radha (as mentioned in Chapter Two). But re-enchanting the landscape on such a scale would take much more than a chapter. It would be another book...

Chapter 12

A Kennet Dreaming

Kenna half-woke to the sound of her grandma chanting. It was the dim light just before day-rise. She could not hear what words Grandma was using but recognised the resonant sound, partway between talking and singing, that carried over the distance even while the words themselves were lost in the trees.

Grandma was, it seemed, down with the boat near the riverbank. They had made a camp just after leaving the big river. As they'd left the winter settlements around the estuary Grandma simply said they were going west, 'All the way to the setting sun.' Kenna knew she looked at her Grandma in surprise. 'We just follow the river all the way there, my dear,' was all she said. Kenna was not sure this reassured her.

Above all Kenna really wanted to know *why* they were going to the setting sun – and what they would be doing when they got there. But she had long since learnt that it was no good asking questions of Grandma. In a slightly put-out voice she would only ever answer 'All in due time, my dear', or 'You'll see when we get there, my dear', and other equally unhelpful answers.

Kenna had little doubt that Grandma was able to find her way anywhere. She had said more than once that 'All you need to do is remember the story. If you follow the story then the places appear in the right order.' But just occasionally Grandma had also remarked, 'Well the stories of the land don't seem to help, we'd better wait till it gets dark and follow the stories of the sky.' Grandma's remarks could be very perplexing at times, thought Kenna.

Sometimes indeed Grandma did tell Kenna about plants and places as they passed by. But Grandma's conversations seemed to raise more questions in Kenna's mind than she ever got explanations or answers. 'It's your age, my dear,' Grandma had recently said to her. 'I was like that too when I was your age.' Kenna found it hard to imagine Grandma ever being any age except old.

~~~~~~~~~~~~~~~~~~~~

Swans by Alan Haylock.

Kenna had gone to sleep dreaming of the sky goddess – can you go to sleep dreaming she wondered? – wearing a dress made of stars. Sometimes, Grandma had said, the sky goddess took the shape of a swan, flying high above the northern sky, and the earth god came to her in the shape of a bull. The sky goddess later laid a golden egg from which came a goose known as the Great Gaggler whose honking had broken the original silence.

At least that's sort-of what Grandma had told her after they'd eaten and the fire died down to a glimmer and the stars came out. Grandma's story had lots more details, but it was difficult for Kenna to remember where they all fitted in. Grandma's stories were often about shape-shifting, especially the stars, but her stories too seemed to shift their shape with each telling – and certainly when Kenna tried to retell them to herself.

Kenna had seen the sky goddess in the night sky often enough. Whenever the clouds parted, there she was like a night-time rainbow running from one horizon to the other, almost to the top of the sky. She knew that some of the kin in the settlements called these stars the Way of the Souls. Some even said that each star was a soul – countless souls just waiting. But were they old souls who had gone off to the summerlands Kenna wondered, or new souls coming to the about-to-be-born? No one had told her before about the goddess becoming a swan and meeting the earth god as a bull – but this must mean it is the Way of the New Souls, Kenna surmised.

Grandma had stopped chanting and was making her way back to the camp. Kenna had barely got to her feet before Grandma said 'Good, up and all ready to get on our way then, my dear?' Kenna answered 'Oh, yes' in a rather unconvincing manner.

~~~~~~~~~~~~~~~~~~~

By that afternoon the river had narrowed considerably. This made it easier to paddle than when the river had been wider and flowing faster – though they almost always kept to the outside of the bends where the current was slower. They passed places where those travelling before had worked hard to shift fallen trees to one side – places where a fallen tree could easily reach from one bank to the other. Where the banks were further apart there were gravelly small islands where plants were re-growing, and the water in between was shallow. A few times the boat scraped around one of the gravel islands, and they pushed their oars against the river bottom instead of paddling. The further up the river they went the more the plants grew. Where bull rushes came within easy reach of the boat Grandma waded into the water with a stick to dig out the roots. Last night's meal had been mostly roasted bull rush roots And there was a growing large pile in the boat – clearly many more such rather tasteless meals in the next week or more Kenna thought, disapprovingly.

Kenna was in her usual place towards the front of the boat. She reached out and grabbed a handful of white flowers with yellow centres. 'Kenna, put them back in the water now, and apologise to the Lady for taking her flowers,' her Grandma's stern voice said behind her. 'But...' said Kenna, turning round to where her Grandma sat at the stern, beyond all the food and skins they used for the camps. 'No buts', interrupted Grandma, 'They are all sacred to the Lady whose land this belongs to. Didn't I tell you that yellow and white are her colours?' 'Yes, but I only wanted to put some in my hair.' 'Not those flowers, Kenna. Now apologise to the Lady. Her name hereabouts is Havern. Bad will come to you if you do not.'

Kenna looked at the dense woods to either side of the river. Whoever Havern was she couldn't be afraid of boars or wild cattle, or even wolves and bears, thought Kenna with a slight shudder. After placing the handful of flowers back in the water – in the midst of yet another large area of just such plants – and making a somewhat perfunctory apology, Kenna couldn't stop asking 'Who is Havern and why does she want to live in this scary place?' 'Well, I don't know about whether she *wants* to live in this place,' replied Grandma. 'After all, the Sovereign of the Land cannot *choose* where she dwells. And she has no reason to think of it as scary – why should she be scared of her own creatures? She and her hounds – wonderful pure white, every one of them, apart from the insides of their ears which are quite pink – she is the sovereign of the land and all the animals around here.'

'A sovereign? Of the land?' What do you mean Grandma?'

'Ah, so many questions, my dear. There is so much I need to tell you. But there is plenty of time. Every place has its Lady of the Land – its Sovereign as I like to think. We are only passing through Havern's lands to get to the land of Kenevar – the White Lady herself. But I will tell you more about her when you are about to meet her.'

'I will meet a Sovereign,' blurted out Kenna, not sure whether it was a question or not. 'I mean, did you really say I would meet a Sovereign of the Land? But isn't that…'

'Oh, do stop getting excited and remember to paddle, my dear. I can't do all the work of getting upstream from back here. Yes of course. Why would we be going all the way to the summerlands of the setting sun if not?'

Kenna wasn't sure she had even the slightest idea about the answer to her Grandma's question but thought it best to concentrate on paddling.

'Did I ever tell you how these lands came to be made, Kenna?' Kenna wasn't quite sure what Grandma meant. Hadn't the land always been here? She stopped herself from asking the question out loud and simply said, 'I don't think so, Grandma.' 'Oh, I'm sure someone must have told you.' After a short pause she continued, 'But I forget your mother died before you could really remember.'

That's not true, thought Kenna, but knew better than to contradict her Grandma. She could remember her mother's face. But no, she could not clearly remember her mother's voice, still less anything she'd ever said to her. This would be the fourth summer since her mother died. Her young brother Kwenton would have been four summer's old now. Mother only lived for a few days after he was born. As the snows melted this last winter Kwent too had died, coughing and blue-faced. She shuddered and tried to think of something that would stop her from crying again.

Grandma realised she that even a passing mention of Kenna's mother was still likely to make Kenna break out into tears. And she herself was not above still shedding one or two for the little lad who her daughter never saw grow, and who will never grow into a man, though he had all the makings of a fine fellow. To distract them both she began to chant:

> The birds circled around and around
> The birds circled around and around
> Nowhere could they land
>
> Constantly flying in circles
> Constantly flying in circles
> Before there was any land
>
> Circles as big as an ocean
> Circles as big as an ocean
> Never able to land
>
> Some circled all day one way
> Some circled the day the other way
> At dusk they all met again
>
> Some circled all night one way
> Some circled the night the other way
> At dawn they all met again
>
> One by one each bird began to whoop
> One by one each bird began to trumpet.
> One by one the sound got louder
>
> After a while every bird was honking
> After a while every bird was hollering
> Untold numbers of birds across the oceans
>
> From all directions a distant sound like deep thunder
> From above the sounds of birds still circling, still honking
> It sounded like the whole universe was squabbling with itself
>
> So loud was the sound the ocean began to tremble
> Waves started to form on the surface of the water
> Deep waves, the tops foamed with spermy white
>
> The sound got louder and louder
> The waves got deeper and deeper
> The birds kept flying around and around
>
> Except one bird. One bird alone was mute.
> The one bird which was perfectly white
> Perfectly white apart from its yellow beak

Where the circling birds crossed their ways
This one bird looked down into the waters.
Deep and deeper still into the water

Where the birds' flights crossed dawn and dusk
Looking to the bottom of the deepest waves
There it saw something white like itself

Down below the waves it dived.
Up it came with spermy, milky whiteness in its beak
Down it went again and back up again.

This bird silently brought to the surface white sperm
This bird silently brought to the surface white mud
Where the birds came back dawn and dusk

From this white mud it made a small mound
From this small mound it made a large mound
From the large mound it made the whole of the land.

'And that is how the land came to be made,' announced Grandma, as if pleased with her own story. Quite a while since she'd told it and some of the lines she knew were not quite as she had been told, but it would do for now.

Kenna was not quite sure if this helped her understand how the land came to be made. As always, what Grandma told her seemed to raise so many more questions. But, as the river got ever narrower, she knew she needed to concentrate on positioning the front of the boat so it eased around the many shallows. Not the time to be asking questions.

After a few moments of silence, Grandma spoke again. 'At the start of this river is the pool where the swan dived down. At least that is what our people have always told. Some say it is also where the sky goddess laid her golden egg. So it is also Kenevar's quim. It all depends which story you tell. But for any – and all – these reasons this river is especially sacred. It is more sacred than the south-flowing river used by the people of the south coast and the south-west lands where they make crockery and delve for the stone to make the best axes, the ones the lads spend hours polishing and telling tall tales at each other's expense.'

'But the summerlands – as we call them – are all sacred too. They are the body of Kenevar. We are nearly at her toes now and soon the river will run between her legs. Look out for a flat-topped ridge shaped like an over-turned boat just to the north. The rounded end of ridge runs right down to the river's edge, where it is wide and shallow. Beyond there is Kenevar's quim.'

Kenna looked briefly to her left and then her right trying to remember which was north. As if reading her mind, Grandma gently admonished her. 'Learn to always be aware where you are heading, even when the sun is hidden, my dear. Here it is easy as, give or take the wriggles, this river flows from the west. Beyond the source is where the summerlands are, the home of the souls of the dead, living out their days where they loved best. To the north is the realm of the spirits of place in all their shape-shifting ways of shining or simply being there unseen. The east has been behind us on our journey. Think of it not as where we spend the winters once the biting flies have died off but as the place of inspiration, the home of the souls of the unborn, all that is yet to make itself fully manifest.'

Kenna had heard Grandma describe the directions in this sort of way a number of times before. She knew that Grandma would now describe south as the place where everything had its greatest energy – like the sun at noon – and was most manifest, most evident. But when the sun was not out she still had to think about where the directions were. 'As you get older and are nearly a woman, you will find it easier to orient yourself,' Grandma reassured, even though Kenna was sure she had not voiced her thoughts out loud.

She looked briefly to the north and shuddered at the thought that this is where the unseen spirits lived. They could be seen clearly enough at night in her dreams, and when she found herself in that half-way place between waking and sleep. 'Daydreaming again, my dear', her Grandma said all too often. But Grandma seemed entirely comfortable when she was chanting to these spirits, or talking to them, asking them for their advice. Kenna hoped she too would be more like Grandma one day. When she was old would she too be less scared of these spirits that darted like foxes into her mind? Yet she liked foxes really. Only when they came into her thoughts like foxes was she sometimes scared. But not as often as she used to be, she realised. Over the winter Grandma had told her many things about foxes, although most of the time she seemed to be talking less about real foxes and more about spirit foxes. Kenna could not see how spirit foxes could be her helpers, as Grandma had said she should, but if they were really her helpers – and Kenna was still not really sure about this – then perhaps she should be less scared when they visited.

'We have reached the toes of Kenevar,' Grandma announced. Kenna looked around but could see nothing that looked like toes. The only difference was that from bank to bank, as far as the next gentle bend, the whole width of the river was taken up with the plant with white flowers with yellow centres. 'This is where the Lady washes her feet. We must do likewise and wade with the boat, my dear,' spoke Grandma. 'How can I wade through all those sacred flowers and not break some off?', asked Kenna, 'The Sovereign Lady will make something awfully bad happen to me.'

'No, not at all, my dear', replied Grandma. 'She knows we come to honour her. And anyway Kenevar is a much better-tempered Sovereign than Havern. And I was worried back then because only I had done the chants to honour Havern – you were still asleep. I should have woken you so we both honoured her but decided to let you sleep longer. Here you will be honouring Kenevar with us all.'

'Does the Sovereign Lady *know* we are coming?' Kenna's mind brimmed with questions. 'Well, in a manner of speaking. You will understand, all in due time, my dear.' Which, once again, hardly stopped Kenna from wondering but she took the cue that any more questions would be more brusquely rebuffed. Grandma was telling her which side of the boat to wade while they made their way through the water plants, Kenna at the front of the boat dragging on plaited thongs and Grandma pushing at the stern, while stopping the vessel from turning over when Kenna stumbled and pulled a little too hard to one side.

Kenna was so involved in keeping her footing and making sure the boat did not tip she had not looked up for several minutes. There it was! The flat-topped hill with the trees coming down to the water's edge in a rounded shape just like the front of the boat she was pulling. She looked ahead, trying to see the quim of Kenevar. But the course of the river and the trees blocked her view.

'Look towards the south of the river, my dear. No, not that far.' Not really to the south but through the trees she could see a clearing on a hill top. And on the summit, silhouetted against the sky, was the home of the dead, the mound where the elders travelled to the realm of the dead to talk with their ancestors.

'We'll camp here, my dear,' said Grandma. 'But aren't we going any further today Grandma? It doesn't seem time to make camp yet.' 'Yes, we made good time today, my dear. I was expecting the water to be lower already and we would have to drag the boat through more shallows. And you did well helping.' Praise or thanks from Grandma was rather rare and never frivolous. For a moment Kenna took pride that she had done well enough to get thanked. 'But we are nearly at Kenevar's quim, my dear. The river goes no further. And no one takes a boat there. Above all, we need to get ready for the preparations.' And as Grandma was speaking, Kenna began to notice several other boats pulled up on the river bank, and small camps among the trees. Other people were here already. She would have smelled the smoke of their embers but the gentle wind was blowing from an unusual direction so was taking the smoke away from where she was.

They began to make camp and Grandma went off to take some embers from the nearest fire, even though there was no one to ask. 'Oh that's all right, Kait and her kin would willingly give it to me if they were here.' Kenna wondered how Grandma knew whose camp it was – presumably she recognised the decorations on the hides of the shelters. Before she could ask, Grandma gave instructions to tend the fire and start roasting the bull rush roots that they had collected while they were wading, and then strode off purposefully.

After a few minutes Kenna could hear the sound of Grandma greeting and joking with other people further away in the trees than Kait's hearth. One woman broke out into a greeting song. That would be Kait. Kenna liked Kait. She looked even older than Grandma but Kait could improvise little songs for almost any occasion. Trouble was she expected you to remember the songs she'd invented for you! And, although Kait had always sung to Kenna songs praising her flax-coloured hair and good looks, she knew that Kait sometimes made one or other of the lads sing back rather rude songs she had made up about their lack of appeal to women – or what seemed to be

A crock as big as the world.

even ruder words. She knew they must be rude because everyone else began that sort of laugh when someone was being embarrassed and couldn't escape.

By the time Grandma came back the water on the fire had been warm long enough that it had started to evaporate, so the big crock was much less full than it should be – Kenna knew she should have topped it up. But Grandma seemed not to notice – although Kenna did think that she actually had noticed but was in such a good mood after meeting the others that she'd chosen not to say anything. Instead of topping up the water, Grandma added some of the grains they'd carried on the boat in a hide bag, and herbs that she'd come back with from the other kins' camps.

While the food finished cooking Grandma passed on to Kenna some of the news about other kinfolk who were there. Kenna couldn't help but think that she'd not known Grandma to be in such a good mood for a long time. Kenevar was clearly a benevolent sort of Sovereign if she could make Grandma happier. While the trees and plants seemed similar to those elsewhere along the river, she realised that the earth beneath her feet must be different here. And, although it still looked like earth on the surface, just beneath must be the flesh of the Lady. Hadn't Grandma said that the river here flowed between her legs – and if her quim was near, then this must be near her knees, or even her thighs. Indeed the hills to either side here did close in more tightly than anywhere else. Were they between Kenevar's thighs, she wondered? But now did not seem the right time to ask Grandma while they were eating.

'Think of the big crock as a smaller version of a huge crock from which everything originates,' suddenly said Grandma as the food had nearly gone. 'Remember I told you about the birds circling over the ocean? Well some say it was not an ocean but a crock of milk and barley simmering over a fire. A very large crock, a crock as large as the world, I suppose. Anyone who could have looked in – although there were no people then to look in it – would have seen the inside as deep darkness, full of mysterious things that had yet to have names. Nothing knew what it was, there were no stars, no sun or moon, no spirits of west and east, south and north. Nothing knew where it was, nothing knew its place. Everything was yet to emerge.'

Kenna looked up at her Grandma. How did she know such things if no one was there to see? But her Grandma ignored the quizzical look on Kenna's face and continued.

'In a few days, when the lads with the cattle arrive, we will all take our crocks, and gently heat up corn grains with water from Kenevar's quim, and creamy milk from the cattle – but not the sheep, of course – and mix it with new-laid eggs and as much honey and herbs as we can find. And while it is slowly cooking we shall all chant the original sound that the birds make. The deep sound like distant thunder. Everyone chants over and over the letters O – U – M.'

Her voice changed to her chanting voice, lower in pitch, with the pitch lowering further with the U and even more with the M. ' But everyone does it differently, in their own time, so the sounds all mix together. But you and the other youngsters, your voices are high-pitched like swans. You will honk and whoop. Kait may even ask you to play the swan-bone which sounds like the swan's own cries.'

The thought of being with Kait – of Kait asking her to play a swan bone – jolted Kenna out of her sleepy thoughts. But the warm food after a hard day of paddling and wading meant that she fell into sleep long before night rise. Grandma covered her where she lay, rather too close to the river. It seemed unlikely that it would rain. She would wake Kenna and move her only if it did.

Kenna slept hearing the babbling of the river in the shallows. But in her dreams it was the babble of the spirits of this place, the same size as her, friendly and welcoming, beckoning her to come and play, to change shape like they could. She played all night with these fair-skinned little folk. The sound of her Grandma chanting interrupted their play and Kenna opened her eyes. The sun was lighting up the sky from the north-east, although their valley was still deep in shadow. She looked around for her little friends, and was not at all sure she had only been dreaming.

~~~~~~~~~~~~~~~~~~~~

That day Kenna was kept busy. Very busy. 'Why so many preparation?' she had been tempted to ask Grandma but knew better. First she had to twist flax into twine. 'But we already brought twine on the boat, Grandma', she protested. 'Yes, but that's not made of flax, my dear,' was the reply, as if that explained everything. 'Remember when you make the two threads to twist one sun-wise and the other against the sun. Then when they are twinned the opposites will unite and not come undo. They will be as inseparable as day and night.'

Grandma then asked her to grind down soft white rock. There were plenty of large almost flat rocks around here – indeed Kenna found she could often hop from one to the next without stepping to the ground – and some had depressions the right shape to use for grinding. Grandma brought some small pieces of yellow rock from one of the bundles on the boat and pounded those on a rock nearby. Kenna was pleased that Grandma had not asked her to grind those stones – she was making much more white powder than Grandma was making with her stones, despite the muscles and sinews on Grandma's arms showing that this was not easy stone to break down.

'What is the white and yellow to be used for?' she asked when her curiosity got the better of her. 'You will see, my dear', started Grandma in her typically enigmatic manner. 'It will make the goose fat visible.' Grandma smiled, knowing she was teasing. 'Do you remember how we brought a crock of fat from the geese and swans we cooked over the winter?' Kenna indeed remembered that Grandma had Kenna take special care packing this into the heather they kept to store and move crocks. And it was a crock that Kenna liked to hold – it was smaller than the others and the grooves around the outside made it feel as it it was alive, like she was running her hands over the rows of scars which decorated her father's chest and back.

Grandma could see that Kenna was off in her own thoughts. 'Well, we're about to take that special fat and mix it with these special colours. That way we will become one with the sky goddess.' Grandma paused, knowing she had now got Kenna's full attention. Before Kenna could decide which of so many questions in her mind she wanted to ask Grandma, the older woman continued. 'Everyone – well, all the women – will be painted with the fat of the goddess's birds, in the colours of the goddess. And, yes, you will get to wear those white and yellow flowers which grow in the river. And you must tie them together with flax twine. The men will paint themselves with deep red mixed with cattle fat, of course.'

Kenna had no idea what Grandma meant by 'of course'. But she continued with the preparations with more enthusiasm. Being painted as the sky goddess sounded really important – and didn't Grandma say they would become one with the goddess? Would they have to fly into the night sky? Grandma seemed to make anything seem possible. Or would the sky goddess come to them? That didn't sound very likely either, but seemed to Kenna just a little bit more likely.

~~~~~~~~~~~~~~~~~~~~

When Grandma told Kenna that the soft white rocks were from the bones of the Lady she stopped grinding. 'Well, in a way of speaking, they are,' she continued, making Kenna even less certain what she meant. 'They came from the side of the hill beyond there,' Grandma said waving her yellow-stained hand over the hill nearest to there. 'And this yellow is from another Sovereign, many day's travel from here. I have never been to their lands but her kinfolk exchanged it for some of our food while we were at the estuary.'

They continued grinding in silence, and Grandma walked away leaving Kenna still pounding. When the last of the bones of the Lady had been ground down – with a little bit more care than when Kenna had thought of it as just soft white rock – Kenna realised no one would miss her if she walked to the side of the hill where Grandma had indicated. As she left the ground nearest the river she realised that the earth between the plants was indeed quite white. The further she walked she kept noticing small lumps of white like the ones she had been grinding. And, where there were clearings between the trees – the sort of places you might come across deer grazing, although there were none to be seen today – there were brilliant yellow flowers, brighter than the yellow of a rainbow. So many dozens of them Kenna could not even begin to think how many. Her first inclination was to start picking some to put in her hair. But as her hand reached out and grasped one, she remembered her Grandma's admonishment back at the river. White and yellow are the Lady's colours, you cannot pick her flowers without upsetting her.

Kenna stood, frozen in mid-movement as the realisation came. She was standing on the Lady – the white soil under her feet was indeed her bones, just as Grandma had said, although Kenna had never thought she really meant it. And these flowers had been chosen by the Lady to decorated her own hair – if you, as Kenna thought you could, think of the grass and plants as hair.

Kenna knelt and put her palms on the ground. She sat, rather overwhelmed that Grandma had indeed brought her to the land of the Lady, where the land and the Lady were one. She struggled to remember if Grandma had ever chanted a song in praise of this Lady, of Kenevar. But she guessed that these were the sort of chants that Grandma did when she was just out of earshot. The only words she could bring to mind were 'Kenevar, I love you. Kenevar I love being with you. Kenevar please love me too.' She repeated them over and over until they seemed the worlds to say themselves and she forgot herself. There was only the here and now, and she and the land were as one.

~~~~~~~~~~~~~~~~~~~~

When she eventually came back to the camp Kenna realised that ever since they'd arrived she'd only seen the women of her kinfolk. She knew her father and his brothers, with all the lads her age and older were bringing the cattle and animals along the valley – and that would be very slow going compared to the way she and Grandma had come by boat. But what about the old men, the ones Grandma just called 'elders'? Would they be here too?

'Just look at those birds!', instructed Grandma. Kenna followed her gaze to where two buzzards were circling close to each other. One was bigger than the other. In fact, at first she thought it was a rook mobbing a buzzard. But even rooks only mobbed buzzards when they were together in groups. 'That's a good sign,' Grandma pronounced, 'The ritual will be a good one. And they don't say the swan's feathers grow on me without good reason.' And Kenna realised that the smaller bird was not mobbing the other, but they were wheeling around each other in a love dance, the smaller father bird persistently trying to get the attention of the mother bird.

Grandma had often said that the swan's feathers grew on her. Kenna didn't think it wasn't really true – or at least not in a way that she could see – but it was something Grandma said when she made some sort of prophecy. And the activities of birds seemed to be just the sort of occasion when Grandma would say this. Indeed, only moments after they had got in the boat to start their journey a few days ago – though it already seemed a lot longer – several swans had taken off together in front of the boat. All that running on the water, all that splashing of their feet, and the noisy beating of wings! It was always exciting to see one swan take off, but being alongside three or four taking off on each side of the boat, racing to get ahead and fly off upstream, that was really exciting, remembered Kenna. But Grandma had seemed excited for other reasons – 'Oh, I think we're going to have a very beneficial trip, my dear,' Kenna remembered her saying. She still wondered in what ways a journey could be beneficial, but Grandma had just said, unhelpfully, 'Oh, we shall see, my dear, all in due course.'

~~~~~~~~~~~~~~~~~~~~

Night rise was almost upon them by the time they ate that evening. 'Put your hands over your ears, my dear,' Grandma suddenly instructed. 'Those sounds are for the men folk only.' Kenna became aware of deep throbbing sounds, then several such deep humming noises, stopping and starting but always with several sounding at once. Truth be told the deep sound only slightly diminished when she put her hands over her ears. Grandma seemed to be only putting her hands near her ears, as if symbolically shutting out the sound, without really trying. Kenna allowed her palms to move away from her ear lobes, just a little bit, but not so it showed in the half-light. It helped her to hear what Grandma was saying. 'The wind is blowing from the house of the dead, where the elders are. We women are told we must not hear them call up the bull god. But the sound carries so well, it is difficult not to hear, don't you think, my dear?'

'What are they doing up there, Grandma?' 'Oh, you and I will never know, my dear. It's a secret. All I can tell you is that if you – or any other woman – see the masks and roarers then the men are under oath to kill you.' Grandma smiled ruefully and continued. 'I suppose that means I should have been killed several times. Can't imagine what they would have to do to make amends for killing one of the swan goddess's own, mind you. Such things are greater than the men's oaths of secrecy.'

'But if they're secret, how do you know?', Kenna blurted out before she could stop herself. Rather expecting Grandma to chide her, she was surprised when instead she smiled again. 'Ah, well, some things are more secret than others. And anyway, secrets need to be told to someone – else how can they be remembered after your spirit has passed on?' Kenna could see the contradiction. 'I will tell you many things that are secrets between you and me, in the same way they were secret between me and my mother, and with her and her grandmother, and all they way back to her grandmother's grandmother and the beginnings of all our kin with the Lady herself. We are all one blood and one bone.'

Kenna pondered on the expression 'One blood and one bone.' Grandma had used it many times before. But that was before Kenna had seen the bones of the Lady when she wandered away. Was she indeed one with the Lady, the land beneath her feet? Grandma interrupted her thoughts. 'The men too have their secrets. That is what they are doing at the house of the dead. The elders are passing on the secrets of the bull god to the lads who are their grandsons. Squatting in the darkness, struggling to keep warm, chanting the hunting songs over and over, repeating the same drama of transformation that goes back till time out of mind. They will spend the night as stags, they will walk as wolves, and they will see the dead.' She paused again. 'Oh yes, they will see the dead all right. Three nights walled up in their house with no food and I guess anyone would see them – and quite a few are never the same again.'

'Will I go into the house of the dead?' asked Kenna, in a worried tone of voice. 'Well, of course, my dear,' Grandma replied, sounding mildly disgruntled. 'We will all visit the house of the dead after the cattle sacrifice just before we leave the summerlands. We will pay our respects, as we always do. But, no, you will not do what the lads do. You will not spend the night as stags or spend three nights and days in there – not that the days are any different to the nights in the darkness. We have our own ways of seeing the dead, our own ways of talking with them, don't we, my dear?' Kenna looked more than a little perplexed but didn't think it was the right moment to say she wasn't at all sure what Grandma meant.

'I forget how much I still need to tell you,' Grandma said, as if reading Kenna's mind. 'The ways of the swan goddess – the secrets of the swan maidens, if you like – are the ways of our kinfolk, at least the women kinfolk. There is much you need to know.' Grandma paused. 'But you learn well, my dear.' Kenna did not miss the unexpected praise, and her face brightened. 'And you seem to know already, even when you don't realise,' said Grandma, as much to herself as her granddaughter. Yes, she said silently, Kenna was certainly one of them, one who would grow up to talk with the swan goddess.

Yes, she continued silently to herself, Kenna is certainly one of Kenevar's own. The men may mock us and call to us 'Daughters of the Old Woman' but they know there is a truth in those words. I need to show Kenna so much more, but it is as if she is already as one with the Lady who knows what shall come about, what shall become, and what shall happen. When I surrender my spirit it will be Kenna who takes my place on the high seat, on the top of the Headland, and speaks with the Lady to learn what the future has in store.

~~~~~~~~~~~~~~~~~~~~

She walked away from the camp where Kenna had started to doze. The night air was still, the bull roarers had fallen silent. She disturbed a bird from its roost and the sound of its wings broke the silence. She stood near the banks of the Kennet and began to chant.

> May there be peace in the heavens, peace in the skies and peace on earth.
>
> May the waters be plentiful.
>
> May the grasses and herbs bring peace to all creatures, and may the plants be at peace also.
>
> May the beneficent beings bring us peace, and may the way of all creation bring peace throughout the world.
>
> May all things be peaceful, and may that peace itself bring further peace.
>
> May we also bring peace to all.

References

Armstrong, Edward A., 1959, *The Folklore of Birds*, Riverside.

Baker, Ian, 2004, *The Heart of the World: A journey to the last secret place,* Penguin 2004; UK edition Souvenir 2006.

Barnes, Jonathan, 1982, *The Presocratic Philosophers* (2nd edn; 1st edn 1972), Routledge.

Barrett, John C,, 1994, *Fragments from Antiquity: An archaeology of social life in Britain, 2900–1200 BC,* Blackwell.

Basso, Keith H., 1996, 'Wisdom sits in places: Notes on a western Apache landscape', in *Senses of Place* Steven Feld and Keith H. Basso (eds), School of American Research Press.

Bates, Brian, 1983, *The Way of Wyrd*, Century.

Bennett, Martyn, *circa* 1997, 'Bothy culture'; online at www.martynbennett.com/album_02_bothyculture_01.html

Bernal-García, María Elena, 2007, 'The dance of time, the procession of space at Mexico-Tenochtitlan's desert garden' in M. Conan (ed), *Sacred Gardens and Landscapes: Ritual and agency*, Dumbarton Oaks Research Library and Collection.

Bey, Hakim (a.k.a. Peter Lamborn Wilson), no date, *Overcoming Tourism;* first published as *Voyage Intentionnel,* 1994; numerous online English translations.

Binchy, D.A., 1958, 'The Fair of Tailtiu and the Feast of Tara', *Eriu* Vol. 18, p113–38.

Blacker, Carmen, 1975, *The Catalpa Bow: A study of shamanistic practices in Japan*, Allen and Unwin; paperback edition 1986.

Blair, John, 1995, 'Anglo-Saxon pagan shrines and their prototypes', in *Anglo-Saxon Studies in Archaeology and History,* Vol. 8, p1–28.

Bolvin, Nicole, 2004, 'Rock art and rock music: petroglyphs of the south Indian Neolithic', *Antiquity*, Vol. 78 (299).

Bord, Janet and Colin Bord, 1972, *Mysterious Britain*, Garnstone.

Bord, Janet, 2004, *Footprints in Stone: The significance of foot- and hand-prints and other imprints left by early men, giants, heroes, devils, saints, animals, ghosts, witches, fairies and monsters*, Heart of Albion.

Branston, Brian, 1980, *Gods of the North* (2nd edn), Thames and Hudson.

Bray, Daniel, 1999, 'Sacral elements of Irish kingship' in C.M. Cusack and P. Oldmeadow (eds), *This Immense Panorama: Studies in Honour of Eric John Sharpe*, School of Studies in Religion University of Sydney; online at escholarship.usyd.edu.au/journals/index.php/SSR/article/viewFile/660/640

Briggs, Keith, 2009, 'OE and ME *cunte* in place-names', *Journal of the English Place-name Society* 41, 26–39; online at keithbriggs.info/documents/cunte_04.pdf

Brown, G. Spencer, 1972, *Laws of Form*, Allen and Unwin.

Burl, Aubrey, 1976, *The Stone Circles of the British Isles*, Yale UP.

Burl, Aubrey, 1979, *Prehistoric Avebury*, Yale UP; 2nd edn 2002.

Cameron , Kenneth, 1988, *English Place Names,*(rev. edn), Batsford.

Camphausen, Rufus C., 1989, 'The Ka'bah at Mecca', *Bres* (Holland) No.139.

Chatwin, Bruce, 1987, *The Songlines,* Jonathan Cape; page references to 1988 Picador edition.

Childe, V.G., 1958, *The Prehistory of European Society*, Penguin.

Classen, Constance, 1993, *Worlds of Sense: Exploring the senses in history and across cultures*, Routledge.

Cleal, Ros, 2009, *Avebury*, The National Trust,

Coates, Richard, 2004, 'Invisible Britons: the view from linguistics', paper at 'Britons in Anglo-Saxon England' conference, Manchester, 14–16 April 2004; published online at www.sussex.ac.uk/linguistics/documents/rc_britons.pdf

Cole, Ann, 2007, *The Place-name Evidence for a Routeway Network in Early Medieval England* (2 vols), unpublished PhD thesis (Kellog College, University of Oxford).

Collins, Andrew, 2008, *The Cygnus Mystery* (2nd end; 1st edn 2006), Watkins.

Cowan, James, 1989, *Mysteries of the Dream-Time: The spiritual life of the Australian Aborigines*, Prism.

Crawford, O.G.S., 1957, *The Eye Goddess*, Phoenix House.

Cummings, Vicki and Robert Johnston (eds), 2007, *Prehistoric Journeys,* Oxbow.

Dames, Michael, 1976, *The Silbury Treasure*, Thames and Hudson.

Dames, Michael, 1977, *The Avebury Cycle*, Thames and Hudson.

Dames, Michael, 1992, *Mythic Ireland*, Thames and Hudson.

Dames, Michael, 2002, *Merlin and Wales: A magician's landscape*, Thames and Hudson.

Dames, Michael, 2006, *Taliesin's Travels: A demi-god at large,* Heart of Albion.

Daniel, Glynn, 1958, *The Megalith Builders of Western Europe*, Hutchinson.

Danser, Simon, 2005, *The Myths of Reality*, Alternative Albion.

Devereux, Paul, 1990, *Places of Power: Secret energies at ancient sites – a guide to observed or measured phenomena*, Batsford.

Devereux, Paul, 2001, *Stone Age Soundtracks: The acoustic archaeology of ancient sites*, Vega.

Devereux, Paul, 2002, 'Soundings', *3rd Stone*, No. 44, p28–32.

Devereux, Paul, 2003, *Spirit Roads: An exploration of otherworldly routes,* Vega; page references to Collins and Brown.2007 edition.

Devereux, Paul, 2004, 'Spirits in the stones', *Fortean Times*, No. 188, p46–50.

Devereux, Paul, 2008, 'The association of prehistoric rock-art and rock selection with acoustically significant landscape locations' in George Nash and George Children (eds) *The Archaeology of Semiotics and the Social Order of Things* Archaeopress.

Devereux, Paul, 2009, 'Archaeology with balls – *Time Stands Still:* new light on megalithic science' *Time and Mind* Vol 2:1.

Devereux, Paul and R.G. Jahn, 1996, 'Preliminary investigations and cognitive considerations of the acoustical resonances of selected archaeological sites', *Antiquity*, 70 (269), 665–6.

Dickinson, Bob, 1990a, 'Sacred resonance', *Markstone*, No. 4, p12–16.

Dickinson, Bob, 1990b, 'Sounding the landscape', *Markstone*, No. 4, p17–21.

Dickinson, Bob, 1998a, 'Sounding the landscape', *At the Edge*, No. 9, p33–7.

Dickinson, Bob, 2001, *Music and the Earth Spirit*, Capall Bann.

Dodds, Eric R., 1951, *The Greeks and the Irrational*, University of California Press.

Edmonds, Mark, 1999, *Ancestral Geographies of the Neolithic: Landscape, monuments and memory*, Routledge.

Eliade, Mircea, 1964, *Shamanism: Archaic techniques of ecstasy*, Pantheon.

Eliot, T.S., 1943, 'The Dry Salvages' in *Four Quartets*, Harcourt Brace.

Erlmann, Veit, 2004, 'But what of the ethnographic ear? Anthropology, sounds, and the senses', in V. Erlmann (ed), *Hearing Culture: Essays on sound, listening and modernity*, Berg.

Ewing, Thor, 2008, *Gods and Worshippers in the Viking and Germanic World*, The History Press.

Fagg, Bernard, 1957, 'Rock gongs and slides', *Man*, Vol. 57, p30–2.

Favret-Saada, Jeanne, 1981, *Deadly Words: Witchcraft in the Bocage,* Cambridge UP; free downloads online.

Field, David, 2008, *Use of Land in Central Southern England During the Neolithic and Early Bronze Age*, BAR British Series.

Garner, Alan, 2010, *By Seven Firs and Goldenstone: An account of the legend of Alderley*, Temenos Academy.

Gell, Alfred, 1995, 'The language of the forest: landscape and phonological iconism in Umeda', in E. Hirsch and M. O'Hanlon (eds), *The Anthropology of Landscape: Perspectives on place and space*, Oxford UP.

Gelling, Margaret and Ann Cole, 2000, *The Landscape of Place-names,* Shaun Tyas.

Gelling, Margaret, 1961, 'Place-names and Anglo-Saxon paganism', *University of Birmingham Historical Journal*, Vol. 8.

Gelling, Margaret, 1984, *Place-names in the Landscape*, Dent.

Gelling, Margaret, 1988, *Signposts to the Past* (2nd edn), Phillimore,

Gilchrist, Cherry, 2007, *Explore Alchemy*, Explore Books.

Gillings, M., J. Pollard, D.W. Wheatley and R. Peterson, 2008, *Landscape of the Megaliths: Excavation and fieldwork on the Avebury Monuments 1997–2003,* Oxbow.

Girardot, N.J., 1983, *Myth and Meaning in Early Taoism*, University of California Press.

Glosecki, Stephen, 1989, *Shamanism and Old English Poetry*, Garland.

Govinda, Anagaraika, 1960, *Foundations of Tibetan Mystery*, Rider; page references to 1969 edition.

Grinsell, Leslie V., 1976, *Folklore of Prehistoric Sites in Britain*, David and Charles.

Guthrie, W.K.C., 1962, *A History of Greek Philosophy* (Vol. 1), Cambridge UP.

Gyrus, 1999, 'Form and meaning in altered states and rock art'; online at dreamflesh.com/essays/rockform/

Haland, Evy Johanne, 2008, 'Interactions with the sacred during the Tauros festival of Agios Charalampos', *Cosmos*, Vol.24, p133–55.

Hall, Alaric, 2007, *Elves in Anglo-Saxon England: Matters of belief, health, gender and identity*, Boydell; the PhD thesis on which this is based is online at www.alarichall.org.uk/phd.php

Hall, David L., 1982, *The Uncertain Phoenix: Adventures towards a post-cultural sensibility*, Fordham UP.

Handy, Nathaniel, 2010, 'Chap off the old block', *Songlines No.* 66, p38–9.

Harte, Jeremy, 2008, *English Holy Wells: A sourcebook* (vol 1), Heart of Albion.

Harte, Jeremy, 2010, 'The Devil's chapels: fiends, fear and folklore at prehistoric sites', in J. Parker (ed), *Written On Stone: The cultural reception of prehistoric monuments,* Cambridge Scholars Publishing.

Harte, Jeremy, 2011, 'An Edge of contention', *Northern Earth*, No. 126, p28–9.

Heyd, Thomas, 2008, 'Interpreting Bash--o's *Narrow Road to the Interior* as a journey to the depths of being', in George Nash and George Children (eds), *The Archaeology of Semiotics and the Social Order of Things,* Archaeopress.

Hooke, Della, 1998, *The Landscape of Anglo-Saxon England,* Leicester UP.

Hutchins, Roger B., 2011, 'Stone rows: a practical solution', *Northern Earth,* No. 126, p12–15.

Hutton, Ronald, 1991, *The Pagan Religions of the Ancient British Isles: Their nature and legacy,* Basil Blackwell.

Hutton, Ronald, 1996, *The Stations of the Sun,* Oxford UP.

Ingold, Tim, 2007, *Lines: A brief history,* Routledge.

Jahn, R.G., P. Devereux, M. Ibson, 1996, 'Acoustical resonances of assorted ancient structures', *Journal of the Acoustical Society of America,* Vol. 99:2.

Jahn, Robert George, 1995, 'The old stones speak', *The Ley Hunter,* No. 123, p1–8.

Johnson, Nathan and Robert Wallis. 2005, *Galdrbok: Practical heathen runecraft, shamanism and magic,* Wykeham Press.

Johnston, Sarah Iles, 2008, *Ancient Greek Divination,* Wiley-Blackwell.

Jolly, Karen Louise, 1996, *Popular Religion in Late Saxon England,* University of North Carolina Press.

Jordan, Peter, 2001, 'Cultural landscapes in colonial Siberia: Khanty settlements of the sacred, the living and the dead', *Landscapes* Vol. 2:2, p83–105.

Kahn, C.H., 1979, *The Art and Thought of Heraclitus,* Cambridge UP.

Kauffmann, Friedrich, 1903, *Northern Mythology,* Dent.

Kieckhefer, Richard, 1990, *Magic in the Middle Ages,* Cambridge UP.

Knight, Peter, 2011, *West Kennett Long Barrow: Landscape, shamans and the cosmos,* Stone Seeker Publishing.

Kohn, Livia, 1992, *Early Chinese Mysticism: Philosophy and soteriology in the Taoist tradition,* Princeton UP.

Lakoff, George and Mark Johnson, 1980, *Metaphors We Live By,* University of Chicago, (revised edn 2003).

Lakoff, George and Mark Johnson, 1999, *Philosophy in the Flesh: The embodied mind and its challenge to Western thought,* Basic Books.

Lakoff, George, 1987, *Women, Fire and Dangerous Things: What categories reveal about the mind,* University of Chicago Press.

Lawrence, John Shelton and Robert Jewett, 2002, *The Myth of the American Superhero,* William B. Eerdmans Publishing.

Lawson, Graeme, 2003, paper at Acoustics, Space and Intentionality conference, MacDonald Institute, Cambridge, 27–29 June.

Leary, Jim, and David Field, 2010, *The Story of Silbury Hill,* English Heritage.

Lucas, George R., Jr., 1989, *The Reclamation of Whitehead: An analytic and historical assessment of process philosophy,* State University of New York Press.

Marshall, Steve, 2010, 'The flint that roared', *British Archaeology*, No. 112, p32–4.

Martinez, Helios de Rosario, 2010, 'Fairy and elves in Tolkien and traditional literature.' The Free Library; online at www.thefreelibrary.com/Fairy+and+Elves+in+Tolkien+and+traditional+literatur e.-a0227196959

Meaden, Terence, 1999, *Secrets of the Avebury Stones: Britain's Greatest Megalithic Temple*, Souvenir.

Meyer, Kuno, 1919, 'Der irische Totengott und die Toteninsel' in *Sitzungberichte der preussischen Akademie der Wissenschaften*, Akademie der Wissenschaften, p537–46.

Mortimer, Neil, 2003, 'Acoustics, space and intentionality: McDonald Institute, Cambridge, 27–29 June 2003', *3rd Stone*, No. 47, p7.

Mountford, Charles, 1968, *Winbaraku and the Myth of Jarapiri*, Rigby.

Mysliwiec, Karol, 2004, *Eros on the Nile*, Cornell UP.

Nicholl, Charles, 1980, *The Chemical Theatre*, RKP.

Nicholson, Lewis E., 1988, 'Beowulf and the pagan cult of the stag', *Studi Medievali* No.27, p637–69.

Noble, Gordon, 2007, 'Monumental journeys', in Vicki Cummings and Robert Johnston (eds), *Prehistoric Journeys,* Oxbow.

Noë, Alva, 2004, *Action in Perception*, MIT Press.

North, John, 1996, *Stonehenge, Neolithic Man and the Cosmos,* Harper Collins.

North, Richard, 1997, *Heathen Gods in Old English Literature*, Cambridge UP.

O Duinn, Sean, 2008, 'Mythology and folklore of Lough Gur: practices and stories' in *Cosmos* Vol. 24, p211–20

Ong, Walter J., 1982, *Orality and Literacy*, Routledge.

Pantos, A. and S.J. Semple, 2004, 'Introduction' in *Assembly Places and Practices in Medieval Europe,* A. Pantos and S.J. Semple (eds), Four Courts Press.

Parker Pearson, M, and Ramilisonina, 1998 'Stonehenge for the ancestors: the stones pass on the message'. *Antiquity* Vol. 72, p308–26.

Pennick, Nigel, 2010, 'Pines on the horizon' *Silver Wheel Annual* No 2, p97–101.

Pennick, Nigel, 2011, *In Field and Fen*, Lear Books.

Pitts, Mike, 2002, 'Stonehenge Landscapes and Stone Circles: A combined review', *Internet Archaeology* No. 11; online at intarch.ac.uk/journal/issue11/reviews/pitts.html

Poikalainen, Väino, 1999, 'Some statistics about rock-carvings of Lake Onega, *Folklore* 11; online at www.folklore.ee/folklore/vol11/pdf/carvings.pdf

Pollard, Josh and Andrew Reynolds, 2002, *Avebury: The biography of a landscape,* Tempus.

Pollington, Stephen, 2000, *Leechcraft: Early English charms, plant-lore and healing,* Anglo-Saxon Books.

Pope, Rob, 2005, *Creativity: Theory, history, practice,* Routledge.

Reith, Sara, 2008, 'Through the "eye of the skull": memory and tradition in a Travelling landscape', *Cultural Analysis,* Vol. 7; online at socrates.berkeley.edu/~caforum/volume7/pdf/reith.pdf

Rifkin, Riaan, 2009, 'Engraved art and acoustic resonance: exploring ritual and sound in north-western South Africa', *Antiquity* Vol. 83, p585–601.

Robertson, Stanley, 1988, *Exodus to Alford,* Balnain Books.

Robertson, Stanley, 2009, *Reek Roon a Camp Fire*, Birlinn.

Roe, David, and Jerry Taki, 1991, 'Living with the stones: people and the landscape in Erromango, Vanuata', in P.J. Ucko and R. Layton (eds), *The Archaeology and Anthropology of Landscape*, Routledge.

Rundle Clark, R.T., 1959, *Myth and Symbol in Ancient Egypt*, Thames and Hudson.

Russell, James C., 1994, *The Germanization of Early Medieval Christianity*, Oxford UP.

Saher, P.J., 1969, *Eastern Wisdom and Western Thought*, Allen and Unwin.

Sanmark, A. and S.J. Semple, 2008, 'Places of assembly: new discoveries in Sweden and England', *Fornvännen*, Vol. 103, p245–59.

Sanmark, A. and S.J. Semple, 2010. 'The topography of outdoor assembly sites in Europe with reference to recent field results from Sweden', in *Perspectives in Landscape Archaeology*. H. Lewis and S.J. Semple (eds) British Archaeological Reports. BAR International Series 2103.

Sanmark, Alexandra, 2002, *Power and Conversion: a comparative study of Christianization in Scandinavia*, unpublished PhD thesis University College London; online at
uhi.academia.edu/AlexandraSanmark/Papers/195381/Power_and_Conversion_a_Comparative_Study_of_Christianization_In_Scandinavia

Scarre, Chris, 2008, 'Shrines of the land and places of power: religion and the transition to farming in Western Europe', in Kelley Hays-Gilpin and David S. Whitley (eds), *Belief in the Past: Theoretical Approaches to the Archaeology of Religion*, Left Coast Press.

Schama, Simon, 1995, *Landscape and Memory*, HarperCollins.

Semple, Sarah, 1998, 'A fear of the past: the place of prehistoric burial mounds in the ideology of middle and later Anglo-Saxon England', *World Archaeology*, Vol. 30:1, p109–126.

Semple, Sarah, 2007, 'Defining the OE *hearg*: a preliminary archaeological and topographic examination of *hearg* place names and their hinterlands', *Early Medieval Europe*, Vol. 15:4, p364–85.

Shakespeare, Nicholas, 2000, *Bruce Chatwin*, Vintage.

Singh, Raghubir, 1974, *Ganga: Sacred river of India*, Perennial Press.

Singh, Raghubir, 1992, *The Ganges*, Thames and Hudson.

Skeates, Robin, 2008, 'Making sense of the Maltese Temple Period: an archaeology of sensory experience and perception', *Time and Mind*, Vol. 1:2, p207–38.

Stenton, Frank, 1941, *Anglo-Saxon England*, Frank Stenton, Oxford UP; 3rd edn 1971.

Stoller, Paul, 1989, *The Taste of Ethnographic Things: The sense in anthropology*, University of Pennsylvania Press.

Stoller, Paul, and Cheryl Olkes, 1987, *In Sorcery's Shadow*, University of Chicago Press.

Stone, Alby, 1997, *Ymir's Flesh: North European creation mythologies*, Heart of Albion.

Stone, Alby, 1998a, *Straight Track, Crooked Road: leys, spirit paths and shamanism*, Heart of Albion.

Stone, Alby, 1998b, 'The road that makes things disappear', *Fortean Studies* Vol. 5.

Stone, Alby, 2005, 'Infernal watchdogs', in B. Trubshaw (ed), *Explore Phantom Black Dogs*, Explore Books.

Stone, C.J., 2009, 'The Way of the Pilgrim', *Kindred Spirit* No.100; online at www.kindredspirit.co.uk/articles/article-detail/787

Stout, Adam, 2008, *Creating Prehistory: Druids, Ley Hunters and Archaeologists in Pre-war Britain*, Blackwell.

Sullivan, Lawrence, 1997, 'Enchanting powers: an introduction', in L.E. Sullivan (ed), *Enchanting Powers: Music in the world's religions*, Harvard UP.

Sundqvist, Olof, 2001, 'Features of pre-Christian inauguration rituals in medieval Swedish laws', in Johannes Hoops and Heinrich Beck (eds), *Reallexikon der Germanischen Altertumskunde*, Walter de Gruyter.

Tambiah, Stanley J., 1990, *Magic, Science, Religion and the Scope of Rationality*, Cambridge UP.

Thorn, Richard, 1997, 'Hearing is believing', *Resonance*, Vol. 5:2, p11–14 (reprinted *At the Edge*, No. 9 (1998), p27–32.

Tilley, Christopher, 1994, *A Phenomenology of Landscape*, Berg.

Tilley, Christopher, 2008, *Body and Image: Explorations in landscape phenomenology*, Left Coast Press.

Tim Ingold, 2000, *The Perception of the Environment: Essays on livelihood, dwelling and skill*, Routledge.

Toop, David, 2010, *Sinister Resonance: The mediumship of the listener*, Continuum.

Torma, Thomas, 2002, 'Imbolc, Candlemas, and the Feast of St Brigit', *Cosmos* Vol. 18, p77–85.

Travers, Nicholas, 2002, *Going Too Far: Travel lying in Bruce Chatwin's* In Patagonia *and* The Songlines, unpublished MA thesis, University of British Columbia; online at circle.ubc.ca/bitstream/handle/2429/12231/ubc_2002-0271.pdf

Trevarthen, Geo Athena, 2008a, 'Editorial', *Cosmos* Vol. 24, p1–8.

Trevarthen, Geo Athena, 2008b, 'Heaven must be missing an angel: romantic relationships with the divine', *Cosmos* Vol. 24, p221–45.

Trubshaw, Bob (ed.), 2005b, *Explore Phantom Black Dogs*, Explore Books.

Trubshaw, Bob, 1993, 'The Black Stone: the omphalos of the goddess', *Mercian Mysteries* No.14; online at www.indigogroup.co.uk/edge/blstone.htm

Trubshaw, Bob, 2002, *Explore Folklore*, Explore Books.

Trubshaw, Bob, 2005a, *Sacred Places: Prehistory and popular imagination*, Heart of Albion.

Twomey, Michael, 2004, 'Travels with Sir Gawain', online at www.ithaca.edu/faculty/twomey/travels/

Venkatesh, M.R., 2004, 'In Shiva's temple, pillars make music', *Telegraph India*, July 26.

Walens, Stanley, 1981, *Feasting with Cannibals: An essay on Kwakiutl cosmology*, Princeton UP.

Waller, Steven, 1993a, 'Sound and rock art', *Nature*, Vol. 363, p501.

Waller, Steven, 1993b, 'Sound reflection as an explanation for the content and context of rock art', *Rock Art Research*, Vol. 10:2, [p91–101.

Watson, Aaron and David Keating, 1999, 'Architecture and sound: an acoustic analysis of megalithic monuments in prehistoric Britain', *Antiquity*, Vol. 73 (280), p325–36.

Watson, W. and D. Keating, 2000, 'The architecture of sound in Neolithic Orkney', in A. Ritchie (ed),*Neolithic Orkney in its European Context*, McDonald Institute Monographs.

Watts, Alan, 1976, *Tao: The Watercourse Way*, Jonathan Cape (1st USA edn 1975).

Welander, R., David J. Breeze and Thomas Owen Clancy (eds), 2003, *The Stone of Destiny: Artefact and icon*, Society of Antiquaries of Scotland.

West, Martin Litchfield, 1971, *Early Greek Philosophy and the Orient*, Clarendon.

Westwood, Jennifer and Jacqueline Simpson, 2005, *The Lore of the Land: A guide to England's legends from Spring-heeled Jack to the Witches of Warboys*, Penguin.

Whitley, James, 2002, 'Too many ancestors', *Antiquity*, Vol. 76, p119–26; online at antiquity.ac.uk/Ant/076/0119/Ant0760119.pdf

Wilby, Emma, 2005, *Cunning Folk and Familiar Spirits*, Sussex Academic Press.

Wilby, Emma, 2010, *The Visions of Isobel Gowdie: Magic, witchcraft and dark shamanism in seventeenth-century Scotland*, Sussex Academic Press.

Williams, Mike, 2010, *Prehistoric Belief: Shamans, trance and the afterlife*, The History Press.

Wilson, David, 1985, 'A note on OE *hearg* and *w-eoh* as place-name elements representing different types of pagan Saxon worship sites', in S. Chadwick Hawkes, J. Campbell and D. Brown (eds), *Anglo-Saxon Studies in Archaeology and History* Vol.4, Oxford Committee for Archaeology.

Wilson, David, 1992, *Anglo-Saxon Paganism*, Routledge.

Winkelman, Michael, 2008, 'Shamanism from biogenetic perspectives' in Kelley Hays-Gilpin and David S. Whitley (eds), *Belief in the Past: Theory and the Archaeology of Religion*. Left Coast Press.

Wright, Brian, 2009, *Brigid: Goddess, druidess and saint*, The History Press.

Index

Numbers shown in **bold** refer to illustrations.

Places in England are listed under county. Places in other countries are listed by country.

Sacred Places
Prehistory and popular imagination
Bob Trubshaw

Sacred Places asks why certain types of prehistoric places are thought of as sacred, and explores how the physical presence of such sacred sites is less important than what these places signify. So this is not another guide book to sacred places but instead provides a unique and thought-provoking guide to the mental worlds – the mindscapes – in which we have created the idea of prehistoric sacred places.

Recurring throughout this book is the idea that we continually create and re-create our ideas about the past, about landscapes, and the places within those landscapes that we regard as sacred. For example, although such concepts as 'nature', 'landscape', 'countryside', 'rural' and the contrast between profane and sacred are all part of our everyday thinking, in this book Bob Trubshaw shows they are all modern cultural constructions which act as the 'unseen' foundations on which we construct more complex myths about places.

Key chapters look at how earth mysteries, modern paganism and other alternative approaches to sacred places developed in recent decades, and also outline the recent dramatic changes within academic archaeology. Is there now a 'middle way' between academic and alternative approaches which recognises that what we know about the past is far less significant than what we believe about the past?

Bob Trubshaw has been actively involved with academic and alternative approaches to archaeology for most of the last twenty years. In 1996 he founded *At the Edge* magazine to popularise new interpretations of past and place.

> '*Sacred Places*... is a very valuable addition to the small body of thoughtful work on the spiritual landscapes of Great Britain and therefore recommended reading.' Nigel Pennick *Silver Wheel*

> 'One of the best books in the field I have ever read.'
> D J Tyrer *Monomyth Supplement*

ISBN 1 872883 67 2. 2005. 245 x 175 mm, 203 + xiv pages, 43 b&w illustrations and 7 line drawings, paperback. **£16.95**

'Highly recommended'
Folklore Society Katharine Briggs Award 2003

Explore Folklore

Bob Trubshaw

**'A howling success, which plugs
a big and obvious gap'**

Professor Ronald Hutton

There have been fascinating developments in the study of folklore in the last twenty-or-so years, but few books about British folklore and folk customs reflect these exciting new approaches. As a result there is a huge gap between scholarly approaches to folklore studies and 'popular beliefs' about the character and history of British folklore. *Explore Folklore* is the first book to bridge that gap, and to show how much 'folklore' there is in modern day Britain.

Explore Folklore shows there is much more to folklore than morris dancing and fifty-something folksingers! The rituals of 'what we do on our holidays', funerals, stag nights and 'lingerie parties' are all full of 'unselfconscious' folk customs. Indeed, folklore is something that is integral to all our lives – it is so intrinsic we do not think of it as being 'folklore'.

The implicit ideas underlying folk lore and customs are also explored. There might appear to be little in common between people who touch wood for luck (a 'tradition' invented in the last 200 years) and legends about people who believe they have been abducted and subjected to intimate body examinations by aliens. Yet, in their varying ways, these and other 'folk beliefs' reflect the wide spectrum of belief and disbelief in what is easily dismissed as 'superstition'.

Explore Folklore provides a lively introduction to the study of most genres of British folklore, presenting the more contentious and profound ideas in a readily accessible manner.

ISBN 1 872883 60 5. 2002. Demy 8vo (215x138 mm), 200 pages, illustrated, paperback **£9.95**

Also from Heart of Albion Press

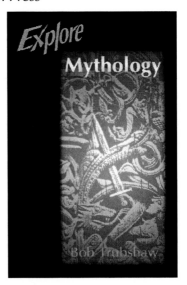

Explore Mythology

Bob Trubshaw

Myths are usually thought of as something to do with 'traditional cultures'. The study of such 'traditional' myths emphasises their importance in religion, national identity, hero-figures, understanding the origin of the universe, and predictions of an apocalyptic demise. The academic study of myths has done much to fit these ideas into the preconceived ideas of the relevant academics.

Only in recent years have such long-standing assumptions about myths begun to be questioned, opening up whole new ways of thinking about the way such myths define and structure how a society thinks about itself and the 'real world'.

These new approaches to the study of myth reveal that, to an astonishing extent, modern day thinking is every bit as 'mythological' as the world-views of, say, the Classical Greeks or obscure Polynesian tribes. Politics, religions, science, advertising and the mass media are all deeply implicated in the creation and use of myths.

Explore Mythology provides a lively introduction to the way myths have been studied, together with discussion of some of the most important 'mythic motifs' – such as heroes, national identity, and 'central places' – followed by a discussion of how these ideas permeate modern society. These sometimes contentious and profound ideas are presented in an easily readable style of writing.

ISBN 1 872883 62 1. Published 2003.
Perfect bound. Demi 8vo (215 x 138 mm), 220 + xx pages, 17 line drawings. **£9.95**

*Winner of the Folklore Society
Katharine Briggs Award 2005*

Explore Fairy Traditions

Jeremy Harte

We are not alone. In the shadows of our countryside there lives a fairy race, older than humans, and not necessarily friendly to them. For hundreds of years, men and women have told stories about the strange people, beautiful as starlight, fierce as wolves, and heartless as ice. These are not tales for children. They reveal the fairies as a passionate, proud, brutal people.

Explore Fairy Traditions draws on legends, ballads and testimony from throughout Britain and Ireland to reveal what the fairies were really like. It looks at changelings, brownies, demon lovers, the fairy host, and abduction into the Otherworld. Stories and motifs are followed down the centuries to reveal the changing nature of fairy lore, as it was told to famous figures like W.B. Yeats and Sir Walter Scott. All the research is based on primary sources and many errors about fairy tradition are laid to rest.

Jeremy Harte combines folklore scholarship with a lively style to show what the presence of fairies meant to people's lives. Like their human counterparts, the secret people could kill as well as heal. They knew marriage, seduction, rape and divorce; they adored some children and rejected others. If we are frightened of the fairies, it may be because their world offers an uncomfortable mirror of our own.

> '... this is the best and most insightful book on fairies generally available... ' John Billingsley *Northern Earth*

> '*Explore Fairy Traditions* is an excellent introduction to the folklore of fairies, and I would highly recommend it.' Paul Mason *Silver Wheel*

ISBN 1 872883 61 3. 2004. Demy 8vo (215 x 138 mm), 171 + vi pages, 6 line drawings, paperback. **£9.95**

Stonehenge:
Celebration and Subversion

Andy Worthington

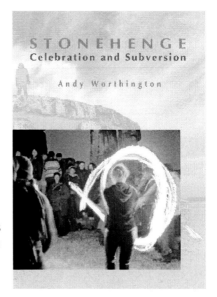

This innovative social history looks in detail at how the summer solstice celebrations at Stonehenge have brought together different aspects of British counter-culture to make the monument a 'living temple' and an icon of alternative Britain. The history of the celebrants and counter-cultural leaders is interwoven with the viewpoints of the land-owners, custodians and archaeologists who have generally attempted to impose order on the shifting patterns of these modern-day mythologies.

The story of the Stonehenge summer solstice celebrations begins with the Druid revival of the 18th century and the earliest public gatherings of the 19th and early 20th centuries. In the social upheavals of the 1960s and early 70s, these trailblazers were superseded by the Stonehenge Free Festival. This evolved from a small gathering to an anarchic free state the size of a small city, before its brutal suppression at the Battle of the Beanfield in 1985.

In the aftermath of the Beanfield, the author examines how the political and spiritual aspirations of the free festivals evolved into both the rave scene and the road protest movement, and how the prevailing trends in the counter-culture provided a fertile breeding ground for the development of new Druid groups, the growth of paganism in general, and the adoption of other sacred sites, in particular Stonehenge's gargantuan neighbour at Avebury.

The account is brought up to date with the reopening of Stonehenge on the summer solstice in 2000, the unprecedented crowds drawn by the new access arrangements, and the latest source of conflict, centred on a bitterly-contested road improvement scheme.

> 'Stonehenge Celebration and Subversion contains an extraordinary story. Anyone who imagines Stonehenge to be nothing but an old fossil should read this and worry. [This book is] ... the most complete, well-illustrated analysis of Stonehenge's mysterious world of Druids, travellers, pagans and party-goers'. Mike Pitts *History Today*

ISBN 1 872883 76 1. 2004. Perfect bound, 245 x 175 mm, 281 + xviii pages, 147 b&w photos, **£14.95**

The Enchanted Land

Myths and Legends of Britain's Landscape

Revised, fully illustrated edition

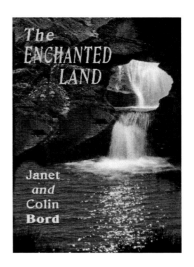

Janet and Colin Bord

Britain's landscape is overlain by a magic carpet of folklore and folktales, myths and legends. Enchantment and legend still lurk in places as diverse as hills and mountains, rivers and streams, caves and hollows, springs and wells, cliffs and coasts, pools and lakes, and rocks and stones.

The dramatic stories woven around these places tell of sleeping knights, beheaded saints, giants, dragons and monsters, ghosts, King Arthur, mermaids, witches, hidden treasure, drowned towns, giant missiles, mysterious footprints, visits to Fairyland, underground passages, human sacrifices, and much more.

The 'Places to Visit' section locates and describes in detail more than 50 sites.

This revised edition is fully illustrated, with around 130 photographs and illustrations.

Janet and Colin Bord live in North Wales, where they run the Fortean Picture Library. They have written more than 20 books since their first successful joint venture, *Mysterious Britain* in 1972.

From reviews of the first edition:

'Janet's own enthusiasm for a number of the sites is conveyed vividly and lends credibility to the notion that Britain is still an enchanted land.'
Mercian Mysteries

ISBN 1 872883 91 5. 2006. 245 x 175 mm, over 200 illustrations, paperback
£16.95

Heart of Albion

Publishing folklore, mythology and
local history since 1989

Further details of all Heart of Albion titles online at
www.hoap.co.uk

All titles available direct from Heart of Albion Press.

Heart of Albion Press

113 High Street, Avebury
Marlborough, SN8 1RF

Phone: 01672 539077
email: albion@indigogroup.co.uk
Web site: www.hoap.co.uk